THE ROMANCE OF WORDS

THE ROMANCE OF WORDS

BY ERNEST WEEKLEY, M.A.

" Vous savez le latin, sans doute ? "—
" Oui, mais faites comme si je ne le savais pas."

(MOLIÈRE, *Le Bourgeois Gentilhomme,* ii. 6.)

DOVER PUBLICATIONS, INC.
NEW YORK,   NEW YORK

422
W394r

Manufactured in the United States of America

Dover Publications, Inc.
180 Varick Street
New York 14, N. Y.

Dedicated to the memory of the author,

ERNEST WEEKLEY
(1865 – 1954)
lexicographer, etymologist, and, incidentally,
a keen student of the American language.

PREFACE

A LONG and somewhat varied experience in language teaching has convinced me that there are still, in spite of the march of science, many people who are capable of getting intellectual pleasure from word-history. I hope that to such people this little book, the amusement of occasional leisure, will not be unwelcome. It differs, I believe, from any other popular book on language in that it deals essentially with the origins of words, and makes no attempt to enforce a moral. My aim has been to select especially the unexpected in etymology, "things not generally known," such as the fact that *Tammany* was an Indian chief, that *assegai* occurs in Chaucer, that *jilt* is identical with *Juliet*, that *brazil* wood is not named from *Brazil*, that to *curry favour* means to comb down a horse of a particular colour, and so forth. The treatment is made as simple as possible, a bowing acquaintance with Latin and French being all that is assumed, though words from many other languages are necessarily included. In the case of each word I have traced the history just so far back as it is likely to be of interest to the reader who is not a philological specialist.

I have endeavoured to state each proposition in its simplest terms, without enumerating all the reservations and indirect factors which belong to the history of almost every word.

The chapter headings only indicate in a general way the division of the subject matter, the arrangement of which has been determined rather by the natural association which exists between words. The quotations are, with few exceptions, drawn from my own reading. They come from very varied sources, but archaic words are exemplified, when possible, from authors easily accessible, generally Shakespeare or Milton, or, for revived archaisms, Scott. In illustrating obsolete meanings I have made much use of the earliest dictionaries[1] available.

It seemed undesirable to load a small work of this kind with references. The writer on word-lore must of necessity build on what has already been done, happy if he can add a few bricks to the edifice. But philologists will recognise that this book is not, in the etymological sense, a mere compilation,[2] and that a considerable portion of the information it contains is here printed for the first time in a form accessible to the general reader.[3] Chapter VII., on Semantics, is, so far as I know, the first attempt at a simple treatment of a science which is now admitted to an equality with phonetics, and which to most people is much more interesting.

Throughout I have used the *New English Dictionary*, in the etymological part of which I have for some years had a humble share, for purposes of verification. Without the materials furnished by the historical method of that great national work, which is now complete from A to R, this book would not have been attempted. For words in S to Z, I have referred chiefly to

---

[1] For a list of these see p. xii.

[2] *Compilatio*, " pillage, polling, robbing " (Cooper).

[3] Among words on which the reader will find either entirely new information or a modification of generally accepted views are *akimbo, anlace, branks, caulk, cockney, felon* (a whitlow), *foil, kestrel, lugger, mulligrubs, mystery* (a craft), *oriel, patch, petronel, salet, sentry, sullen, tret*, etc.

Professor Skeat's *Etymological Dictionary* (4th ed., Oxford, 1910).

It is not many years since what passed for etymology in this country was merely a congeries of wild guesses and manufactured anecdotes. The persistence with which these crop up in the daily paper and the class-room must be my excuse for "slaying the slain" in Chapter XIII. Some readers may regret the disappearance of these fables, but a little study will convince them that in the life of words, as in that of men, truth is stranger than fiction.

ERNEST WEEKLEY.

NOTTINGHAM, *January* 1912.

CONTENTS

CHAP.   PAGE

I. OUR VOCABULARY I

II. WANDERINGS OF WORDS 15

III. WORDS OF POPULAR MANUFACTURE . . 26

IV. WORDS AND PLACES 43

V. PHONETIC ACCIDENTS 49

VI. WORDS AND MEANINGS 66

VII. SEMANTICS 79

VIII. METAPHOR 97

IX. FOLK-ETYMOLOGY 104

X. DOUBLETS 128

XI. HOMONYMS 144

XII. FAMILY NAMES 157

XIII. ETYMOLOGICAL FACT AND FICTION . . 171

INDEX 191

xi

The following dictionaries are quoted without further reference :—

Palsgrave, French and English (1530).
Cooper, Latin and English (1573).
Percyvall, Spanish and English (1591).
Florio, Italian and English (1598).
Cotgrave, French and English (1611).
Hexham, Dutch and English (1660).
Ludwig, German and English (1716).

THE ROMANCE OF WORDS

THE ROMANCE OF WORDS

CHAPTER I

OUR VOCABULARY

THE bulk of our literary language is Latin, and consists of words either borrowed directly or taken from "learned" French forms. The every-day vocabulary of the less educated is of Old English, commonly called Anglo-Saxon, origin ; and from the same source comes what we may call the machinery of the language, *i.e.*, its inflexions, numerals, pronouns, prepositions, and conjunctions. Along with Anglo-Saxon, we find a considerable number of words from the related Norse languages, this element being naturally strongest in the dialects of the north and east of England. The third great element of our working vocabulary is furnished by Old French, *i.e.*, the language naturally developed from the spoken Latin of the Roman soldiers and colonists, generally called Vulgar Latin. To its composite character English owes its unequalled richness in expression. For most ideas we have three separate terms, or groups of terms, which, often starting from the same metaphor, serve to express different shades of meaning. Thus a deed done with malice *prepense* (an Old French compound from Lat. *pensare*, to weigh), is *deliberate* or *pondered*, both Latin words which mean literally "weighed"; but the four words convey four distinct shades of meaning. The Gk. *sympathy* is Lat. *compassion*, rendered in English by *fellow-feeling*.

Sometimes a native word has been completely supplanted by a loan word, *e.g.*, Anglo-Sax. *here*, army (*cf.* Ger. *Heer*), has given way to Fr. *armée*, a past participle like Span. *armada*, and *host* (see p. 147). *Here* has survived in *Hereford*, *harbour* (p. 122), *harbinger* (p. 83), etc., and in the verb *harry* (*cf.* Ger. *verheeren*, to harry). Or a native word may persist in some special sense, e.g., *weed*, a general term for garment in Shakespeare—

> "And there the snake throws her enamel'd skin,
> *Weed* wide enough to wrap a fairy in."
> (*Midsummer Night's Dream*, ii. 2.)

survives in "widow's *weeds*." *Chare*, a turn of work—

> "the maid that milks
> And does the meanest *chares*."
> (*Antony and Cleopatra*, iv. 15.)

survives in *charwoman*, and in American *chore*—

> "Sharlee was . . . concluding the post-prandial *chores*."
> (H. S. HARRISON, *Queed*, Ch. 17.)

Sake, cognate with Ger. *Sache*, thing, cause, and originally meaning a contention at law, has been replaced by *cause*, except in phrases beginning with the preposition *for*. See also *bead* (p. 68). *Unkempt*, uncombed, and *uncouth*, unknown, are fossil remains of obsolete verb forms.

In addition to these main constituents of our language, we have borrowed words, sometimes in considerable numbers, sometimes singly and accidentally, from almost every tongue known to mankind, and every year sees new words added to our vocabulary. The following chapters deal especially with words borrowed from Old French and from the other Romance languages, their origins and journeyings, and the various accidents that have befallen them in English. It is in such words as these that the romance of language is best exemplified, because we can usually trace their history from Latin to modern English, while the earlier history of Anglo-Saxon words is a matter for the philologist.

Words borrowed directly from Latin or Greek lack this intermediate experience, though the study of their original meanings is full of surprises. This, however, is merely a question of opening a Latin or Greek dictionary, if we have not time for the moment's reflexion which would serve the same purpose. Thus, to take a dozen examples at hazard, to *abominate* is to turn shuddering from the evil *omen*, a *generous* man is a man of "race" (*genus*), an *innuendo* can be conveyed "by nodding," to *insult* is to "jump on," a *legend* is something "to be read," a *manual* is a "*hand*-book," an *obligation* is essentially "binding," to *relent* is to "go slow," *rivals* are people living by the same *stream* (*rivus*), a *salary* is an allowance for "salt" (*sal*), a *supercilious* man is fond of lifting his *eyebrows* (*supercilium*), and a *trivial* matter is so commonplace that it can be picked up at the meeting of "three ways" (*trivium*). *Dexterity* implies skill with the "right" hand (*dexter*), while *sinister* preserves the superstition of the ill-omened "left."

It may be remarked here that the number of Latin words used in their unaltered form in every-day English is larger than is generally realised. Besides such phrases as *bona-fide, post-mortem, viva-voce,* or such abbreviations as A.M., *ante meridiem,* D.V., *Deo volente,* and L. s. d., for *libræ, solidi, denarii,* we have, without including scientific terms, many Latin nouns, e.g., *animal, genius, index, odium, omen, premium, radius, scintilla, stimulus, tribunal,* and adjectives, e.g., *complex, lucifer, miser, pauper, maximum, senior,* and the ungrammatical *bonus.* The Lat. *veto,* I forbid, has been worked hard of late. The stage has given us *exit,* he goes out, and the Universities *exeat,* let him go out, while law language contains a number of Latin verb forms, e.g., *affidavit* (late Latin), he has testified, *caveat,* let him beware, *cognovit,* he has recognised—

> "You gave them a *cognovit* for the amount of your costs after the trial, I'm told."
>
>   (*Pickwick,* Ch. 46.)

due to the initial words of certain documents. Similarly *item,* also, is the first word in each paragraph of an inventory. With this we may compare the *purview* of a statute, from the Old Fr. *pourveu* (*pourvu*), provided, with which it used to begin. A *tenet* is what one "holds." *Fiat* means "let it be done." When Mr Weller lamented, "Vy worn't there a *alleybi?*" it is safe to say that he was not consciously using a Latin adverb, nor is the printer who puts in a *viz.* always aware that this is an old abbreviation for *videlicet,* i.e., *videre licet,* it is permissible to see. A *nostrum* is "our" unfailing remedy, and *tandem,* at length, instead of side by side, is a university joke.

Sometimes we have inflected forms of Latin words. A *rebus*[1] is a word or phrase represented "by things." *Requiem,* accusative of *requies,* rest, is the first word of an antiphon used in the mass for the dead, "*Requiem* æternam dona eis, Domine," while *dirge* is the Latin imperative *dirige,* in another antiphon, "*Dirige,* Dominus

---

[1] But the word comes to us from French. In the 16th century such puzzles were called *rébus de Picardie,* because of their popularity in that province.

meus, in conspectu tuo vitam meam." The spelling
dirige was once common—

"Also I byqwethe to eche of the paryshe prystys beying at my
dyryge and masse xiid."

(Will of John Perfay, of Bury St. Edmunds, 1509.)

Query was formerly written *quære*, seek, and *plaudit* is
for *plaudite*, clap your hands. *Debenture* is for *debentur*,
there are owing. *Dominie* is the Latin vocative *domine*,
formerly used by schoolboys in addressing their master,
while *pandy*, a stroke on the hand with a cane, is from
pande palmam, hold out your hand. *Parse* is the Lat.
pars, occurring in the question *Quæ pars orationis?*
What part of speech? *Omnibus*, for all, is a dative
plural. *Limbo* is the ablative of Lat. *limbus*, an edge,
hem, in the phrase "in *limbo* patrum," where *limbus*
is used for the abode of the Old Testament saints on
the verge of Hades. It is already jocular in Shakespeare—

"I have some of 'em in *limbo* patrum, and there they are like
to dance these three days."

(*Henry VIII.*, v. 3.)

Folio, quarto, etc., are ablatives, from the phrases *in folio,
in quarto*, etc., still used in French. *Premises*, earlier
premisses, is a slightly disguised Lat. *præmissas*, the
aforesaid, lit. sent before, used in deeds to avoid
repeating the full description of a property. It is thus
the same word as logical *premisses*, or assumptions.
Quorum is from a legal formula giving a list of persons
"of whom" a certain number must be present. A
teetotum is so called because it has, or once had, on one
of its sides, a *T* standing for *totum*, all. It was also
called simply a *totum*. The other three sides also bore
letters to indicate what share, if any, of the stake they
represented. Cotgrave has *totum* (*toton*), "a kind of

game with a whirle-bone." In spite of the interesting anecdote about the temperance orator with an impediment in his speech, it was probably *teetotum* that suggested *teetotaller.*

We have also a few words unaltered from Greek, e.g., *analysis, aroma, atlas,* the world-sustaining demi-god whose picture used to decorate map-books, *colon, comma, dogma, epitome, miasma, nausea,* lit. sea-sickness, *nectar,* whence the fruit called a *nectarine—*

> " *Nectarine* fruits which the compliant boughs
> Yielded them, sidelong as they sat recline."
>
> (*Paradise Lost,* iv., 332.)

pathos, python, pyx, synopsis, etc. ; but most of our Greek words have passed through French *via* Latin, or are newly manufactured scientific terms, often most unscientifically constructed.

Gamut contains the Gk. *gamma* and the Latin conjunction *ut.* Guy d'Arezzo, who flourished in the 11th century, is said to have introduced the method of indicating the notes by the letters *a* to *g.* For the note below *a* he used the Gk. *gamma.* To him is attri-buted also the series of monosyllables by which the notes are also indicated. They are supposed to be taken from a Latin hymn to St John—

> *Ut* queant laxis *re*sonare fibris
> *Mi*ra gestorum *fa*muli tuorum
> *Sol*ve polluti *la*bii reatum
> Sancte *Io*hannes.

Do is sometimes substituted for *ut* in French, and always in modern English.

In considering the Old French element in English, one has to bear in mind a few elementary philological facts. Nearly all French nouns and adjectives are derived from the accusative. I give, for simplicity, the nominative, adding the stem in the case of imparisyllabic words. The foundation of French is Vulgar Latin, which differs considerably from that we study at school. I only give Vulgar Latin forms where it cannot be avoided. For instance, in dealing with *culverin* (p. 34), I connect Fr. *couleuvre*, adder, with Lat. *cólŭber*, a snake. Every Romance philologist knows that it must represent Vulgar Lat. * *colóbra*; but this form, which, being conjectural, is marked with an asterisk, had better be forgotten by the general reader.

Our modern English words often preserve a French form which no longer exists, or they are taken from dialects, especially those of Normandy and Picardy, which differ greatly from that of Paris. The word *caudle* illustrates both these points. It is the same word as modern Fr. *chaudeau*, "a *caudle;* or, warme broth" (Cotgrave), but it preserves the Old French[1] *-el* and the Picard *c-* for *ch-*. An uncomfortable bridle which used to be employed to silence scolds was called the *branks*. It is a Scottish word, originally applied to a bridle improvised from a halter with a block of wood each side to prevent it from slipping. These blocks correspond to the two parallel levers called the "branches" of a bridle, and *brank* is the Norman *branque*, branch. All the meanings of *patch* answer to those of Fr. *pièce*. It comes from the Old French dialect form *peche*, as *match* comes from *mèche*, and *cratch*, a manger, from *crèche*, of German origin, and ultimately the same word as *crib*. *Pew* is from Old Fr. *puy*, a stage, eminence, Lat. *podium*, which survives in *Puy de Dôme*, the mountain in Auvergne on which Pascal made his experiments with the barometer. *Dupuy*

---

[1] For simplicity the term Old French is used here to include all words not in modern use. Where a modern form exists it is given in parenthesis.

is a common family name in France, but the *Depews*
of the West Indies have kept the older pronunciation.

Many Old French words which live on in England
are obsolete in France. *Chime* is Old Fr. *chimbe* from
Greco-Lat. *cymbalum.* Minsheu (1617) derived *dismal*
from Lat. *dies mali*, evil days. This, says Trench,
" is exactly one of those plausible etymologies which
one learns after a while to reject with contempt." But
Minsheu is substantially right, if we substitute Old
Fr. *dis mal*, which is found as early as 1256. Old Fr.
di, a day, also survives in the names of the days of the
week, *lundi*, etc. In *remainder* and *remnant* we have the
infinitive and present participle of an obsolete Old French
verb derived from Lat. *remanēre. Manor* and *power* are
also Old French infinitives, the first now only used
as a noun (*manoir*), the second represented by *pouvoir.*
Misnomer is the Anglo-French infinitive, " to misname."

In some cases we have preserved meanings now
obsolete in French. *Trump*, in cards, is Fr. *triomphe*,
" the card game called ruffe, or *trump ;* also, the ruffe,
or *trump* at it " (Cotgrave), but the modern French
word for trump is *atout*, to all. *Rappee* is for obsolete
Fr. (tabac) *râpé*, pulverised, rasped. Fr. *talon*, heel,
from Vulgar Lat. * *talo, talon-*, for *talus*, was applied by
falconers to the heel claw of the hawk. This meaning,
obsolete in French, has persisted in English. The *mizen*
mast is the rearmost of three, but the Fr. *mât de misaine*
is the fore-mast, and both come from Ital. *mezzana*,
which means " middle."

As in the case of Latin, we have some inflected
French forms in English. *Lampoon* is from the
archaic Fr. *lampon*, " a drunken song " (Miège, *French
Dict.*, 1688). This is coined from the imperative
lampons, let us drink, regularly used as a refrain
in seditious and satirical songs. We may compare

American *vamoose*, from Span. *vamos*, let us go. The
military *revelly* is the French imperative *réveillez*, wake
up, but in the French army it is called the *diane*. The
gist of a matter is the point in which its importance
really "lies." *Ci-gît* for *ci-gist*, Lat. *jacet*, here lies,
is seen on old tombstones. *Tennis*, says Minsheu,
is so called from Fr. *tenez*, hold, "which word the
Frenchmen, the onely tennis-players, use to speake
when they strike the ball." This etymology, for a
long time regarded as a wild guess, has been shewn
by recent research to be quite correct. The game was
played by French knights in Italy a century before we
find record of it in English. Erasmus tells us that the
server called out *accipe*, to which his opponent replied
mitte, and as French, and not Latin, was certainly the
language of the earliest tennis-players, we may infer
that the spectators named the game from the foreign
word with which each service began. The French
name is *paume*, palm of the hand ; cf. *fives*, also a slang
name for the hand. The archaic *assoil*, Scot. *assoilzie*—

"'God *assoilzie* her,' ejaculated old Elspeth."
(*Antiquary*, Ch. 26.)

is the present subjunctive of the Old Fr. *asoldre*
(*absoudre*), to absolve, used in the stereotyped phrase
Dieus vos asoile, may God absolve you.

A linguistic invasion such as that of English by Old
French is almost unparalleled. We have instances of
the expulsion of one tongue by another, *e.g.*, of the
Celtic dialects of Gaul by Latin and of those of Britain
by Anglo-Saxon. But a real blending of two languages
can only occur when a large section of the population
is bilingual for centuries. This, as we know, was the
case in England. The Norman dialect, already familiar
through inevitable intercourse, was transplanted to

England in 1066. It developed further on its own lines into Anglo-Norman, and then, mixed with other French dialects, for not all the invaders were Normans, and political events brought various French provinces into relation with England, it produced Anglo-French, a somewhat barbarous tongue which was the official language till 1362, and with which our legal jargon is saturated. We find in Anglo - French many words which are unrecorded in continental Old French, among them one which we like to think of as essentially English, viz., *dueté*, duty, an abstract formed from the past participle of Fr. *devoir*.

No dictionary can keep up with the growth of a language. The *New English Dictionary* had done the letter *C* before the *cinematograph* arrived, but got it in under *K*. Words of this kind are manufactured in such numbers that the lexicographer is inclined to wait and see whether they will catch on. In such cases it is hard to prophesy. The population of this country may be divided into those people who have been operated for *appendicitis* and those who are going to be. Yet this word was considered too rare and obscure for insertion in the first volume of the *New English Dictionary* (1888), the greatest word-book that has ever been projected. *Sabotage* looks, unfortunately, as if it had come to stay. It is a derivative of *saboter*, to scamp work, from *sabot*, a wooden shoe, used contemptuously of an inferior article. The great French dictionaries do not know it in this sense, and the *New English Dictionary*, which finished *Sa-* last year, has just missed it. *Hooligan* is not recorded by the *New English Dictionary*. The original *Hooligans* were a spirited Irish family of that name whose proceedings enlivened the drab monotony of life in Southwark about fourteen years ago. The word is younger than the Australian *larrikin*, of doubtful origin (see p. 177), but older than Fr. *apache*. The adoption of the Red Indian name *Apache* for a modern Parisian street ruffian is a curious parallel to the 18th-century use of *Mohock* (Mohawk) for an aristocratic London ruffler.

Heckle is first recorded in its political sense for 1880. The *New English Dictionary* quotes it from *Punch* in connection with the Fourth Party. In Scottish, however, it is old in this sense, so that it is an example of a dialect word that has risen late in life. Its southern form *hatchell* is common in Mid. English in its proper sense of ".teasing" hemp or flax, and the metaphor is exactly the same. *Tease,* earlier *toose,* means to pluck or pull to pieces, hence the name *teasel* for the thistle used by wool-carders. The older form is seen in the derivative *tousle*, the family name *Tozer*, and the dog's name *Towser*. *Feckless*, a common Scottish word, was hardly literary English before Carlyle. It is now quite familiar— " Thriftless, shiftless, *feckless*." (Mr Lloyd George, in the House, 1st November 1911). There is a certain appropriateness in the fact that almost the first writer to use it was James I. It is for *effectless*. I never heard of a *week-end* till I paid a visit to Lancashire in 1883. It has long since invaded the whole island. An old *geezer* has a modern sound, but it is the medieval *guiser*, *guisard*, mummer, which has persisted in dialect and re-entered the language.

The fortunes of a word are sometimes determined by accident. *Glamour* (see p. 134) was popularised by Scott, who found it in old ballad literature. *Grail* would be much less familiar but for Tennyson. *Mascot*, from a Provençal word meaning sorcerer, dates from Audran's operetta *La Mascotte* (1880). *Jingo* first appears in conjurors' jargon of the 17th century. It has been conjectured to represent Basque *jinko*, God, picked up by sailors. If this is the case, it is probably the only pure Basque word in English. The Ingoldsby derivation from St Gengulphus, "sometimes styled 'The Living Jingo,' from the great tenaciousness of vitality exhibited by his severed members," is of course a joke. In 1878, when war with Russia seemed imminent, a music-hall singer, the great Macdermott, delighted large audiences with—

> "We don't want to fight, but, by *Jingo*, if we do,
>   We've got the ships, we've got the men, we've got the
>   money too."

Hence the name *jingo* applied to that ultra-patriotic section of the population which, in war-time, attends to the shouting. Fr. *chauvin*, a jingo, is the name of a real Napoleonic veteran introduced into Scribe's play *Le Soldat Laboureur*. *Barracking* is known to us only through the visits of English cricket teams to Australia. It is said to come from a native Australian word meaning derision. The American *caucus* was first applied (1878) by Lord Beaconsfield to the Birmingham Six Hundred. In 18th-century American it means meeting or discussion. It is probably connected with a North American Indian (Algonkin) word meaning counsellor, an etymology supported by that of *pow-wow*, a palaver or confab, the Algonkin for a medicineman. With these words may be mentioned *Tammany*, now used of a corrupt political body, but, in the 18th century, of a society named after the patron saint of Pennsylvania. The original Tammany was an Indian chief with whom William Penn negotiated for grants of land about the end of the 17th century. *Littoral* first became familiar in connection with Italy's ill-starred Abyssinian adventure, and *hinterland* marks the appearance of Germany as a colonial power—

"'Let us glance a moment,' said Mr Queed, 'at Man, as we
see him first emerging from the dark *hinterlands* of history.'"
(H. S. HARRISON, *Queed*, Ch. 17.)

Sometimes the blunder of a great writer has
enriched the language. Scott's *bartisan*—

> "Its varying circle did combine
> Bulwark, and *bartisan*, and line
> And bastion, tower . . . "
>
> (*Marmion*, vi. 2.)

is a mistake for *bratticing*, timber-work, a word of
obscure origin. It is rather a favourite with writers of
"sword and feather" novels. Other sham antiques are
slug-horn, Chatterton's absurd perversion of the Gaelic
slogan, war-cry, copied by William Morris, and Scott's
extraordinary misuse of *warison*, security, a doublet of
garrison, as though it meant "war sound"—

> "Or straight they sound their *warison*,
> And storm and spoil thy garrison."
>
> (*Lay*, iv. 21.)

Scott also gave currency to *niddering*, a coward—"faith-
less, mansworn,[1] and *niddering*" (*Ivanhoe*, Ch. 43),
which has been copied by Lytton and Kingsley, and
elaborated into *nidderling* by Mr Crockett. It is a
misprint in an early edition of William of Malmesbury
for *niding* or *nithing*, cognate with Ger. *Neid*, envy.
This word, says Camden, is mightier than *Abracadabra*,[2]
for "it hath levied armies and subdued rebellious
enemies." *Derring-do* is used several times by Spenser,

---

[1] From Anglo-Sax. *mān*, deceit, cognate with the first syllable of Ger.
Meineid, perjury.

[2] This word, which looks like an unsuccessful palindrome, belongs to
the language of medieval magic. It seems to be artificially elaborated from
ἀβραξάς, a word of Persian origin used by a sect of Greek gnostics. Its
letters make up the magic number 365, supposed to represent the number
of spirits subject to the supreme being.

who explains it as "manhood and chevalrie." It is due to his misunderstanding of a passage in Lidgate, in which it is an imitation of Chaucer, complicated by a misprint. Scott took it from Spenser—

> "'Singular,' he again muttered to himself, 'if there be two who can do a deed of such *derring-do*.'" (*Ivanhoe*, Ch. 29.)

and from him it passed to Bulwer Lytton and later writers.

Such words as these, the illegitimate offspring of genius, are to be distinguished from the "ghost words" which dimly haunt the dictionaries without ever having lived (see p. 188). Speaking generally, we may say that no word is ever created *de novo*. The names invented for commercial purposes are not exceptions to this law. *Bovril* is compounded of Lat. *bos*, ox, and *vril*, the mysterious power which plays so important a part in Lytton's *Coming Race*, while *Tono-Bungay* suggests *tonic*. The only exception to this is *gas*, the arbitrary coinage of the Belgian chemist Van Helmont in the 17th century. But even this is hardly a new creation, because we have Van Helmont's own statement that the word *chaos* was vaguely present to his mind. *Chortle* has, however, secured a limited currency, and is admitted by the *New English Dictionary*—

> "O frabjous day! Callooh! callay!
> He *chortled* in his joy."
> (*Through the Looking-Glass.*)

and, though an accurate account of the *boojum* is lacking, most people know it to be a dangerous variety of *snark*.

CHAPTER II

WANDERINGS OF WORDS

IN assigning to a word a foreign origin, it is necessary to show how contact between the two languages has taken place, or the particular reasons which have brought about the borrowing. A Chinese word cannot suddenly make its appearance in Anglo-Saxon, though it may quite well do so in modern English. No nautical terms have reached us from the coast of Bohemia (*Winter's Tale*, iii. 3), nor is the vocabulary of the wine trade enriched by Icelandic words. Although we have words from all the languages of Europe, our direct borrowings from some of them have been small. The majority of High German words in English have passed through Old French, and we have taken little from modern German. On the other hand, commerce has introduced a great many words from the old Low German dialects of the North Sea and the Baltic.

The Dutch[1] element in English supplies a useful object lesson on the way in which the borrowing of words naturally takes place. As a great naval power, the Dutch have contributed to our nautical vocabulary a number of words, many of which are easily recognised as near relations; such are *boom* (beam), *skipper*

[1] This includes Flemish, spoken in a large part of Belgium and in the North East of France.

(shipper), *orlop* (over leap).   *Yacht*, properly a "hunting" ship, is cognate with Ger. *Jagd*, hunting, but has
no English kin.   Hexham has *jaght*, zee-roovers schip,
"pinace, or pirats ship."   The modern Dutch spelling is
jacht.   We should expect to find art terms from the
country of Hobbema, Rubens, Vandyke, etc.   See *easel*
(p. 35), *etch* (p. 123), *lay-figure* (p. 154), *sketch* (p. 20).
Landscape, earlier *landskip*, has the suffix which in
English would be *-ship.*   In the 16th century Camden
speaks of "a *landskip*, as they call it."   The Low
Countries were for two centuries the cockpit of Europe,
and many military terms were brought back to England
by Dugald Dalgetty and the armies which "swore
terribly in Flanders."   Such are *cashier* (p. 146), *forlorn
hope* (p. 119), *tattoo* (p. 150).   Other interesting military
words are *leaguer* (lair), recently re-introduced from
South Africa as *laager*, and *furlough*, formerly pronounced to rime with *cough*, from Du. *verlof* (for leave);
cf. archaic Ger. *Verlaub*, now replaced by *Urlaub.*
Knapsack,[1] a food sack, comes from colloquial Du. *knap*,
food, or what the Notts colliers call *snap.*   We also
find it called a *snapsack.*   *Roster* (roaster) is the Dutch
for gridiron ; for a somewhat similar metaphor cf. *cancel*
(p. 80).   The pleasant fiction that—

> "The children of Holland take pleasure in making
>   What the children of England take pleasure in breaking,"

confirms the derivation of *toy* from Du. *tuig*, implement,
thing, stuff, etc., a word, like its German cognate *Zeug*,
with an infinity of meanings.   We now limit *toy* to the
special sense represented by Du. *speel-tuig*, play-thing.
   Our vocabulary dealing with war and fortification is
chiefly French, but most of the French terms come from
Italian.   Addison wrote an article in No. 165 of *The*

---

[1] *Haversack*, oat sack, comes through French from German.

Spectator ridiculing the Frenchified character of the military language of his time, and, in the 16th century, Henri Estienne, patriot, printer, and philologist, lamented that future historians would believe, from the vocabulary employed, that France had learnt the art of war from Italy. As a matter of fact she did. The earliest writers on the new tactics necessitated by villainous saltpetre were Italians trained in condottiere warfare. They were followed by the great French theorists and engineers of the 16th and 17th centuries, who naturally adopted a large number of Italian terms which thus passed later into English.

A considerable number of Spanish and Portuguese words have reached us in a very roundabout way (see pp. 20-4). This is not surprising when we consider how in the 15th and 16th centuries the world was dotted with settlements due to the Portuguese and Spanish adventurers who had a hundred years' start of our own.

There are very few Celtic words either in English or French. In each country the result of conquest was, from the point of view of language, complete. A few words from the Celtic languages have percolated into English in comparatively recent times, but many terms which we associate with the picturesque Highlanders are not Gaelic at all.[1] *Tartan* comes through French from the *Tartars* (see p. 43); *kilt* is a Scandinavian verb, "to tuck up," and *dirk*,[2] of unknown origin, first appears about 1600. For *trews* see p. 109.

A very interesting part of our vocabulary, the *canting*, or rogues', language, dates mostly from the 17th

---

[1] This applies also to some of the clan names, e.g., *Macpherson*, son of the parson, *Macnab*, son of the abbot.

[2] My own conviction is that it is identical with Dan. *dirik, dirk*, a picklock. See *dietrich* (p. 38). An implement used for opening an enemy may well have been named in this way. *Cf.* Du. *opsteeker* (up sticker), "a picklock, a great knife, or a dagger" (Sewel, 1727).

and 18th centuries, and includes contributions from most of the European languages, together with a large Romany element. The early dictionary makers paid great attention to this aspect of the language. Elisha Coles, who published a fairly complete English dictionary in 1676, says in his preface, "'Tis no disparagement to understand the canting terms: it may chance to save your throat from being cut, or (at least), your pocket from being pick'd."

Words often go long journeys. *Boss* is in English a comparatively modern Americanism. But, like many American words, it belongs to the language of the Dutch settlers who founded New Amsterdam (New York). It is Du. *baas*, master, which has thus crossed the Atlantic twice on its way to England. A number of Dutch words have become familiar to us in recent years in consequence of the South African war. One of them, *slim*, 'cute, seems to have been definitely adopted. It is cognate with Ger. *schlimm*, bad, and Eng. *slim*, slender, and the latter word has for centuries been used in the Eastern counties in the very sense in which it has now been re-introduced.

Apricot is a very travelled word. It comes to us from Fr. *abricot*, while the Shakespearean *apricock* (*Richard II.*, iii. 4) represents the Spanish or Portuguese form. Ger. *Aprikose* comes, *via* Dutch, from the French plural. The word was adopted into the Romance languages from Arab. *al-barkok*, where *al* is the definite article (*cf.* examples on p. 106), while *barkok* comes, through medieval Greek, from Vulgar Lat. *præcoquum*, for *præcox*, early-ripe. Thus the word first crossed the Adriatic, passed on to Asia Minor or the North coast of Africa, and then travelling along the Mediterranean re-entered Southern Europe.

Many other Arabic trade words have a similar history. *Carat* comes to us, through French, from Italian *carato*,

"a waight or degree called a *caract*" (Florio). The
Italian word is from Arabic, but the latter is a corruption of Gk. κεράτιον, fruit of the locust tree, lit. little
horn, also used of a small weight. The verb to *garble*,
now used only of confusing or falsifying,[1] meant originally to sort or sift, especially spices—

"*Garbler* of spices is an officer of great antiquity in the city of
London, who may enter into any shop, warehouse, etc., to view
and search drugs, spices, etc., and to *garble* the same and make
them clean."—(Cowel's *Interpreter.*)

It represents Span. *garbellar*, from *garbello*, a sieve.
This comes from Arab. *garbil*, a sieve, borrowed
from Lat. *cribellum*, diminutive of *cribrum*. *Quintal*,
an old word for hundredweight, looks as if it had
something to do with five. Fr. and Span. *quintal* are
from Arab. *qintar*, hundredweight, which is Lat. *cen-
tenarium* (whence directly Ger. *Zentner*, hundredweight).
The French word passed into Dutch, and gave, with a
diminutive ending, *kindekijn*, now replaced by *kinnetje*,
a firkin.[2] We have adopted it as *kilderkin*. With these
examples of words that have passed through Arabic may
be mentioned *talisman*, not a very old word in Europe,
from Arab. *telsam*, magic picture, ultimately from Gk.
τελεῖν, to initiate into mysteries, lit. to accomplish, and
effendi, a Turkish corruption of Gk. αὐθέντης, a master,
cognate with *authentic*.

Hussar seems to be a late Latin word which
passed into Greece and then entered Central Europe
via the Balkans. It comes into 16th-century German
from Hungar. *huszar*, freebooter. This is from a

---

[1] "It was a wholly *garbled* version of what never took place" (Mr
Birrell, in the House, 26th Oct. 1911). The bull appears to be a laudable
concession to Irish national feeling.

[2] Formerly *ferdekin*, a derivative of Du. *vierde*, fourth ; cf. *farthing*, a
little fourth.

Servian word which means also pirate. It represents medieval Gk. κουρσάριος, a transliteration of Vulgar Lat. *cursarius*, from *currere*, to run, which occurs also with the sense of pirate in medieval Latin. *Hussar* is thus a doublet of *corsair*. The immediate source of *sketch* is Du. *schets*, "draught of any picture" (Hexham), from Ital. *schizzo*, "an ingrosement or first rough draught of anything" (Florio), whence also Fr. *esquisse* and Ger. *Skizze*. The Italian word represents Greco-Lat. *schedium*, an extempore effort.

Assassin and *slave* are of historic interest. *Assassin*, though not very old in English, dates from the Crusades. Its oldest European form is Ital. *assassino*, and it was adopted into French in the 16th century. Henri Estienne, whose fiery patriotism entered even into philological questions, reproaches his countrymen for using foreign terms. They should only adopt, he says, Italian words which express Italian qualities hitherto unknown to the French, such as *assassin, charlatan, poltron!* *Assassin* is really a plural, from the *hachaschin*, eaters of *haschish*, who executed the decrees of the Old Man of the Mountains. It was one of these who stabbed Edward Longshanks at Acre. The first *slaves* were captive *Slavonians*. We find the word in most of the European languages. The fact that none of the Western tribes of the race called themselves *Slavs* or *Slavonians* shows that the word could not have entered Europe *via* Germany, where the Slavs were called Wends. It must have come from the Byzantine empire *via* Italy.

Some Spanish words have also come to us by the indirect route. The *cocoa*, which is grateful and comforting, was formerly spelt *cacao*, as in French and German. It is a Mexican word. The *cocoa* of *cocoa-nut* is for *coco*, a Spanish baby word for an ugly face or bogie-man. The black marks at one end of the nut give it, especially before the removal of the fibrous husk, some resemblance to a ferocious face. Stevens (1706) explains *coco* as " the word us'd to fright children ; as we say the Bulbeggar."

Mustang seems to represent two words, *mestengo y mostrenco*, "a straier" (Percyvall). The first appears to be connected with *mesta*, "a monthly fair among herdsmen ; also, the laws to be observed by all that keep or deal in cattle" (Stevens), and the second with *mostrar*, to show, the finder being expected to advertise a stray. The original *mustangs* were of course descended from the strayed horses of the Spanish *conquistadors*. *Ranch*, Span. *rancho*, a row (of huts), is a doublet of *rank*, from Fr. *rang*, old Fr. *reng*, Old High Ger. *hring*, a ring. Thus what is now usually straight was once circular, the ground idea of ar*r*ange-ment surviving. Another doublet is Fr. *harangue*, due to the French inability to pronounce *hr* (see p. 50), a speech delivered in the ring. *Cf.* also Ital. *aringo*, "a riding or carreering place, a liste for horses, or feates of armes : a declamation, an oration, a noise, a common loud speech " (Florio), in which the " ring " idea is also prominent.

Other "cow-boy" words of Spanish origin are the less familiar *cinch*, girth of a horse, Span. *cincha*, from Lat. *cingula*, also used metaphorically—

" The state of the elements enabled Mother Nature ' to get a *cinch*,' on an honourable æstheticism."—(Snaith, Mrs Fitz, Ch. 1.)

and the formidable riding-whip called a *quirt*, Span. *cuerda*, cord. We have the same transference of mean-ing in Span. *reata*, a rope, from the verb *reatar*, to bind together, Lat. *re-aptare*. This means a tethering rope in Bret Harte, but in contemporary novels of Californian life it is used for a whip. Combined with the definite article, *la reata*, it has given *lariat*, a familiar word in literature of the Buffalo Bill character. *Lasso*, Span. *lazo*, Lat. *laqueus*, snare, is a doublet of Eng. *lace*.

When, in the *Song of Hiawatha*—

> "Gitche Manito, the mighty,
> Smoked the *calumet*, the Peace-pipe,
> As a signal to the nations,"

he was using an implement with a French name. *Calumet* is an Old Norman word for *chalumeau*, reed, pipe, a diminutive from Lat. *calamus*. It was naturally applied by early French voyagers to the "long reed for a pipe stem." English *shawm* is the same word without the diminutive ending. Another Old French word, once common in English, but now found only in dialect, is *felon*, a whitlow. It is used more than once by Mr Hardy—

> "I've been visiting to Bath because I had a *felon* on my thumb."—(*Far from the Madding Crowd*, Ch. xxxiii.)

This is still an everyday word in Canada and the United States. It is a metaphorical use of *felon*, a fell villain. A whitlow was called in Latin *furunculus*, "a little theefe; a sore in the bodie called a *fellon*" (Cooper), whence Fr. *furoncle*, or *froncle*, "the hot and hard bumpe, or swelling, tearmed, a *fellon*" (Cotgrave). Another Latin name for it was *tagax*, "a *felon* on a man's finger" (Cooper), lit. thievish. One of its Spanish names is *padrastro*, lit. step-father. I am told that an "agnail" was formerly called a "step-mother" in Yorkshire. This is a good example of the semantic method in etymology (see pp. 92-6).

Some of the above instances show how near to home we can often track a word which at first sight appears to belong to another continent. This is still more strikingly exemplified in the case of Portuguese words, which have an almost uncanny way of pretending to be African or Indian. Some readers will, I think, be surprised to hear that *assegai* occurs in Chaucer, though in a form not easily recognisable. It is a Berber word, which passed through Spanish and Portuguese into French and English. We find Fr. *archegaie* in the 14th century, *azagaie* in Rabelais, and the modern form *zagaie* in Cotgrave, who describes it as "a fashion of slender, long, and long-headed pike, used by the Moorish horsemen." In Mid. English *l'archegaie* was corrupted by folk etymology (see p. 106) into *lancegay*, *launcegaye*, the form used by Chaucer. The use of this weapon was prohibited by statute in 1406, hence the early disappearance of the word.

Another "Zulu" word which has travelled a long way is *kraal*. This is a contracted Dutch form from Port. *curral*, a sheepfold (*cf.* Span. *corral*, a pen, enclosure). Both *assegai* and *kraal* were taken to South East Africa by the Portuguese and then adopted by the Boers and Kafirs.[1] *Sjambok* occurs in 17th-century accounts of India in the form *chawbuck*. It is a Persian word, spelt *chabouk* by Moore, in *Lalla Rookh*. It was adopted by the Portuguese as *chabuco*, "(in the Portuguese India) a whip or scourge"[2] (Vieyra, *Port. Dict.*, 1794). *Fetish*, an African idol, first occurs in the records of the early navigators, collected and published by Purchas and Hakluyt. It is the Port. *feitiço*, Lat. *factitius*, artificial, applied by the Portuguese explorers

---

[1] *Kafir* (Arab.) means infidel.

[2] Eng. *chawbuck* is used in connection with the punishment we call the *bastinado*. This is a corruption of Span. *bastonada*, "a stroke with a club or staff" (Stevens, 1706). On the other hand, we extend the meaning of *drub*, the Arabic word for *bastinado*, to a beating of any kind.

to the graven images of the heathen. The corresponding Old Fr. *faitis* is rather a complimentary adjective, and everyone remembers the lady in Chaucer who spoke French fairly and *fetousli*. *Palaver*, also a travellers' word from the African coast, is Port. *palavra*, word, speech, Greco-Lat. *parabola*. It is thus a doublet of *parole* and *parable*, and is related to *parley*. *Ayah*, an Indian nurse, is Port. *aia*, nurse, of unknown origin. *Caste* is Port. *casta*, pure, and a doublet of *chaste*. *Tank*, an Anglo-Indian word of which the meaning has narrowed in this country, is Port. *tanque*, a pool or cistern, Lat. *stagnum*, whence Old Fr. *estang* (*étang*) and provincial Eng. *stank*, a dam, or a pond banked round. *Cobra* is the Portuguese for snake, cognate with Fr. *couleuvre*, Lat. *coluber* (see p. 7). We use it as an abbreviation for *cobra de capello*, hooded snake, the second part of which is identical with Fr. *chapeau* and cognate with *cape*, *chapel* (p. 141), *chaplet*, a garland, and *chaperon*, a "protecting" hood. From still further afield than India comes *joss*, a Chinese god, a corruption of Port. *deos*, Lat. *deus*. Even *mandarin* comes from Portuguese, and not Chinese, but it is of Eastern origin, probably Malay.

The word *gorilla* is perhaps African, but more than two thousand years separate its first appearance from its present use. In the 5th or 6th century, B.C., a Carthaginian navigator named Hanno sailed beyond the Pillars of Hercules along the west coast of Africa. He probably followed very much the same route as Sir Richard Dalyngridge and Saxon Hugh when they voyaged with Witta the Viking. He wrote in Punic a record of his adventures, which was received with the incredulity usually accorded to travellers' tales. Among the wonders he encountered were some hairy savages called *gorillas*. His work was translated into

Greek and later on into several European languages, so that the word became familiar to naturalists. In 1847 it was applied to the giant ape, which had recently become known to naturalists.

The origin of the word *silk* is a curious problem. It is usually explained as from Greco-Lat. *sericum*, a name derived from an Eastern people called the *Seres*, presumably the Chinese. It appears in Anglo-Saxon as *seolc*. Now, at that early period, words of Latin origin came to us by the overland route and left traces of their passage. But all the Romance languages use for silk a name derived from Lat. *sæta*, bristle, and this name has penetrated even into German (*Seide*) and Dutch (*zijde*). The derivatives of *sericum* stand for another material, *serge*. Nor can it be assumed that the *r* of the Latin word would have become in English always *l* and never *r*. There are races which cannot sound the letter *r*, but we are not one of them. As the word *silk* is found also in Old Norse, Swedish, Danish, and Old Slavonian, the natural inference is that it must have reached us along the north of Europe, and, if derived from *sericum*, it must, somewhere in Asia, have passed through a language which had no *r*.

CHAPTER III

WORDS OF POPULAR MANUFACTURE

IN a sense, all nomenclature, apart from purely scientific language, is popular. But real meanings are often so rapidly obscured that words become mere labels and cease to call up the image or the poetic idea with which they were first associated. To take a simple instance, how many people realise that the *daisy* is the "day's eye?" In studying that part of our vocabulary which especially illustrates the tendencies shown in popular name-giving, one is struck by the keen observation and imaginative power shown by our far-off ancestors, and the lack of these qualities in later ages.

Perhaps in no part of the language does this appear so clearly as in the names of plants and flowers. The most primitive way of naming a flower is from some observed resemblance, and it is curious to notice the parallelism of this process in various languages. Thus our *crowfoot, crane's bill, larkspur, monkshood, snapdragon*, are in German *Hahnenfuss* (cock's foot), *Storchschnabel* (stork's bill), *Rittersporn* (knight's spur), *Eisenhut* (iron hat), *Löwenmaul* (lion's mouth). I have purposely chosen instances in which the correspondence is not absolute, because examples like *Löwenzahn* (lion's tooth), *dandelion* (Fr. *dent de lion*) may be suspected of being mere translations. I give the names in most general use, but the provincial variants are numerous, though usually of the same type. The French names of the flowers mentioned are still more like the English. The more learned words which sometimes replace the above are, though now felt as mere symbols, of similar origin, e.g., *geranium* and *pelargonium*, used for the cultivated *crane's bill*, are derived from the Greek for crane and stork respectively. So also in *chelidonium*, whence our *celandine* or *swallow-wort*, we have the Greek for swallow.

In the English names of plants we observe various tendencies of the popular imagination. We have the crudeness of *cowslip* for earlier *cowslop*, cow-dung, and many old names of unquotable coarseness, the quaintness of *Sweet William, lords and ladies, bachelors' buttons, dead men's fingers*, and the exquisite poetry of *forget-me-not, heart's ease, love in a mist, traveller's joy*. There is also a special group named from medicinal properties, such as *feverfew*, a doublet of *febrifuge, tansy*, Fr. *tanaisie*, from Greco-Lat. *athanasia*, immortality. We may compare the learned *saxifrage*, stone-breaker, of which the Spanish doublet is *sassafras*. The German name is *Steinbrech*.

There must have been a time when a simple instinct for poetry was possessed by all nations, as it still is by uncivilised races and children. Among European nations this instinct appears to be dead for ever. We can name neither a mountain nor a flower. Our Mount Costigan, Mount Perry, Mount William cut a sorry figure beside the peaks of the Bernese Oberland, the Monk, the Maiden, the Storm Pike, the Dark Eagle Pike. Occasionally a race which is accidentally brought into closer contact with nature may have a happy inspiration, such as the *Drakenberg* (dragon mountain) or *Weenen* [1] (weeping) of the old *vortrekkers.* But the Cliff of the Falling Flowers, the name of a precipice over which the Korean queens cast themselves to escape dishonour, represents an imaginative realm which is closed to us.[2] The botanist who describes a new flower hastens to join the company of Messrs *Dahl, Fuchs, Lobel, Magnol* and *Wister,* while fresh varieties are used to immortalise a florist and his family.

The names of fruits, perhaps because they lend themselves less easily to imaginative treatment, are even duller than modern names of flowers. The only English names are the *apple* and the *berry.* New fruits either retained their foreign names (*cherry, peach, pear, quince*) or were violently converted into *apples* or *berries,* usually the former. This practice is common to the European languages, the *apple* being regarded as the typical fruit. Thus the orange is usually called in North Germany *Apfelsine,* apple of China, with which we may compare our "China orange." In South Germany it was called *Pomeranze* (now used especially of the Seville orange), from Ital. *pomo,* apple, *arancia,* orange. Fr. *orange* is folk-etymology (*or,* gold) for * *arange,* from Arab. *narandj,* whence Span. *naranja.* *Melon* is simply the Greek for "apple," and has also given us *marmalade,* which comes, through French, from Port. *marmelada,* quince jam, a derivative of Greco-Lat. *melimelum,* quince, lit. honey-apple. *Pine-apple* meant "fir-cone" as late as the 17th century, as Fr. *pomme de pin* still does. The fruit (Fr. *ananas*) was named from its shape, which closely resembles that of a fir-cone.

---

[1] A place where a large number of settlers with their wives and children were massacred by the Zulus.

[2] "Two mountains near Dublin, which we, keeping in the grocery line, have called the Great and the Little Sugarloaf, are named in Irish the Golden Spears."—(Trench, *On the Study of Words.*)

Pomegranate means "apple with seeds." We also find the apricot, lemon (*pomcitron*), peach, and quince all described as apples.

At least one fruit, the *greengage*, is named from a person, Sir William Gage, a gentleman of Suffolk, who popularised its cultivation early in the 18th century. It happens that the French name of the fruit, *reine-claude* (pronounced *glaude*), is also personal, from the wife of Francis I.

Animal nomenclature shows some strange vagaries. The resemblance of the *hippopotamus*, lit. river-horse, to the horse, hardly extends beyond their common possession of four legs. The lion would hardly recognise himself in the *ant-lion* or the *sea-lion*, still less in the *chameleon*, lit. earth-lion, the first element of which occurs also in *camomile*, earth-apple. The *guinea-pig* is not a pig, nor does it come from Guinea (see p. 47). *Porcupine* means "spiny pig." It has an extraordinary number of early variants, and Shakespeare wrote it *por-pentine*. One Mid. English form was *porkpoint*. The French name has hesitated between *spine* and *spike*. The modern form is *porc-épic*, but Palsgrave has "*porkepyn* a beest, *porc espin*." *Porpoise* is from Old Fr. *porpeis*, for *porc peis* (Lat. *porcus piscis*), pig-fish. The modern French name is *marsouin*, from Ger. *Meerschwein*, sea-pig; *cf.* the name *sea-hog*, formerly used in English. Old Fr. *peis* survives also in *grampus*, Anglo-Fr. *grampais* for *grand peis*, big fish, but the usual Old French word is *craspeis* or *graspeis*, fat fish.

The *caterpillar* seems to have suggested in turn a cat and a dog. Our word is corrupted by folk-etymology from Old Fr. *chatepeleuse*, "a corne-devouring mite, or weevell" (Cotgrave). This probably means "woolly cat," just as a common species is popularly called *woolly bear*, but it was understood as being connected with the

French verb *peler*, "to *pill*, pare, barke, unrinde, unskin" (Cotgrave). The modern French name *chenille* is a derivative of *chien*, dog. It has also been applied to a fabric of a woolly nature; *cf.* the botanical *catkin*, which is in Fr. *chaton*, kitten.

Some animals bear nicknames. *Dotterel* means "dotard," and *dodo* is from the Port. *doudo*, mad. *Ferret* is from Fr. *furet*, a diminutive from Lat. *fur*, thief. *Shark* was used of a sharper or greedy parasite before it was applied to the fish. This, in the records of the Elizabethan voyagers, is more often called by its Spanish name *tiburon*, whence Cape Tiburon, in Haiti. The origin of *shark* is unknown, but it appears to be identical with *shirk*, for which we find earlier *sherk*. We find Ital. *scrocco* (whence Fr. *escroc*), Ger. *Schurke*, Du. *schurk*, rascal, all rendered "shark" in early dictionaries, but the relationship of these words is not clear. The *palmer*, *i.e.* pilgrim, worm is so called from his wandering habits. *Ortolan* means "gardener" (Lat. *hortus*, garden). It comes to us through French from Ital. *ortolano*, "a gardener, an orchard keeper. Also a kinde of daintie birde in Italie, some take it to be the linnet" (Florio). We may compare Fr. *bouvreuil*, bull-finch, a diminutive of *bouvier*, ox-herd. This is called in German *Dompfaffe*, a contemptuous name for a cathedral canon. Fr. *moineau*, sparrow, is a diminutive of *moine*, monk. The wagtail is called in French *lavandière*, laundress, from the up and down motion of its tail suggesting the washerwoman's beetle, and *bergeronnette*, little shepherdess, from its habit of following the sheep. *Adjutant*, the nickname of the solemn Indian stork, is clearly due to Mr Atkins, and the *secretary* bird is so named because some of his head feathers suggest a quill pen behind an ear.

The converse process of people being nicknamed

from animals is also common and the metaphor is usually pretty obvious. An interesting case is *shrew*, a libel on a very inoffensive little animal, the *shrew-mouse*, Anglo-Sax. *scrēawa*. Cooper describes *mus araneus* as " a kinde of mise called a *shrew*, which if he go over a beastes backe he shall be lame in the chyne ; if he byte it swelleth to the heart and the beast dyeth." This " information " is derived from Pliny, but the superstition is found in Greek. The epithet was, up to Shakespeare's time, applied indifferently to both sexes. From *shrew* is derived *shrewd*, earlier *shrewed*, the meaning of which has become much milder than when Henry VIII. said to Cranmer—

> " The common voice I see is verified
> Of thee which says, ' Do my lord of Canterbury
> A *shrewd* turn, and he's your friend for ever.' "
>
> (*Henry VIII.*, v. 2.)

The title *Dauphin*, lit. dolphin, commemorates the absorption into the French monarchy, in 1349, of the lordship of Dauphiné, the cognisance of which was three dolphins.

The application of animals' names to diseases is a familiar phenomenon, e.g., *cancer* (and *canker*), crab, and *lupus*, wolf. To this class belongs *mulligrubs*, for which we find in the 17th century also *mouldy grubs*. Its oldest meaning is stomach-ache, still given in Hotten's Slang Dictionary (1864). *Mully* is still used in dialect for mouldy, earthy, and *grub* was once the regular word for worm. The Latin name for the same discomfort was *verminatio*. For the later transition of meaning we may compare *megrims*, from Fr. *migraine*, head-ache, Greco-Lat. *hemicrania*, lit. half skull, because supposed to affect one side only of the head.

A good many names of plants and animals have a

religious origin. *Hollyhock* is for *holy hock*, from Anglo-Sax. *hoc*, mallow: for the pronunciation cf. *holiday*. *Halibut* means *holy butt*, the latter word being an old name for flat fish; for this form of *holy*, cf. *halidom*. *Lady* in names of flowers such as *lady's bedstraw*, *lady's garter*, *lady's slipper*, is for Our Lady. So also in *lady-bird*, called in French *bête à bon Dieu* and in German *Marienkäfer*, Mary's beetle. Here may be mentioned *samphire*, from Old Fr. *herbe de Saint Pierre*, "sampire, crestmarin" (Cotgrave). The *filbert*, earlier *philibert*, is named from St Philibert, the nut being ripe by St Philibert's day (22nd Aug.). We may compare Ger. *Lambertsnuss*, filbert, originally "Lombard nut," but popularly associated with St Lambert's day (17th Sept.).

The application of baptismal names to animals is a very general practice, though the reason for the selection of the particular name is not always clear. The most famous of such names is *Renard* the Fox. The Old French for fox is *goupil*, a derivative of Lat. *vulpes*, fox. The hero of the great beast epic of the Middle Ages is *Renard le goupil*, and the fact that *renard* has now completely supplanted *goupil* shows how popular the Renard legends must have been. *Renard* is from Old High Ger. *regin-hart*, strong in counsel; *cf.* our names *Reginald* and *Reynold*, and Scot. *Ronald*, of Norse origin. From the same source come *Chantecler*, lit. sing clear, the cock, and *Partlet*, the hen, while *Bruin*, the bear, lit. "brown," is from the Dutch version of the epic. In the Low German version, *Reinke de Vos*, the ape's name is *Moneke*, a diminutive corresponding to Ital. *monicchio*, "a pugge, a *munkie*, an ape" (Florio), the earlier history of which is much disputed. The cat was called *Tibert*, whence the allusions to Tybalt's nine lives in *Romeo and Juliet* (iii. 1).

The fact that the donkey was at one time regularly

called *Cuddy* made *Cuthbert* for a long period unpopular as a baptismal name. He is now often called *Neddy*. The hare was called *Wat* (*Walter*) in Tudor times. In the *Roman de Renard* he is *Couard*, whence *coward*, a derivative of Old Fr. *coue* (*queue*), tail, from Lat. *cauda*. The idea is that of the tail between the legs, so that the name is etymologically not very appropriate to the hare. *Parrot*, for earlier *perrot*, means "little Peter." Fr. *pierrot* is still used for the sparrow. The family name *Perrot* is sometimes a nickname, "the chatterer," but can also mean literally "little Peter," just as *Emmot* means "little Emma," and *Marriot* "little Mary." The extension *Poll Parrot* is thus a kind of hermaphrodite. *Petrel* is of cognate origin, with an allusion to St Peter's walking upon the sea; *cf.* its German name, *Sankt Peters Vogel*. Sailors call the petrel *Mother Carey's chicken*, probably a nautical corruption of some old Spanish or Italian name. But in spite of ingenious guesses, this lady's genealogy remains as obscure as that of Davy Jones or the Jolly Roger.

Robin has practically replaced *red-breast*. The *martin* is in French *martinet*, and the name may have been given in allusion to the southward flight of this swallow about Martinmas; but the king-fisher, not a migrant bird, is called *martin-pêcheur*, formerly also *martinet pêcheur* or *oiseau de Saint-Martin*, so that *martin* may be due to some other association. Sometimes the double name survives. We no longer say *Philip sparrow*, but *Jack ass*, *Jack daw*, *Jenny wren*, *Tom tit* (see p. 113), and the inclusive *Dicky bird*, are still familiar. With these we may compare *Hob* (*i.e.* Robert) *goblin*. *Madge owlet*, or simply *Madge*, was once common. For *Mag pie* we find also the diminutive *Maggot pie*. Cotgrave has *pie*, "a pye, pyannat, meggatapie." In Old French it was also called *jaquette*, "a proper name for a woman; also, a piannat, or megatapie."

The connection of this word, Fr. *pie*, Lat. *pica*, with the comestible *pie* is uncertain, but it seems likely that the magpie's habit of collecting miscellaneous trifles caused its name to be given to a dish of uncertain constituents. It is a curious coincidence that the obsolete *chuet* or *chewet* meant both a round pie and a jackdaw. It is uncertain in which of the two senses Prince Hal applies the name to Falstaff (1 *Henry IV.*, v. 1). Fr. *chouette*, screech-owl, formerly meant also "a chough, daw, jack-daw" (Cotgrave).

A *piebald* horse is one *balled* like a magpie. *Ball* is a Celtic word for a white mark, especially on the forehead; hence the tavern sign of the *Baldfaced Stag*. Our adjective *bald* is thus a past participle.

Things are often named from animals. *Crane, kite, donkey-engine, monkey-wrench, pig-iron*, etc., are simple cases. The *crane* picture is so striking that we are not surprised to find it literally reproduced in many other languages. For *kite* we have Fr. *cerf-volant*, flying stag, a name also applied to the stag-beetle, and Ger. *Drachen*, dragon. It is natural that terrifying names should have been given to early fire-arms. Many of these, e.g., *basilisk, serpent, falconet, saker* (from Fr. *sacre*, a kind of hawk), are obsolete. More familiar is *culverin*, Fr. *couleuvrine*, a derivative of *couleuvre*, adder, Lat. *coluber*—

> "And thou hast talk'd
> Of sallies and retires, of trenches, tents,
> Of palisadoes, frontiers, parapets,
> Of basilisks, of cannon, *culverin*."
>
> (1 *Henry IV.*, ii. 3.)

One name for a handgun was *dragon*, whence our

dragoon, originally applied to a kind of mounted infantry or carbineers. *Musket* was the name of a small hawk. Mistress Ford uses it playfully to her page—

> "How now, my eyas [1]-*musket*, what news with you?"
>
> (*Merry Wives*, iii. 3.)

But the hawk was so nicknamed from its small size. Fr. *mousquet*, now replaced in the hawk sense by *émouchet*, is from Ital. *moschetto*, a diminutive from Lat. *musca*, fly. Thus *mosquito* (Spanish) and *musket* are doublets.

Porcelain comes, through French, from Ital. *porcellana*, "a kinde of fine earth called *porcelane*, whereof they make fine china dishes, called *porcellan* dishes" (Florio). This is, however, a transferred meaning, *porcellana* being the name of a particularly glossy shell called the "Venus shell." It is a derivative of Lat. *porcus*, pig. *Easel* comes, with many other painters' terms, from Holland. It is Du. *ezel*, ass, which, like Ger. *Esel*, comes from Lat. *asinus*. For its metaphorical application we may compare Fr. *chevalet*, easel, lit. "little horse," and Eng. "clothes *horse*."

Objects often bear the names of individuals. Such are *albert* chain, *brougham*, *victoria*, *wellington* boot. Middle aged people can remember ladies wearing a red blouse called a *garibaldi*.[2] Sometimes an inventor is immortalised, e.g., *mackintosh* and *shrapnel*, both due to 19th-century inventors. The more recent *maxim* is named from one who, according to the late Lord Salisbury, has saved many of his fellow-men from dying of old age. Other benefactors are commemorated in *derringer*, first recorded in Bret

---

[1] For *eyas*, see p. 105.

[2] To the same period belongs the colour *magenta*, from the victory of the French over the Austrians at Magenta in 1859.

Harte, and *bowie*, which occurs in Dickens' *American Notes*. *Sandwich* and *spencer* are coupled in an old rime—

> "Two noble earls, whom, if I quote,
> Some folks might call me sinner ;
> The one invented half a coat,
> The other half a dinner."

An Earl Spencer (1782-1845) made a short overcoat fashionable for some time. An Earl of Sandwich (1718-1792) invented a form of light refreshment which enabled him to take a meal without leaving the gaming table. It does not appear that *Billy Cock* is to be classed with the above, or with *Chesterfield*, *Chippendale & Co.* The *New English Dictionary* quotes (from 1721) a description of the Oxford "blood" in his "*bully-cocked* hat," worn aggressively on one side. *Pinchbeck* was a London watchmaker (*fl. c.* 1700), and *doily* is from *Doyley*, a linen-draper of the same period. Etienne de *Silhouette* was French finance minister in 1759, but the application of his name to a black profile portrait is variously explained. *Negus* was first brewed in Queen Anne's reign by Colonel Francis Negus.

The first *orrery* was constructed by the Earl of Orrery (*c.* 1700). *Galvani* and *Volta* were Italian scientists of the 18th century. *Mesmer* was a German physician of the same period. *Nicotine* is named from Jean Nicot, French ambassador at Lisbon, who sent some tobacco plants to Catherine de Médicis in 1560. He also compiled the first Old French dictionary. The gallows-shaped contrivance called a *derrick* perpetuates the name of a famous hangman who officiated in London about 1600. It is a Dutch name, identical with *Dietrich*, *Theodoric*, and *Dirk* (Hatteraick). Conversely the Fr. *potence*, gallows, meant originally a

bracket or support, Lat. *potentia*, power. The origin
of *darbies*, handcuffs, is unknown, but the line—

> "To bind such babes in father *Derbies* bands,"
> (GASCOIGNE, *The Steel Glass*, 1576.)

suggests connection with some eminent gaoler or thief-
taker.

Occasionally a verb is formed from a proper name.
On the model of *tantalise*, from the punishment of
Tantalus, we have, *bowdlerise*, from *Bowdler*, who
published an expurgated "family Shakespeare" in
1818; cf. *macadamise*. *Burke* and *boycott* commemorate
a scoundrel and a victim. The latter word, from the
treatment of Captain Boycott of Co. Mayo in 1880,
seems to have supplied a want, for Fr. *boycotter* and
Ger. *boycottieren* are already every-day words. Burke
was hanged at Edinburgh in 1829 for murdering
people by suffocation in order to dispose of their
bodies to medical schools. We now use the verb only
of "stifling" discussion, but in the Ingoldsby Legends
it still has the original sense—

> "But, when beat on his knees,
> That confounded De Guise
> Came behind with the 'fogle' that caused all this breeze,
> Whipp'd it tight round his neck, and, when backward he'd jerk'd
> him,
> The rest of the rascals jump'd on him and *Burk'd* him."
> *(The Tragedy.)*

Jarvey, the slang name for a coachman, was in the
18th century *Jervis* or *Jarvis*, but history is silent as to
this English *Jehu*. A *pasquinade* was originally an
anonymous lampoon affixed to a statue of a gladiator
which still stands in Rome. The statue is said to
have been nicknamed from a scandal-loving cobbler
named Pasquino. Florio has *pasquino*, "a statue in

Rome on whom all libels, railings, detractions, and satirical invectives are fathered." *Pamphlet* is an extended use of Old Fr. *Pamphilet*, the name of a Latin poem by one *Pamphilus* which was popular in the Middle Ages. The suffix *-et* was often used in this way, *e.g.*, the translation of Æsop's fables by Marie de France was called *Ysopet*, and Cato's moral maxims had the title *Catonet*, or Parvus Cato. Modern Fr. *pamphlet*, borrowed back from English, has always the sense of polemical writing. In Eng. *libel*, lit. "little book," we see a converse development of meaning. A three-quarter portrait of fixed dimensions is called a *kitcat*—

"It is not easy to see why he should have chosen to produce a replica, or rather a *kitcat*." (*Journal of Education*, Oct. 1911.)

The name comes from the portraits of members of the *Kitcat* Club, painted by Kneller. *Kit Kat*, Christopher Kat, was a pastrycook at whose shop the club used to dine.

Implements and domestic objects sometimes bear christian names. We may mention spinning-*jenny*, and the innumerable meanings of *jack*. *Davit*, earlier *daviot*, is a diminutive of David. Fr. *davier*, formerly *daviet*, is used of several mechanical contrivances, including a pick-lock. A kind of davit is called in Ger. *Jütte*, a diminutive of Judith. The implement by which the burglar earns his daily bread is now called a *jemmy*, but in the 17th century we also find *bess* and *betty*. The French name is *rossignol*, nightingale. The German burglar calls it *Dietrich*, *Peterchen*, or *Klaus*, and the contracted forms of the first name, *dyrk* and *dirk*, have passed into Swedish and Danish with the same meaning. In Italian a pick-lock is called *grimaldello*, a diminutive of the name Grimaldo.

A kitchen wench was once called a *malkin*

(*Coriolanus*, ii. 1). This is a diminutive of Matilda or Mary, possibly of both. *Grimalkin*, applied to a fiend in the shape of a cat, is for *gray malkin*—

> "I come, *Graymalkin*." (*Macbeth*, i. 1.)

Malkin was also the regular name for a mop. Cotgrave has *escouillon* (*écouvillon*), " a wispe, or dish-clowt; a *maukin*, or drag, to cleanse, or sweepe an oven." *Écouvillon* is a derivative of Lat. *scopa*, broom. Now another French word which means both "kitchen servant" and "dish-clout" is *souillon*, from *souiller*, to soil. What share each of these words, the sense development of which has been the converse of that of *malkin*, has in Eng. *scullion* is hard to say. The only thing certain is that *scullion* is not related to *scullery*, Old Fr. *escuelerie*, a collective from Old Fr. *escuelle* (*écuelle*), dish, from Lat. *scutella*.

A *doll* was formerly called a *baby* or *puppet*. It is the abbreviation of *Dorothy*, for we find it called a *doroty* in Scottish. We may compare Fr. *marionnette*, a double diminutive of Mary, explained by Cotgrave as "little Marian or Mal; also, a puppet." *Little Mary*, in another sense, has been recently, but perhaps definitely, adopted into our language. Another old name for doll is *mammet*. Capulet uses it contemptuously to his daughter—

> "And then to have a wretched puling fool,
> A whining *mammet*, in her fortune's tender,
> To answer : 'I'll not wed,'—' I cannot love.'"
> (*Romeo and Juliet*, iii. 5.)

Its earlier form is *maumet*, meaning "idol," and it is a contraction of Mahomet.

The derivation of *jug* is not capable of proof, but a 17th-century etymologist regards it as identical with the female name *Jug*,[1] for Joan or Jane. This is supported by *jack* used in a similar sense, and by *toby jug* and *demi-john*. The latter word is in French *dame-jeanne*, but both forms are probably due to folk-etymology. A coat of mail was called in English a *jack* and in French *jaque*, " a *jack*, or coat of maile " (Cotgrave); hence the diminutive *jacket*. The German miners gave to an ore which they considered useless the name *kobalt*, from *kobold*, a goblin, gnome. This has given Eng. *cobalt*. Much later is the similarly formed *nickel*, a diminutive of Nicholas. It comes to us from Sweden, but appears earliest in the German compound *Kupfernickel*. Apparently *nickel* here means something like goblin; cf. *Old Nick* and, probably, the *dickens*—

"I cannot tell what the *dickens* his name is my husband had him of.—What do you call your knight's name, sirrah?"

(*Merry Wives*, iii. 2.)

Pantaloons come, *via* France, from Venice. A great many Venetians bore the name of *Pantaleone*, one of their favourite saints. Hence the application of the name to the characteristic Venetian hose. The "lean and slippered pantaloon" was originally one of the stock characters of the old Italian comedy. Torriano (1659) has *pantalone*, " a *pantalone*, a covetous and yet amorous old dotard, properly applyed in comedies unto a Venetian." *Knickerbockers* take their name from Diedrich *Knicker-bocker*, the pseudonym under which Washington Irving wrote his History of Old New York, in which the early Dutch inhabitants are depicted in loose knee-breeches.

Certain christian names are curiously associated with stupidity. In modern English we speak of a

[1] For extraordinary perversions of baptismal names see Chap. XII. It is possible that the rather uncommon family name *Juggins* is of the same origin.

silly Johnny, while the Germans say *ein dummer Peter*
and French uses *Colas* (*Nicolas*), *Nicodème* and *Claude*,
the reason for the selection of the name not always
being clear. English has, or had, in the sense of "fool,"
the words *ninny*, *nickum*, *noddy*, *zany*. *Ninny* is for
Innocent, " Innocent, *Ninny*, a proper name for a man"
(Cotgrave). With this we may compare French *benêt*
(*i.e.* Benedict), "a simple, plaine, doltish fellow ; a noddy
peake, a ninny hammer, a peagoose, a coxe, a silly
companion" (Cotgrave). *Nickum* and *noddy* are probably for Nicodemus or Nicholas, both of which are
used in French for a fool. The reader will remember
that Noddy Boffin was christened Nicodemus. *Noddypeak*, *ninny-hammer*, *nickumpoop*, now *nincompoop*, seem
to be arbitrary elaborations. *Zany*, formerly a con-
juror's assistant, is *zanni*, an Italian diminutive of
Giovanni, John. With the degeneration of *Innocent*
and *Benedict* we may compare Fr. *crétin*, idiot, an
Alpine patois form of *chrétien*, Christian, and Eng. *silly*,
which once meant blessed, a sense preserved by its
German cognate *selig*. *Dunce* is a libel on the disciples
of the great medieval schoolman John Duns Scotus,
born at Dunse in Berwickshire.

Dago, now usually applied to Italians, was used by
the Elizabethans, in its original form *Diego*, of the
Spaniards. The derivation of *guy* and *bobby* (peeler) is
well known. *Jockey* is a diminutive of the north
country *Jock*, for *Jack*. The history of *jackanapes* is
obscure. The earliest record of the name is in a
satirical song on the unpopular William de la Pole,
Duke of Suffolk, who was beheaded at sea in 1450.
He is called *Jack Napes*, the allusion being apparently
to his badge, an ape's clog and chain. But there also
seems to be association with Naples ; cf. *fustian-anapes*
for Naples fustian. A poem of the 15th century tells

us that from Italy came "apes and japes and marmus-
ettes tayled." *Dandy* is Scottish for *Andrew*; cf.
Dandie Dinmont.

Jilt was once a stronger epithet than at present. It
is for earlier *jillet*, which is a diminutive of *Jill*, the
companion of Jack. *Jill*, again, is short for *Gillian*, i.e.
Juliana, so that *jilt* is a doublet of Shakespeare's
sweetest heroine. *Termagant*, like *shrew* (p. 31), was
formerly used of both sexes. In its oldest sense of
a Saracen god it regularly occurs with *Mahound*
(Mahomet)—

> "Marsilies fait porter un livre avant :
>   La lei i fut Mahum e *Tervagan*." [1]
>
> (*Chanson de Roland*, ll. 610-11.)

Ariosto has *Trivigante*. Being introduced into the
medieval drama, the name became synonymous with a
stage fury—

> "I would have such a fellow whipped for o'erdoing *Termagant*."
>
> (*Hamlet*, iii. 2.)

Falstaff calls Douglas "that hot *termagant* Scot"
(1 *Henry IV.*, v. 4). The origin of the word is unknown, but its sense development is strangely different
from that of Mahomet (p. 39).

---

[1] "Marsil has a book brought forward: the law of Mahomet and
Termagant was in it."

CHAPTER IV

WORDS AND PLACES

A VERY large number of wares are named from the places from which they come. This is especially common in the case of woven fabrics, and the origin is often obvious, e.g., *arras, cashmere* (by folk-etymology, *kerseymere*) *damask, holland*. The following are perhaps not all so evident—*frieze* from *Friesland;*[1] *fustian*, Old Fr. *fustaine* (*futaine*), from *Fustat*, a suburb of Cairo; *muslin*, Fr. *mousseline*, from *Mosul* in Kurdistan; *shalloon* from *Châlons*-sur-Marne; *lawn* from *Laon*; *jean*, formerly *jane*, from *Genoa* (French *Gênes*[2]); *cambric* from *Kamerijk*, the Dutch name of Cambrai (*cf.* the obsolete *dornick*, from the Dutch name of *Tournay*); *tartan* from the *Tartars* (properly *Tatars*), used vaguely for Orientals; *sarcenet* from the Saracens; *sendal*, ultimately from *India* (*cf.* Greco-Lat. *sindon*, Indian cloth); *tabby*, Old Fr. *atabis*, from the name of a suburb of Bagdad, now chiefly used of a cat marked something like the material in question.

[1] Whence also *cheval de frise*, a contrivance used by the Frieslanders against cavalry. The German name is *die spanischen Reiter*, explained by Ludwig as "a bar with iron-spikes; *cheval de frise*, a warlick instrument, to keep off the horse."

[2] The form *jeans* appears to be usual in America, *e.g.*, "His hands were thrust carelessly into the side pockets of a gray *jeans* coat." (Meredith Nicholson, *War of the Carolinas*, Ch. 15.)

Brittany used to be famous for hempen fabrics, and the villages of *Locrenan* and *Daoulas* gave their names to *lockram* (*Coriolanus*, ii. 1) and *dowlas*—

> *Hostess.* You owe me money, Sir John; and now you pick a quarrel to beguile me of it: I bought you a dozen of shirts to your back.
>
> *Falstaff. Dowlas,* filthy dowlas; I have given them away to bakers' wives, and they have made bolters of them.
>
> (1 *Henry IV.,* iii. 3.)

Duffel is a place near Antwerp—

> "And let it be of *duffil* gray,
> As warm a cloak as man can sell."
> (WORDSWORTH, *Alice Fell.*)

and *Worstead* is in Norfolk. Of other commodities *majolica* comes from *Majorca*, called in Spanish *Mallorca*, and in medieval Latin *Majolica*; *bronze* from *Brundusium* (Brindisi), *delf* from *Delft*, the *magnet* from *Magnesia*, the *shallot*, Fr. *échalotte*, in Old French also *escalogne*, whence archaic Eng. *scallion*, from *Ascalon;* the *sardine* from *Sardinia*. A *milliner*, formerly *milaner*, dealt in goods from *Milan*. *Cravat* dates from the Thirty Years' War, in which the *Croats*, earlier *Cravats*, played a part. *Ermine* is in medieval Latin *mus Armenius*, Armenian mouse, but comes, through Fr. *hermine*, from Old High Ger. *harmo*, weasel. *Buncombe*, more usually *bunkum*, is the name of a county in North Carolina. To make a speech "for Buncombe" means, in American politics, to show your constituents that you are doing your best for your £400 a year or its American equivalent. Cf. *Billingsgate* and *Limehouse*.

The adjective *spruce* was formerly *pruce* and meant Prussia. Todd quotes from Holinshed, "Sir Edward Howard then admirall, and with him Sir Thomas Parre in doubletts of crimsin velvett, etc., were apparelled after the fashion of Prussia or *Spruce.*" Of similar origin are *spruce-leather*, *spruce-beer*, and the *spruce-fir*, of which Evelyn says, " Those from Prussia (which we call *spruce*) and Norway are the best."

Among coins the *bezant* comes from *Byzantium*, the *florin* from *Florence*, and Shylock's *ducat*, chiefly a Venetian coin, from the *ducato* d'Apuglia, the Duchy of Apulia, where it was first coined in the 12th century. The *dollar* is the Low Ger. *daler*, for Ger. *Taler*, originally called a *Joachimstaler*, from the silver-mine of Joachimstal, Joachim's dale, in Bohemia. Cotgrave registers a curious Old French perversion *jocondale*, " a *daller*, a piece of money worth about 3s. sterl." Some fruits may also be mentioned, *e.g.*, the *damson* from *Damascus*, through Old Fr. *damaisine*, "a damascene or damsen plum" (Cotgrave); the *currant* from *Corinth*, and the *peach*, Fr. *pêche*, from Vulgar Lat. *pessica*, for *Persica*.

A *polony* was originally a *Bolonian* sausage, from *Bologna*. Parchment, Fr. *parchemin*, is the adjective *pergamenus*, from *Pergamus*, in Asia Minor. *Spaniel* is the Old Fr. *espagneul* (*épagneul*), lit. Spanish. We have the adjective *Moorish* in *morris pike*—

" He that sets up his rest to do more exploits with his mace than a *morris pike*." (*Comedy of Errors*, iv. 3.)

In *morris dance*, Fr. *danse mauresque*, the same adjective is used with something of the vagueness to be noticed in connection with India and Turkey (p. 47). Shakespeare uses the Spanish form—

"I have seen him
Caper upright, like to a wild *morisco*,
Shaking the bloody darts as he his bells."
(2 *Henry VI.*, iii. 1.)

Other "local" dances are the *polka*, which means " Polish woman"; *mazurka*, woman of Massovia; and the obsolete *polonaise, cracovienne*, from Cracow, and *varsovienne*, from Warsaw. The *tarantella*, like the *tarantula* spider, takes its name from Taranto, in Italy, Lat. *Tarentum.* There is said to be some pathological connection between the spider and the dance, *e.g.*, Florio has *tarantola*, "a serpent called an eft or an evet. Some take it to be a flye whose sting is perillous and deadly, and nothing but divers sounds of musicke can cure the patient."

The town of *Troyes* has given its name to *troy* weight. The armourers of *Bilbao*, in Spain, made swords of such perfect temper that they could be bent point to hilt. Hence Falstaff describes himself in the buck-basket as—

"Compassed, like a good *bilbo*, in the circumference of a peck, hilt to point, heel to head." (*Merry Wives*, iii. 5.)

The *Andrea Ferrara*, or Scottish broadsword, carried by Fergus M'Ivor, bears, according to some authorities, the name of an armourer of Ferrara, in Italy. According to others, *Andrea Ferrara* was a swordmaker at Belluno. I have heard it affirmed by a Scottish drill-sergeant that this genius, whose real name was *Andrew Ferrars*, belonged to the same nationality as other great men.

An *argosy*, formerly also *ragusye*, was named from the Adriatic port of *Ragusa*, and a *lateen* sail is a *Latin*, *i.e.* Mediterranean, sail; *gamboge* is the Fr. *Cambotge*, Cambodia, and *indigo* is from Span. *indico*, Indian. Of wines, *malmsey*, chiefly remembered in connection with George of Clarence, and *malvoisie* are doublets, from *Monemvasia* in the Morea. *Port* is named from *Oporto*, i.e. *o porto*, the harbour (cf. *le Havre*), and *sherry* (see p. 107) from *Xeres*, Lat. *Cæsaris* (urbs); cf. *Saragossa*, from *Cæsarea Augusta.*

But it is possible to be mistaken in connecting countries with products. *Brazil* wood is not named from the country, but *vice versâ*. It was known as a dye-wood as early as the 12th century, and the name is found in many of the European languages. The Portuguese navigators found large quantities of it in South America and named the country accordingly. They christened an island *Madeira*, timber, Lat. *materia*, for a similar reason. The *canary* comes from the Canary Islands, but its name is good Latin. The largest of these islands, *Canaria*, was so called by the Romans from the dogs found there. The *guinea*-fowl and *guinea* gold came first from the west coast of Africa, but the *guinea-pig* is a native of Brazil. The name probably came from the Guinea-men, or slave-ships, which regularly followed a triangular course. They sailed outward to the west coast of Africa with English goods. These they exchanged for slaves, whom they transported to the West Indies, the horrible "middle passage," and finally they sailed homeward with New World produce, including, no doubt, *guinea-pigs* brought home by sailors. The turkey is also called *guinea-fowl* in the 17th century, probably to be explained in the same way. The German name for guinea-pig, *Meerschweinchen*, seems to mean little pig from over the sea.

Guinea was a vague geographical expression in the 17th century, but not so vague as India or Turkey. *Indian ink* comes from China (Fr. *encre de Chine*), and *Indian corn* from America. The names given to the *turkey* are extraordinary. We are not surprised that, as an American bird, it should be naturally connected with India; *cf.* West Indies, Red Indian, etc. *Turk* was in the 16th and 17th centuries a vague term for non-Christians, "Jews, *Turks*, infidels, and hereticks"

(Collect for Good Friday), and we find also *Turkey wheat* for maize. The following names for the turkey, given in a *Nomenclator* in eight languages, published in Germany in 1602, do not exhaust the list:—

German. — *Indianisch* oder *Kalekuttisch* [1] oder *Welsch* [2] Hun.

Dutch.—*Calcoensche* oft *Turckische* Henne.

French.—Geline ou poulle d'*Inde*, ou d'*Africque*.

Italian.—Gallina d'*India*.

Spanish.—Pavon (peacock) de las *Indias*.

English.—Cok off Inde !

No doubt the turkey was confused with other birds, for we find Fr. *geline d'Inde* before the discovery of America. *D'Inde* has become *dinde*, whence a new masculine *dindon* has been formed.

The early etymologists were fond of identifying foreign wares with place-names. They connected *diaper* with Yprès, *gingham* with Guingamp (in Brittany), *drugget* with Drogheda, and the *sedan* chair with Sedan. Such guesses are almost always wrong. The origin of *diaper* is doubtful, that of *drugget* quite unknown, and *gingham* is Malay. As far as we know at present, the *sedan* came from Italy in the 16th century, and it is there, among derivatives of Lat. *sedere*, to sit, that its origin must be sought, unless indeed the original *Sedan* was some mute, inglorious Hansom.

---

[1] Calicut, not Calcutta.　　　[2] See *walnut* (p. 140).

CHAPTER V

PHONETIC ACCIDENTS

THE history of a word has to be studied from the double point of view of sound and sense, or, to use more technical terms, phonetics and semantics. In the logical order of things it seems natural to deal first with the less interesting aspect, phonetics, the physical processes by which sounds are gradually transformed. Speaking generally, it may be said that phonetic changes are governed by the law of least resistance, a sound which presents difficulty being gradually and unconsciously modified by a whole community or race. With the general principles of phonetics I do not propose to deal, but a few simple examples will serve to illustrate the great general law on which this science is based.

The population of this country is educationally divided by the letter *h* into three classes, which we may describe as the confident, the anxious, and the indifferent. The same division existed in imperial Rome, where educated people sounded the aspirate, which completely disappeared from the everyday language of the lower classes, the so-called Vulgar Latin from which the Romance languages are descended, so far as their working vocabulary is concerned. The anxious class was also represented. A Latin epigrammatist[1] remarks that since Arrius, prophetic name, has visited the Ionic islands, they will probably be henceforth known as the *Hionic* islands. To the disappearance of the *h* from Vulgar Latin is due the fact that the Romance languages have no aspirate. French still writes the initial *h* in some words by etymological reaction, e.g., *homme* for Old Fr. *ome*, and also at one time really had an aspirate in the case of words of Germanic origin, e.g., *la honte*, shame. But this *h* is no longer sounded, although it still, by tradition, prevents elision and *liaison*, mistakes in which are regarded much in the same way as a misplaced aspirate in English. The "educated" *h* of modern English is largely an artificial restoration; *cf.* the modern *hotel*-keeper with the older word *ostler* (see p. 152), or the family name *Armitage* with the restored *hermitage*.

We have dropped the *k* sound in initial *kn*, as in *knave*, still sounded in German *Knabe*, boy. French gets over the difficulty by inserting a vowel between the two consonants, e.g., *canif* is a Germanic word cognate with Eng. *knife*. This is a common device in French when a word of Germanic origin begins with two consonants. *Cf.* Fr. *dérive*, drift, Eng. *drive*; Fr. *varech*, sea-weed, Eng. *wrack*. *Harangue*, formerly *harengue*, is Old High Ger. *hring*, Eng. *ring*, the allusion being to the circle formed by the audience. Fr. *chenapan*, rogue, is Ger. *Schnapphahn*, robber, lit. fowl-stealer. The *shallop* that "flitteth silken-sail'd, skimming down to Camelot," is Fr. *chaloupe*, from Du. *sloep*, sloop.

The general dislike that French has for a double

---

[1] "Nec sibi postilla metuebant talia verba,
    Cum subito adfertur nuntius horribilis,
  Ionios fluctus, postquam illuc Arrius isset,
    Iam non *Ionios* esse, sed *Hionios*."

                          (*Catullus*, 84.)

consonant sound at the beginning of a word appears also in the transformation of all Latin words which began with *sc*, *sp*, *st*, e.g., *scola* > *escole* (*école*), *spongia* > *esponge* (*éponge*), *stabulum* > *estable* (*étable*). English words derived from French generally show the older form, but without the initial vowel, *school*, *sponge*, *stable*. The above are very simple examples of sound change. There are certain less regular changes, which appear to work in a more arbitrary fashion and bring about more picturesque results. Three of the most important of these are assimilation, dissimilation, and metathesis.

Assimilation is the tendency of a sound to imitate its neighbour. The tree called the *lime* was formerly the *line*, and earlier still the *lind*. We see the older form in *linden* and in such place-names as *Lyndhurst*, lime wood. *Line* often occurred in such compounds as *line-bark*, *line-bast*, *line-wood*, where the second component began with a lip consonant. The *n* became also a lip consonant because it was easier to pronounce, and by the 17th century we generally find *lime* instead of *line*. We have a similar change in *Lombard* for Ger. *lang-bart*, long-beard. For *Liverpool* we find also *Litherpool* in early records. If the reader attempts to pronounce both names rapidly, he will be able to form his own opinion as to whether it is more natural for *Liverpool* to become *Litherpool* or *vice versa*, a vexed question with philologists. Fr. *vélin*, a derivative of Old Fr. *veel* (*veau*), calf, and *venin*, Lat. *venenum*, have given Eng. *vellum* and *venom*, the final consonant being in each case assimilated[1] to the initial labial. So also *mushroom*, Mid. Eng. *muscheron*, Fr. *mousseron*, from *mousse*, moss.

---

[1] Apart from assimilation, there is a tendency in English to substitute -*m* for -*n*, e.g. *grogram* for *grogran* (see p. 62). In the family name *Hansom*, for *Hanson*, the son of Hans, we have dissimilation of *n* (see p. 52).

Vulgar Lat. *circare* (from *circa*, around) gave Old Fr. *cerchier*, Eng. *search*. In modern Fr. *chercher* the initial consonant has been influenced by the medial *ch*. The *m* of the curious word *ampersand*, variously spelt, is due to the neighbouring *p*. It is applied to the sign &. I thought it obsolete till I came across it on successive days in two contemporary writers—

"One of my mother's chief cares was to teach me my letters, which I learnt from big A to *Ampersand* in the old hornbook at Lantrig." (QUILLER COUCH, *Dead Man's Rock*, Ch. ii.)

"Tommy knew all about the work. Knew every letter in it from A to *Emperzan*." (PETT RIDGE, *In the Wars*.)

Children used to repeat the alphabet thus — "A per se A, B per se B," and so on to "*and per se and*." The symbol & is an abbreviation of Lat. *et*, written *&*.

Dissimilation is the opposite process. The archaic word *pomander*—

"I have sold all my trumpery; not a counterfeit stone, not a riband, glass, *pomander*, brooch, . . . to keep my pack from fasting." (*Winter's Tale*, iv. 3.)

was formerly spelt *pomeamber*. It comes from Old Fr. *pome ambre*, apple of amber, a ball of perfume once carried by the delicate. In this case one of the two lip consonants has been dissimilated. A like change has occurred in Fr. *nappe*, cloth, from Latin *mappa*, whence our *napkin*, apron (p. 104), and the family name *Napier*.

The sounds most frequently affected by dissimilation are those represented by the letters *l*, *n*, and *r*. Fr. *gonfalon* is for older *gonfanon*. Chaucer uses the older form, Milton the newer—

"Ten thousand thousand ensigns high advanc'd,
Standards and *gonfalons*, 'twixt van and rear,
Stream in the air."

(*Paradise Lost*, v. 589.)

Gonfanon is of Germanic origin. It means literally "battle-flag," and the second element is cognate with English *fane* or *vane* (Ger. *Fahne*). Eng. *pilgrim* and Fr. *pèlerin*, from Lat. *peregrinus*, illustrate the change from *r* to *l*, while the word *frail*, an osier basket for figs, is due to a change from *l* to *r*, which goes back to Roman times. A grammarian of imperial Rome named Probus compiled, about the 3rd or 4th century, A.D., a list of cautions as to mispronunciation. In this list we find "*flagellum*, non *fragellum*." In the sense of switch, twig, *fragellum* gave Old Fr. *freel*, basket made of twigs, whence Eng. *frail;* while the correct *flagellum* gave Old Fr. *fleel* (*fléau*), whence Eng. *flail*. A Vulgar Lat. **mora*, mulberry, from Lat. *morus*, mulberry tree, has given Fr. *mûre*. The *r* of *berry* has brought about dissimilation in Eng. *mulberry* and Ger. *Maulbeere*. *Colonel* has the spelling of Fr. *colonel*, but its pronunciation points rather to the dissimilated Spanish form *coronel* which is common in Elizabethan English. Cotgrave has *colonel*, "a *colonell*, or *coronell;* the commander of a regiment."

Sometimes dissimilation leads to the disappearance of a consonant, *e.g.*, Eng. *feeble*, Fr. *faible*, represents Lat. *flebilis*, lamentable, from *flere*, to weep. *Fugleman* was once *fluglelman*, from Ger. *Flügelmann*, wing man, *i.e.*, a tall soldier on the right wing who exaggerated the various movements of musketry drill for the guidance of the rest. The female name *Annabel* is a dissimilation of *Amabel*, whence *Mabel*. By an irregular change, of which, however, we have other examples, *Annabel* has become *Arabel* or *Arabella*. Our *level* is Old Fr. *livel*, Vulgar Lat. **libellum*, for *libella*, a plummet, diminutive of *libra*, scales. Old Fr. *livel* became by dissimilation *nivel*, now *niveau*. Many conjectures have been made as to the etymology of *oriel*. It is from Old Fr. *oriol*, a recess, or sanctum, which first occurs in a Norman French poem of the 12th century on Becket. This is from a late Latin diminutive *aulæolum*, a small chapel or shrine, which was dissimilated into *auræolum*.

Metathesis is the transposition of two sounds. A simple case is our *trouble*, Fr. *troubler*, from Lat. *turbulare*. *Maggot* is for Mid. Eng. *maddok*, a diminutive of Anglo-Sax. *maþa; cf.* Ger. *Made*, maggot. *Kittle*, in the phrase "kittle cattle," is identical with *tickle; cf.* Ger. *kitzeln*, to tickle. The only reasonable theory for the origin of *tankard* is that it stands for *cantar, from Lat. *cantharus*, with which it corresponds exactly in meaning; e.g., *cantharus*, "a pot, a jugge, a *tankerd*" (Cooper); *cantharo*, "a *tankard* or jug that houldeth much" (Florio); *canthare*, "a great jugge, or *tankard*" (Cotgrave).

Fr. *moustique*, from Span. *mosquito*, is for earlier *mousquite*. *Tinsel* is Fr. *étincelle*, spark, earlier *estincele*, which supposes a Lat. *stincilla for *scintilla*. The old word *anlace*, dagger, common in Mid. English and revived by Byron and Scott—

> "His harp in silken scarf was slung,
> And by his side an *anlace* hung."
>
> (*Rokeby*, v. 15.)

has provoked many guesses. Its oldest form, *anelas*, is a metathesis of the common Old Fr. *alenas*, dagger. This is formed from *alêne*, of Germanic origin, cognate with *awl; cf. cutlass*, Fr. *coutelas* (p. 116). *Beverage* is from Old Fr. *bevrage*, or *beuvrage*, now *breuvage*, Vulgar Lat. *biberaticum, from *bibere*, to drink. Here, as in the case of *level* (p. 53), and *search* (p. 52), English preserves the older form.

In *Martello* tower, from a fort taken by the British (1794) in *Mortella*, *i.e.*, Myrtle, Bay, Corsica, we have vowel metathesis. *Wattle* and *wallet* are used indifferently in Mid. English for a little bag. Shakespeare no doubt had in mind the *wattles* of a cock or turkey when he made Gonzalo speak of mountaineers—

> "Dew-lapp'd like bulls, whose throats had hanging at them
>   *Wallets* of flesh."   (*Tempest*, iii. 3.)

It goes without saying that such linguistic phenomena are often observed in the case of children and uneducated people. Not long ago the writer was urged by a gardener to embellish his garden with a *ruskit* arch. When metathesis extends beyond one word we have what is known as a *spoonerism*, the original type of which is said to be " *Kinquerings congs their titles take.*"

We have seen (p. 52) that the letters *l*, *n*, *r* are particularly subject to dissimilation and metathesis. But we sometimes find them alternating without apparent reason. Thus *banister* is a modern form for the correct *baluster*.[1] This was not at first applied to the rail, but to the bulging colonets on which it rests. Fr. *balustre* comes, through Italian, from Greco-Lat. *balaustium*, a pomegranate flower, the shape of which resembles the supports of a balustrade. Cotgrave explains *balustres* as " *ballisters* ; little, round and short pillars, ranked on the outside of cloisters, terraces, galleries, etc." *Glamour* is a doublet of *grammar* (see p. 134), and *flounce* was formerly *frounce*, from Fr. *froncer*, now only used of "knitting" the brows—

> "Till civil-suited morn appear,
>   Not trickt and *frounc't* as she was wont
>   With the Attic boy to hunt."
>
>   (MILTON, *Penseroso*, 123.)

Fr. *flibustier*, whence our *filibuster*, was earlier *fribustier*,

---

[1] *Cf.* the similar change in the family name *Banister* (p. 166).

a corruption of Du. *vrijbuiter*, whence directly the Eng. *freebooter*.[1]

All words tend in popular usage to undergo a certain amount of shrinkage. The reduction of Lat. *digitale*, from *digitus*, finger, to Fr. *dé*, thimble (little thumb) is a striking example. The strong tonic accent of English, which is usually on the first, or root, syllable, brings about a kind of telescoping which makes us very unintelligible to foreigners. This is seen in the pronunciation of names such as *Cholmondeley* and *Marjoribanks*. *Bethlehem* hospital, for lunatics, becomes *bedlam;* Mary *Magdalene*, taken as a type of tearful repentance, gives us *maudlin*, now generally used of the lachrymose stage of intoxication. *Sacristan* is contracted into *sexton*. Fr. *paralysie* becomes *palsy*, and *hydropisie* becomes *dropsy*. The fuller form of the word usually persists in the literary language, or is artificially introduced at a later period, so that we get such doublets as *proctor* and *procurator*.

In the case of French words which have a prefix, this prefix is almost regularly dropped in English, e.g., *raiment* for *arrayment;* while suffixes, or final syllables, often disappear, *e.g.*, treasure *trove*, for Old Fr. *trové* (*trouvé*), or become assimilated to some familiar English ending, e.g., *parish*, Fr. *paroisse; skirmish*, Fr. *escarmouche; cartridge*, Fr. *cartouche; partridge*, Fr. *perdrix*. A good example of such shrinkage is the word *vamp*, part of a shoe, Old Fr. *avant-pie* (*pied*), which became Mid. Eng. *vampey*, and then lost its final syllable. We may compare *vambrace*, armour for the forearm, Fr. *avant-bras, vanguard*, Fr. *avant-garde*, often reduced to *van—*

---

[1] It may be noted here that a *buccaneer* was not originally a pirate, but a man whose business was the smoking of beef in the West Indies. The name comes from a native word *boucan*, adopted into French, and explained by Cotgrave as a "woodden-gridiron whereon the cannibals broile pieces of men, and other flesh."

> " Go, charge Agrippa
> Plant those that have revolted in the *van;*
> That Antony may seem to spend his fury
> Upon himself."
>
> (*Antony and Cleopatra*, iv. 6.)

and the obsolete *vaunt-courier*, forerunner—

> "You sulphurous and thought-executing fires,
> *Vaunt-couriers* of oak-cleaving thunderbolts."
>
> (*Lear*, iii. 2.)

When the initial vowel is *a-*, its loss may have been helped by confusion with the indefinite article. Thus for *anatomy* we find *atomy*, for a skeleton or scarecrow figure, applied by Mistress Quickly to the constable (2 *Henry IV.*, v. 4). *Peal* is for *appeal*, call ; *mend* for *amend*, *lone* for *alone*, i.e., *all one*. *Peach*, used by Falstaff—

> " If I be ta'en, I'll *peach* for this."
>
> (1 *Henry IV.*, ii. 2.)

is for older *appeach*, related to *impeach*. *Size*, in all its senses, is for *assize*, Fr. *assise*, with a general meaning of allowance or assessment, from Fr. *asseoir*, to put, lay. *Sizars* at Cambridge are properly students in receipt of certain allowances called *sizings*. With painters' *size* we may compare Ital. *assisa*, "*size* that painters use" (Florio). We use the form *assize* in speaking of the sitting of the judges, but those most familiar with this tribunal speak of being tried at the '*sizes*. The obsolete word *cate*, on which Petruchio plays—

> " For dainties are all *cates*—and therefore, Kate,
> Take this of me, Kate of my consolation."
>
> (*Taming of the Shrew*, ii. 1.)

is for earlier *acate*, an Old French dialect form corresponding to modern Fr. *achat*, purchase. The man entrusted with purchasing was called an *acatour* or *catour* (whence the name *Cator*), later *cater*, now extended to *caterer*, like *poulterer* for *poulter* and *upholsterer* for *upholdster* or *upholder*.[1]

Limbeck has been squeezed out by the orthodox *alembic*—

> "Memory the warder of the brain,
> Shall be a fume, and the receipt of reason
> A *limbeck* only."
>
> (*Macbeth*, i. 7.)

and *prentice* has given way to *apprentice*. *Tire* and *attire* both survive, and *maze* persists by the side of *amaze* with the special sense which I have heard a Notts collier express by *puzzle-garden* (*cf.* Ger. *Irrgarten*). *Binnacle* is a corruption, perhaps due to association with *bin*, of earlier *bittacle*, from Lat. *habitaculum*, a little dwelling. It may have come to us through Fr. *habitacle* or Port. *bitacola*, "the *bittacle*, a frame of timber in the steerage, where the compass is placed on board a ship" (Vieyra, *Port. Dict.*, 1794). As King of Scotland, King George has a household official known as the *limner*, or painter. For *limner*[2] we find in the 15th century *lumner* and *luminour*, which is aphetic for *alluminour*, or *enlumineur*. Cotgrave, s.v. *enlumineur de livres*, says, "we call one that coloureth, or painteth upon, paper, or parchment, an *alluminer*."

But confusion with the article is not necessary in order to bring about aphesis. It occurs regularly in the case of words beginning with *esc*, *esp*, *est*, borrowed from Old French (see p. 51). Thus we have *squire* from *escuyer* (*écuyer*), *skew* from Old Fr. *eschuer*, to

---

[1] *Cf.*, for the specialised sense, *undertaker*, and *stationer*, properly a tradesman with a *station* or stall. *Costermonger* illustrates the converse process. It meant originally a dealer in *costards*, i.e. *apples*.

[2] English *i* often occurs as an attempt at the French and Celtic *u ;* cf. *brisk* from *brusque*, *periwig* (p. 64), and *whisky* (p. 63).

dodge, "eschew," ultimately cognate with Eng. *shy, spice* from *espice* (*épice*), *sprite* from *esprit*, *stage* from *estage* (*étage*), etc.   In some cases we have double forms, e.g., *esquire, eschew ;* cf. *sample* and *example. Fender,* whether before a fireplace or slung outside a ship, is for *defender ; fence* is always for *defence,* either in the sense of a barrier or in allusion to the noble art of self-defence.[1]   The *tender* of a ship or of a locomotive is the *attender,* and *taint* is aphetic for *attaint,* Fr. *atteinte,* touch—

> "I will not poison thee with my *attaint.*"
>
> (*Lucrece,* l. 1072.)

Puzzle was in Mid. Eng. *opposaile, i.e.,* something put before one.   We still speak of "a poser."

Spital, for *hospital,* survives in *Spitalfields,* and *Spittlegate* at Grantham and elsewhere.   *Crew* is for *accrewe* (Holinshed).   It meant properly a reinforcement, lit. on-growth, from Fr. *accroître,* to accrue.   In *recruit,* we have a later instance of the same idea.   Fr. *recrue,* recruit, from *recroître,* to grow again, is still feminine, like many other military terms which were originally abstract or collective.   Cotgrave has *recreuë,* "a supplie, or filling up of a defective company of souldiers, etc." We have *possum* for *opossum,* and *coon* for *racoon,* and this for *arrahacoune,* which I find in a 16th-century record of travel ; cf. American *skeeter* for *mosquito.*   In these two cases we perhaps have also the deliberate intention to shorten (see p. 61), as also in the obsolete

---

[1] Our ancestors appear to have been essentially pacific. With *fence,* for *defence,* we may compare Ger. *schirmen,* to fence, from *Schirm,* screen (cf. *Regenschirm,* umbrella), which, passing through Italian and French, has given us *skirmish, scrimmage, scaramouch* (see p. 131), and Shakespearean *scrimer,* fencer (*Hamlet,* iv. 7).   So also Ger. *Gewehr,* weapon, is cognate with Eng. *weir,* and means defence—

> "Cet animal est très méchant ;
> Quand on l'attaque, il se défend."

Australian *tench*, for the aphetic *'tentiary*, i.e., *penitentiary*. With this we may compare *'tec* for *detective*.

Drawing-room is for *withdrawing room*, and only the final *t* of *saint* is left in *Tooley St.*, famed for its three tailors, formerly *Saint Olave Street*, and *tawdry*. This latter word is well known to be derived from *Saint Audrey's* fair. It was not originally depreciatory—

"Come, you promised me a *tawdry* lace, and a pair of sweet gloves." (*Winter's Tale*, iv. 3.)

and the full form is recorded by Palsgrave, who has *Seynt Andries* (read *Audrie's*) *lace*, "cordon."

In *drat*, formerly *'od rot*, *zounds*, for *God's wounds*, *'sdeath*, *odsbodikins*, etc., there is probably a deliberate avoidance of profanity. The same tendency is seen in *Gogs* (*Shrew*, iii. 2), Fr. *parbleu*, and Ger. *Potz* in *Potztausend*, etc. The verb *vie* comes from Fr. *envi*, Lat. *invitus*, unwilling, in the phrase *à l'envi l'un de l'autre*, "in emulation one of the other" (Cotgrave); cf. *gin* (trap), Fr. *engin*, Lat. *ingenium*. The prefix *dis* or *des* is lost in *Spencer* (see p. 153), *spite*, *splay*, *sport*, *stain*, etc.

This English tendency to aphesis is satirised by a French song of the 14th century, intentionally written in bad French. Thus, in the line—

"Or sont il vint le tans que Glais voura vauchier."

Glais is for *Anglais* and *vauchier* is for *chevauchier* (*chevaucher*), to ride on a foray. The literary language runs counter to this instinct, though Shakespeare wrote *haviour* for *behaviour* and *longing* for *belonging*, while *billiments* for *habiliments* is regular up to the 17th century. Children keep up the national practice when they say *member* for *remember* and *zamine* for *examine*. It is quite certain that *baccy* and *tater* would be recognised literary forms if America had been discovered two centuries sooner or printing invented two centuries later.

Many words are shortened, not by natural and gradual shrinkage, but by deliberate laziness. The national distaste for many syllables appears in *wire* for *telegram*, the Artful Dodger's *wipe* for the clumsy *pocket handkerchief*, *soccer* for *association*, and such portmanteau words as *squarson*, an individual who is at once *squire* and *parson*, or *Bakerloo* for *Baker St. and Waterloo*.

The simplest way of reducing a word is to take the first syllable and make it a symbol for the rest. Of comparatively modern formation are *pub* and *Zoo*, with which we may compare *Bart's*, for Saint Bartholomew's, *Cri*, *Pav*, "half a *mo'*," *bike*, and even *paj*, for *pageant*.

This method of shortening words was very popular in the 17th century, from which period date *cit*(izen), *mob*(ile vulgus) and *pun*(digrion). We often find the fuller *mobile* used for *mob*. The origin of *pundigrion* is uncertain. It may be an illiterate attempt at Ital. *puntiglio*, which, like Fr. *pointe*, was used of a verbal quibble or fine distinction. Most of these clipped forms are easily identified, e.g., *cab*(riolet), *gent*(leman), *hack*(ney), *vet*(erinary surgeon). *Cad* is for Scot. *caddie*, errand boy, now familiar in connection with golf, and *caddie* is from Fr. *cadet*. The word had not always the very strong meaning we now associate with it. Among *Sketches by Boz* is one entitled, " The last Cab driver and the first Omnibus *Cad*," where *cad* means conductor. On *tick*, for on *ticket*, is found in the 17th century. We may compare the more modern *biz* and *spec*. *Brig* is for *brigantine*, Ital. *brigantino*, " a kinde of pinnasse or small barke called a *brigantine*" (Florio). The original meaning is pirate ship; cf. *brigand*. *Wag* has improved in meaning. It is for older *waghalter*. Cotgrave has *baboin* (*babouin*), " a trifling, busie, or crafty knave ; a crackrope, *waghalter*, etc." The older sense survives in the phrase "to play the *wag*," *i.e.* truant. For the "rope" figure we may compare Scot. *hempie*, a minx, and obsolete Ital. *cavestrolo*, a diminutive from Lat. *capistrum*, halter, explained by Florio as "a *wag*, a haltersacke." Modern Ital. *capestro* is used in the same sense. *Crackrope* is shortened to *crack*. Justice Shallow remembered Falstaff breaking somebody's head "when he was a *crack*, not thus high" (2 *Henry IV.*, iii. 2).

Chap is for *chapman*, once in general use for a merchant and still a common family name. It is cognate with *cheap*, *chaffer*, and Ger. *kaufen*, to buy, and probably also with Lat. *caupo*, tavern keeper. We have the Dutch form in *horse-couper*, and also in the word *coopering*, the illicit sale of spirits by Dutch boats to North Sea fishermen. *Merchant* was used by the Elizabethans in the same way as our *chap*. Thus the Countess of Auvergne calls Talbot a "riddling *merchant*" (1 *Henry VI.*, ii. 3). We may also compare Scot. *callant*, chap, from the Picard form of Fr. *chaland*, customer, and our own expression "a rum *customer*," reduced in America to "a rum *cuss*." *Hock*, for *Hochheimer*, wine from Hochheim, occurs as early as Beaumont and Fletcher; and *rum*, spirit, is for earlier *rumbullion*, of obscure origin. *Gin* is for *geneva*, a corruption of Fr. *genièvre*, Lat. *juniperus*, from the berries of which it is distilled. The history of *grog* is more complicated. The stuff called *grogram*, earlier *grograyne*, is from Fr. *gros grain*, coarse grain. Admiral Vernon (18th century) was called by the sailors "Old Grog" from his habit of wearing grogram breeches. When he issued orders that the regular allowance of rum was henceforth to be diluted with water, the sailors promptly baptized the mixture with his nickname.

Sometimes the two first syllables survive. We have *navvy* for *navigator*, *brandy* for *brandywine*, from Du. *brandewyn*, lit. burnt wine, and *whisky* for *usquebaugh*, Gaelic *uisge-beatha*, water of life (cf. *eau-de-vie*), so that the literal meaning of *whisky* is very innocent. Before the 18th century *usquebaugh* is the regular form. "The prime is *usquebaugh*, which cannot be made anywhere in that perfection; and whereas we drink it here in *aqua vitæ* measures, it goes down there by beer-glassfuls, being more natural to the nation." *Canter* is for *Canterbury* gallop, the pace of pilgrims riding to the shrine of St Thomas. John Dennis, known as Dennis the Critic, says of Pope, "Boileau's Pegasus has all his paces. The Pegasus of Pope, like a Kentish post-horse, is always on the *Canterbury*." In *bugle*, for *bugle-horn*, lit. wild-ox-horn, Old Fr. *bugle*, Lat. *buculus*, a diminutive of *bos*, ox, we have perhaps rather an ellipsis, like *waterproof* (coat), than a clipped form—

"Comrades, leave me here a little, while as yet 'tis early morn :
Leave me here, and when you want me, sound upon the *bugle-
  horn*."   (*Locksley Hall*.)

Patter is no doubt for *paternoster*—

> "Fitz-Eustace, you, with Lady Clare,
>   May bid your beads and *patter* prayer."
>   (*Marmion*, vi. 27.)

and the use of the word *marble* for a toy originally made of that stone makes it pretty certain that the *alley*, most precious of marbles, is short for *alabaster*.

Less frequently the final syllable is selected, e.g., *bus* for *omnibus*, *loo* for *lanterloo*, variously spelt in the 17th and 18th centuries. Fr. *lanturelu* was originally the meaningless refrain or "tol de rol" of a popular song in Richelieu's time. *Van* is for *caravan*, a Persian word, properly a company of merchants or ships travelling together, "also of late corruptly used with us for a kind of waggon to carry passengers to and from London" (Blount, *Glossographia*, 1674). *Wig* is for *periwig*, a corruption of Fr. *perruque*, of obscure origin. '*Varsity*, for university, and Sam Weller's '*Tizer*, for *Morning Advertiser*, belong to the 19th century.

Christian names are treated in the same way. *Alexander* gives *Alec* and *Sandy*, *Herbert*, '*Erb* or *Bert*. *Ib* (see p. 160) was once common for *Isabella*, while the modern language prefers *Bella; Maud* for *Matilda* is rather a case of natural shrinkage, while '*Tilda* is perhaps due to unconscious aphesis, like *Denry*—

"She saved a certain amount of time every day by addressing her son as *Denry*, instead of *Edward Henry*" (ARNOLD BENNETT, *The Card*, Ch. i.)

Among conscious word formations may be classed many reduplicated forms, whether riming, as *hurly-burly*, or alliterative, as *tittle-tattle*, though reduplication belongs to the natural speech of children, and in at least one case, Fr. *tante*, from *ante-ante*, Lat. *amita*, the baby word has prevailed. In a reduplicated form only one half as a rule needs to be explained. Thus *seesaw* is from *saw*, the motion suggesting two sawyers at work on a log. *Zigzag* is based on *zag*, cognate with Ger. *Zacke*, tooth, point. *Shilly-shally* is for *shill I, shall I?* *Namby-pamby* commemorates the poet Ambrose Philips, who was thus nicknamed by Pope and his friends. The weapon called a *snickersnee*—

"As he squirmed and struggled
And gurgled and guggled,
I drew my *snickersnee*."

(*The Mikado*, ii.)

is of Dutch origin and means something like "cut and

thrust." It is usually mentioned in connection with the Hollanders—

"Among other customs they have in that town, one is, that none must carry a pointed knife about him; which makes the Hollander, who is us'd to *snik* and *snee*, to leave his horn-sheath and knife a ship-board when he comes ashore." (HOWELL, letter from Florence, 1621.)

The compound does not occur in Dutch. It is rather an English variant on Du. *snee*, cut. Reduplication is also responsible for *pickaback*, earlier *pickpack*, from *pack*, bundle. The modern form is due to popular association with *back*.

CHAPTER VI

WORDS AND MEANINGS

WE have all noticed the fantastic way in which ideas are linked together in our thoughts. One thing suggests another with which it is accidentally associated in memory, the second suggests a third, and, in the course even of a few seconds, we find that we have travelled from one subject to another so remote that it requires an effort to reconstruct the series of links which connects them. The same thing happens with words. A great number of words, despite great changes of sense, retain the fundamental meaning of the original, but in many cases this is quite lost. A truer image than that of the linked chain would be that of a sphere giving off in various directions a number of rays each of which may form the nucleus of a fresh sphere. Or we may say that at each link of the chain there is a possibility of another chain branching off in a direction of its own. In Cotgrave's time to *garble* (see p. 19) and to *canvass, i.e.* sift through *canvas*, meant the same thing. Yet how different is their later sense development.

There is a word *ban*, found in Old High German and Anglo-Saxon, and meaning, as far back as it can be traced, a proclamation containing a threat, hence a command or prohibition. We have it in *banish*, to put under the *ban*. The proclamation idea survives in the *banns* of marriage and in Fr. *arrière-ban*, "a proclamation, whereby those that hold authority of the king in mesne tenure, are summoned to assemble, and serve him in his warres" (Cotgrave). This is folk-etymology for Old Fr. *arban*, Old High Ger. *hari-ban*, army summons. Slanting off from the primitive idea of proclamation is that of rule or authority. The French for outskirts is *banlieue*, properly the "circuit of a league, or thereabouts" (Cotgrave) over which the local authority extended. All public institutions within such a radius were associated with *ban*, e.g., *un four, un moulin à ban*, "a comon oven or mill whereat all men may, and every tenant and vassall must, bake, and grind" (Cotgrave)· The French adjective *banal*, used in this connection, gradually developed from the meaning of "common" that of "common place," in which sense it is now familiar in English.[1]

Bureau, a desk, was borrowed from French in the 17th century. In modern French it means not only the desk, but also the office itself and the authority exercised by the office. Hence our familiar *bureaucracy*, likely to become increasingly familiar. The desk is so called because covered with *bureau*, Old Fr. *burel*, "a thicke course cloath, of a brown russet, or darke mingled, colour" (Cotgrave), whence Mid. Eng. *borel*, rustic, clownish, lit. roughly clad. The source is perhaps Lat. *burrus*, fiery, from Gk. πῦρ, fire.

Romance was originally an adverb. To write in the vulgar tongue, instead of in classical Latin, was called *romanice scribere*, Old Fr. *romanz escrire*. When *romanz* became felt as a noun, it developed a "singular" *roman* or *romant*, the latter of which gave the archaic Eng. *romaunt*. The most famous of Old French romances

---

[1] Archaic Eng. *bannal* already existed in the technical sense.

are the epic poems called *Chansons de geste*, songs of exploits, *geste* coming from the Lat. *gesta*, deeds. Eng. *gèst* or *jest* is common in the 16th and 17th centuries in the sense of act, deed, and *jest*-book meant a story-book. As the favourite story-books were merry tales, the word gradually acquired its present meaning.

A part of our Anglo-Saxon church vocabulary was supplanted by Latin or French words. Thus Anglo-Sax. *ge-bed*, prayer, was gradually expelled by Old Fr. *preiere* (*prière*), Lat. *precaria*. It has survived in *beadsman*—

> "The *beadsman*, after thousand aves told,
> For aye unsought-for slept among his ashes cold."
> (KEATS, *Eve of St Agnes.*)

beadroll, and *bead*, now applied only to the humble device employed in counting prayers.

Not only the Romance languages, but also German and Dutch, adopted, with the Roman character, Lat. *scribere*, to write. English, on the contrary, preserved the native to *write*, *i.e.* to scratch (runes), giving to *scribere* only a limited sense, to *shrive*.

The meaning which we generally give to *pudding* is comparatively modern. The older sense appears in *black pudding*, a sausage made of pig's blood. This is also the meaning of Fr. *boudin*, whence *pudding* comes. A still older meaning of both words is intestine.

A *hearse*, now the vehicle in which a coffin is carried, is used by Shakespeare for a coffin or tomb. Its earlier meaning is a framework to support candles, usually put round the coffin at a funeral. This framework was so named from some resemblance to a harrow,[1] Fr. *herse*, Lat. *hirpex*, *hirpic-*, a rake.

---

[1] This is the usual explanation. It seems possible that the framework suggested a portcullis. See p. 142.

Treacle is a stock example of great change of meaning. In Jeremiah, viii. 22, where the Vulgate has "Numquid *resina* non est in Galaad?" Coverdale's Bible has "There is no more *triacle* at Galaad." Old Fr. *triacle* is from Greco-Lat. *theriaca*, a remedy against poison or snake-bite (θήρ, a wild beast). In Mid. English and later it was used of a sovereign remedy. It has, like *sirup* (p. 135), acquired its present meaning *via* the apothecary's shop.

A *stickler* is now a man who is fussy about small points of etiquette or procedure. In Shakespeare he is one who parts combatants—

> " The dragon wing of night o'erspreads the earth,
>   And, *stickler*-like, the armies separates."
> (*Troilus and Cressida*, v. 8.)

An earlier sense is that of seeing fair-play. The derivation is disputed, but the word has been popularly associated with the *stick*, or staff, used by the umpires in duels. Torriano (1659) gives *stickler* as one of the meanings of *bastoniere*, a verger or mace-bearer.

Infantry comes, through French, from Italian. It means a collection of "infants" or juniors, so called by contrast with the proved veterans who composed the cavalry.

The *pastern* of a horse, defined by Dr Johnson as the knee, from "ignorance, madam, pure ignorance," still means in Cotgrave and Florio "shackle." Florio even recognises a verb to *pastern*, e.g., *pastoiare*, "to fetter, to clog, to shackle, to *pastern*, to give (gyve)." It comes from Old Fr. *pasturon* (*paturon*), a derivative of *pasture*, such shackles being used to prevent grazing horses from straying. *Pester* (p. 155) is connected with it. The modern French word has changed its meaning in the same way.

To *rummage* means in the Elizabethan navigators to stow goods in a hold. A rummager was what we call a *stevedore*.[1] *Rummage* is Old Fr. *arrumage* (*arrimage*), from *arrumer*, to stow, the middle syllable of which is probably cognate with English *room;* cf. *arranger*, to put in "rank."

The Christmas *waits* were originally watchmen, Anglo-Fr. *waite*, Old Fr. *gaite*, from the Old High German form of modern Ger. *Wacht*, watch. Modern French still has the verb *guetter*, to lie in wait for, and *guet*, the watch. *Minstrel* comes from an Old French derivative of Lat. *minister*, servant. Modern Fr. *méné-trier* is only used of a country fiddler who attends village weddings.

The *lumber*-room is supposed to be for *Lombard* room, *i.e.*, the room in which pawnbrokers used to store pledged property. The Lombards introduced the three golden balls into this country.

Livery is thus explained by the poet Spenser : " What *livery* is, we by common use in England know well enough, namely, that it is allowance of horse-meat, as they commonly use the word in stabling ; as, to keep horses at *livery ;* the which word, I guess, is derived of *livering* or *delivering* forth their nightly food. So in great houses, the *livery* is said to be served up for all night, that is, their evening allowance for drink ; and *livery* is also called the upper weed which a serving-man wears ; so called, as I suppose, for that it was *delivered* and taken from him at pleasure." This passage explains also *livery* stable.[2] Our word

---

[1] A Spanish word, Lat. *stipator*, " one that stoppeth chinkes " (Cooper). It came to England in connection with the wool trade.

[2] In " livery and bait " there is pleonasm. *Bait*, connected with *bite*, is the same word as in bear-*baiting* and fishermen's *bait*. We have it also, *via* Old French, in *abet*, whence the aphetic *bet*, originally to egg on.

comes from Fr. *livrée*, the feminine past participle of *livrer*, from Lat. *liberare*, to deliver.

Pedigree was in Mid. English *pedegrew*, *petigrew*, etc. It represents Old Fr. *pie* (*pied*) *de grue*, crane's foot, from the shape of a sign used in showing lines of descent in genealogical charts. The older form survives in the family name *Pettigrew*. Here it is a nickname, like *Pettifer*, ironfoot; cf. *Sheepshanks*.

Fairy is a collective, Fr. *féerie*, its modern use being perhaps due to its occurrence in such phrases as *Faerie Queen*, i.e., Queen of Fairyland. Cf. *paynim*, used by some poets for *pagan*, but really a doublet of *paganism*, occurring in *paynim host*, *paynim knight*, etc. The correct name for the individual *fairy* is *fay*, Fr. *fée*, Lat. *fata*, plural of *fatum*, fate. This appears in Ital. *fata*, "a fairie, a witch, an enchantres, an elfe" (Florio). The *fata morgana*, the mirage sometimes seen in the Strait of Messina, is attributed to the fairy Morgana of Tasso, the Morgan le Fay of our own Arthurian legends.

Many people must have wondered at some time why the *clubs* and *spades* on cards are so called. The latter figure, it is true, bears some resemblance to a spade, but no giant of fiction is depicted with a club with a triple head. The explanation is that we have adopted the French pattern, *carreau* (see p. 150), diamond, *cœur*, heart, *pique*, pike, spear-head, *trèfle*, trefoil, clover-leaf, but have given to the two latter the names used in the Italian and Spanish pattern, which, instead of the pike and trefoil, has the sword (Ital. *spada*) and mace (Ital. *bastone*). Etymologically both *spades* are identical, the origin being Greco-Lat. *spatha*, the name of a number of blade-shaped objects; cf. the diminutive *spatula*.

Wafer, in both its senses, is related to Ger. *Wabe*, honeycomb. We find Anglo-Fr. *wafre* in the sense of a thin cake, perhaps stamped with a honeycomb pattern.

The cognate Fr. *gaufre* is the name of a similar cake which not only has the honeycomb pattern, but is also largely composed of honey. Hence our verb to *goffer*, to give a cellular appearance to a frill.

The meanings of adjectives are especially subject to change. *Quaint* now conveys the idea of what is unusual, and, as early as the 17th century, we find it explained as "strange, unknown." This is the exact opposite of its original meaning, Old Fr. *cointe*, Lat. *cognitus ;* cf., *acquaint*, Old Fr. *acointier*, make known. It is possible to trace roughly the process by which this remarkable *volte - face* has been brought about. The intermediate sense of trim or pretty is common in Shakespeare—

> "For a fine, *quaint*, graceful, and excellent fashion, yours is worth ten on't." (*Much Ado*, iii. 4.)

We apply *restive* to a horse that will not stand still. It means properly a horse that will not do anything else. Fr. *rétif*, Old Fr. *restif*, from *rester*, to remain, Lat. *re-stare*, has kept more of the original sense. Scot. to *reest* means to stand stock-still. Dryden even uses *restive* in the sense of sluggish—

> " So James the drowsy genius wakes
>   Of Britain, long entranced in charms,
>   *Restive*, and slumbering on its arms."
>   (*Threnodia Augustalis*.)

Reasty, used of meat that has "stood" too long, is the same word, (cf. *testy*, Old Fr. *testif*, heady), and *rusty* bacon is probably folk-etymology for *reasty* bacon—

> "And then came haltyng Jone,
>   And brought a gambone
>   Of bakon that was *reasty*."
>   (SKELTON, *Elynour Rummyng*.)

Sterling has a curious history. It is from Old Fr. *esterlin*, a coin which etymologists have until lately connected with the *Easterlings*, or Hanse merchants, who formed one of the great mercantile communities of the Middle Ages; and perhaps some such association is responsible for the meaning that *sterling* has acquired; but chronology shows this traditional etymology to be impossible. We find *unus sterlingus* in a medieval Latin document of 1184, and the Old French *esterlin* occurs in Wace's *Roman de Rou* (Romaunt of Rollo the Sea King), which was written before 1175. Hence it is conjectured that the original coin may have been stamped with a *star* or a *starling*.

When Horatio says—

"It is a nipping and an *eager* air." (*Hamlet*, i. 4.)

we are reminded that *eager* is identical with the second part of vin-*egar*, Fr. *aigre*, sour, Lat. *acer*, keen. It seems hardly possible to explain the modern sense of *nice*, which in the course of its history has traversed nearly the whole diatonic scale between "rotten" and "ripping." In Mid. English and Old French it means foolish. Cotgrave explains it by "lither, lazie, sloathful, idle; faint, slack; dull, simple." It is supposed to come from Lat. *nescius*, ignorant. The transition from *fond*, foolish, which survives in "*fond* hopes," to *fond*, loving, is easy. French *fou* is used in exactly the same way. *Cf.* also to *dote* on, *i.e.*, to be foolish about. *Puny* is Fr. *puîné*, from *puis né*, later born, junior, whence the *puisne* justices. Milton uses it of a minor—

"He must appear in print like a *puny* with his guardian."
(*Areopagitica.*)

Petty, Fr. *petit*, was similarly used for a small boy.

In some cases a complimentary adjective loses its true meaning and takes on a contemptuous or ironic sense. None of us care to be called *bland*, and to describe a man as *worthy* is to apologise for his existence. We may compare Fr. *bonhomme*, which now means generally an old fool, and *bonne femme*, good-wife, goody. *Dapper*, the Dutch for brave (*cf.* Ger. *tapfer*), and *pert*, Mid. Eng. *apert*, representing in meaning Lat. *expertus*, have changed much since Milton wrote of—

"The *pert* fairies and the *dapper* elves." (*Comus*, 118.)

Pert seems in fact to have acquired the meaning of its opposite *malapert*. *Smug*, a variant of Ger. *schmuck*, trim, elegant, beautiful, has its original sense in Shakespeare—

"And here the *smug* and silver Trent shall run
In a new channel, fair and evenly."
(1 *Henry IV.*, iii. 1.)

The degeneration of an adjective is sometimes due to its employment for euphemistic purposes. The favourite substitute for *fat* is *stout*, properly strong,[1] dauntless, etc., cognate with Ger. *stolz*, proud. Precisely the same euphemism appears in French, e.g., *une dame un peu forte*. *Ugly* is replaced by *plain*, or *homely*, "ugly, disagreeable, course, mean" (Kersey's *Dictionary*, 1720). *Homely* has been rehabilitated in English, but in America it still has the sense given by Kersey.

Change of meaning may be brought about by association. A *miniature* is a small portrait, and we even use the word as an adjective meaning "small, on a reduced scale." But the true sense of *miniature* is something painted in *minium*, red lead. Florio explains

---

[1] Hence the use of *stout* for a "strong" beer. *Porter* was once the favourite tap of *porters*, and a mixture of stout and ale, now known as *cooper*, was especially relished by the brewery *cooper*.

miniatura as "a limning (see p. 58), a painting with vermilion." Such paintings were usually small, hence the later meaning. The word was first applied to the ornamental red initial capitals in manuscripts. *Vignette* still means technically in French an interlaced vine-pattern on a frontispiece.[1] Cotgrave has *vignettes*, "vignets; branches, or branch-like borders, or flourishes in painting, or ingravery."

The degeneration in the meaning of a noun may be partly due to frequent association with disparaging adjectives. Thus *hussy*, *i.e.* housewife, *quean*,[2] lit. woman, *wench*, child, have absorbed such adjectives as impudent, idle, light, saucy, etc. Shakespeare uses *quean* only three times, and these three include "cozening *quean*" (*Merry Wives*, iv. 2) and "scolding *quean*" (*All's Well*, ii. 2). With *wench*, still used without any disparaging sense by country folk, we may compare Fr. *garce*, lass, and Ger. *Dirne*, maid-servant, both of which are now insulting epithets, but, in the older language, could be applied to Joan of Arc and the Virgin Mary respectively. *Garce* was replaced by *fille*, which has acquired in its turn a meaning so offensive that it has now given way to *jeune fille*. *Minx*, earlier *minkes*, is probably the Low Ger. *minsk*, Ger. *Mensch*, lit. human, but used also in the sense of "wench." For the consonantal change cf. *hunks*, Dan. *hundsk*, stingy, lit. doggish. These examples show that the indignant "Who are you calling a *woman?*" is, philologically, in all likelihood a case of intelligent anticipation.

Adjectives are affected in their turn by being regularly coupled with certain nouns. A *buxom* help-

---

[1] Folk-etymology for *frontispice*, Lat. *frontispicium*, front view.
[2] Related to, but not identical with, *queen*.

mate was once obedient, the word being cognate with Ger. *biegsam*, flexible, yielding—

> "The place where thou and Death
> Shall dwell at ease, and up and down unseen
> Wing silently the *buxom* air."
>
> (*Paradise Lost*, ii. 840.)

An obedient nature is "buxom, blithe and debonair," qualities which affect the physique and result in heartiness of aspect and a comely plumpness. An *arch* damsel is etymologically akin to an *arch*bishop, both descending from the Greek prefix ἀρχι, from ἀρχή, a beginning, first cause. Shakespeare uses *arch* as a noun—

> "The noble duke my master,
> My worthy *arch* and patron comes to-night."
>
> (*Lear*, ii. 1.)

Occurring chiefly in such phrases as *arch* enemy, *arch* heretic, *arch* hypocrite, *arch* rogue, it acquired a depreciatory sense, which has now become so weakened that *archness* is by no means an unpleasing attribute. The same double meaning is developed in the cognate German prefix *Erz*, so that we find, in Ludwig, as successive entries, *Ertz-dieb*, "an arch-thief, an arrant thief," and *Ertz-engel*, "an arch-angel." The meaning of *arrant* is almost entirely due to association with "thief." It means lit. wandering, vagabond, so that the *arrant* thief is nearly related to the knight *errant*, and to the Justices in *eyre*, Old Fr. *eire*, Lat. *iter*, a way, journey. Fr. *errer*, to wander, stray, is compounded of Vulgar Lat. *iterare*, to journey, and Lat. *errare*, to stray, and it would be difficult to calculate how much of each enters into the composition of *le Juif errant*.

As I have suggested above, association accounts to some extent for changes of meaning, but the process is in reality more complex, and usually a number of factors are working together or in opposition to each other. A low word may gradually acquire right of citizenship. "That article blackguardly called *pluck*" (Scott) is now much respected. It is the same word as *pluck*, the heart, liver, and lungs of an animal—

"During the Crimean war, *plucky*, signifying courageous, seemed likely to become a favourite term in Mayfair, even among the ladies." (HOTTEN'S *Slang Dictionary*, 1864.)

Having become respectable, it is now replaced in sporting circles by the more emphatic *guts*, which reproduces the original metaphor. A word may die out in its general sense, surviving only in some special meaning. Thus the poetic *sward*, scarcely used except with "green," meant originally the skin or crust of anything. It is cognate with Ger. *Schwarte*, "the *sward*, or rind, of a thing" (Ludwig), which now means especially bacon-rind. Related words may meet with very different fates in kindred languages. Eng. *knight* is cognate with Ger. *Knecht*, servant, which had, in Mid. High German, a wide range of meanings, including "warrior, hero." There is no more complimentary epithet than *knightly*, while Ger. *knechtisch* means servile. The degeneration of words like *boor*, *churl*, farmer, is a familiar phenomenon (cf. *villain*, p. 139). The same thing has happened to *blackguard*, the modern meaning of which is a libel on a humble but useful class. The name *black guard* was given collectively to the kitchen detachment of a great man's retinue. The *scavenger* has also come down in the world, rather an unusual phenomenon in the case of official titles. The medieval *scavager*[1] was an

---

[1] English regularly inserts *n* in words thus formed; cf. *harbinger*, *messenger*, *passenger*, *pottinger*, etc.

important official who originally seems to have been a
kind of inspector of customs.   He was called in Anglo-
French *scawageour*, from the noun *scawage*, showing.
The Old French dialect verb *escauwer* is of Germanic
origin and cognate with Eng. *show* and Ger. *schauen*, to
look.   The *cheater*, now usually *cheat*, probably deserved
his fate.   The *escheators* looked after *escheats*, *i.e.*, estates
or property that lapsed and were forfeited.   The origin of
the word is Old Fr. *escheoir* (*échoir*), to fall due, Lat. *ex*
*cadēre for *cadĕre*.   Their reputation was unsavoury, and
cheat has already its present meaning in Shakespeare.
He also plays on the double meaning—

"I will be *cheater* to them both, and they shall be exchequers
to me." (*Merry Wives*, i. 3.)

Beldam implies "hag" as early as Shakespeare, but
he also uses it in its proper sense of "grandmother,"
e.g., Hotspur refers to "old *beldam* earth" and "our
grandam earth" in the same speech (1 *Henry IV.*, iii. 1),
and Milton speaks of "*beldam* nature."   It is of course
from *belle-dame*, used in Old French for "grandmother,"
as *belsire* was for "grandfather."   Hence it is a doublet
of *belladonna*.   The masculine *belsire* survives as a
family name, *Belcher;* and to Jim Belcher, most
gentlemanly of prize - fighters, we owe the *belcher*
handkerchief, which had large white spots with a
dark blue dot in the centre of each on a medium
blue ground.   It was also known to the "fancy" as a
"bird's-eye wipe."

CHAPTER VII

SEMANTICS

THE convenient name semantics has been applied of late to the science of meanings, as distinguished from phonetics, the science of sound. The comparative study of languages enables us to observe and codify the general laws which govern sense development, and to understand why meanings become extended or restricted. One phenomenon which seems to occur normally in language results from what we may call the simplicity of the olden times. Thus the whole vocabulary which is etymologically related to *writing* and *books* has developed from an old Germanic verb that means to *scratch* and the Germanic name for the *beech*. Our earliest books were wooden tablets on which inscriptions were scratched. The word *book* itself comes from Anglo-Sax. *bōc*, beech; *cf.* Ger. *Buchstabe*, letter, lit. beech-stave. Lat. *liber*, book, whence a large family of words in the Romance languages, means the inner bark of a tree, and *bible* is ultimately from Greek βύβλος, the inner rind of the *papyrus*, the Egyptian rush from which *paper* was made.[1]

The earliest measurements were calculated from the human body. All European languages use the *foot*, and

---

[1] Parchment (see p. 45) was invented as a substitute when the supply of papyrus failed.

we still measure horses by *hands*, while *span* survives in table-books. *Cubit* is Latin for *elbow*, the first part of which is the same as *ell*, cognate with Lat. *ulna*, also used in both senses. Fr. *brasse*, fathom, is Lat. *brachia*, the two arms, and *pouce*, thumb, means inch. A further set of measures are represented by simple devices: a *yard* is a small "stick," and the *rod, pole,* or *perch* (cf. *perch* for birds, Fr. *perche*, pole) which gives charm to our arithmetic is a larger one. A *furlong* is a *furrow-long*. For weights common objects were used, *e.g.*, a *grain*, or a *scruple*, Lat. *scrupulus*, "a little sharpe stone falling sometime into a man's shooe" (Cooper), for very small things, a *stone* for heavier goods. Gk. δραχμά, whence our *dram*, means a handful. Our decimal system is due to our possession of ten *digits*, or fingers, and *calculation* comes from Lat. *calculus*, a pebble.

A modern Chancellor of the Exchequer, considering his budget, is not so near the reality of things as his medieval predecessor, who literally sat in his counting-house, counting up his money. For the *exchequer*, named from the Old Fr. *eschequier* (*échiquier*), chess-board, was once the board marked out in squares on which the treasurer piled up the king's taxes in hard cash. This Old Fr. *eschequier*, which has also given *chequer*, is a derivative of Old Fr. *eschec* (*échec*), check. Thus "*check* trousers" and a "*chequered* career" are both directly related to an eastern potentate (see *chess*, p. 111). The *chancellor* himself was originally a kind of door-keeper in charge of a *chancel*, a latticed barrier which we now know in church architecture only. *Chancel* is derived, through Fr. *chancel* or *cancel*, from Lat. *cancellus*, a cross bar, occurring more usually in the plural in the sense of lattice, grating. We still *cancel* a document by drawing such a pattern on it. In German *cancellus* has given *Kanzel*, pulpit. The *budget*, now a document in

which millions are mere items, was the chancellor's
little bag or purse—

> " If tinkers may have leave to live,
>   And bear the sow-skin *budget*,
> Then my account I well may give,
>   And in the stocks avouch it."
>   (*Winter's Tale*, iv. 2.)

Fr. *bougette*, from which it is borrowed, is a diminutive
of *bouge*, a leathern bag, which comes from Lat. *bulga*,
"a male or *bouget* of leather; a purse; a bagge"
(Cooper). Modern French has borrowed back our
budget, together with several other words dealing with
business and finance.

Among the most important servants of the
exchequer were the *controllers*. We now call them
officially *comptroller*, through a mistaken association
with Fr. *compte*, account. The controller had charge of
the *counter-rolls* (cf. *counterfoil*), from Old Fr. *contre-rolle*,
" the copy of a role (of accounts, etc.), a paralell of the
same quality and content, with the originall" (Cotgrave).
In French *contrôle* has preserved the sense of supervision
or verification which it has lost in ordinary English.

A very ancient functionary of the exchequer, the
tally-cutter, was abolished in the reign of George III.
Tallies (Fr. *tailler*, to cut) were sticks "scored" across
in such a way that the notches could be compared for
purposes of verification. Jack Cade preferred those
good old ways—

> "Our fore-fathers had no other books but the *score* and the
> *tally* ; thou hast caused books to be used."
>   (2 *Henry VI.*, iv. 7.)

This rudimentary method of calculation was still in use
in the Kentish hop-fields within fairly recent times ; and
some of us can remember very old gentlemen asking us,

after a cricket match, how many "notches" we had " scored "—

"The scorers were prepared to notch the runs."
(*Pickwick*, Ch. vii.)

This use of *score*, for a reckoning in general, or for twenty, occurs in Anglo-Saxon. The words *score* and *tally*, one native and the other borrowed, were thus originally of identical meaning. They were soon differentiated, a common phenomenon in such cases. For the exchequer *tally* was substituted an "indented cheque receipt." An *indenture*, chiefly familiar to us in connection with apprenticeship, was a duplicate document of which the "indented" or toothed edges had to correspond like the notches of the score or tally. *Cheque*, earlier *check*, is identical with *check*, rebuff. The metaphor is from the game of chess (see p. 111), to check a man's accounts involving a sort of control, or pulling up short, if necessary. The modern spelling *cheque* is due to popular association with *exchequer*, which is etymologically right, though the words have reached their modern functions by very different paths.

The development of the meaning of *chancellor* can be paralleled in the case of many other functionaries, once humble but now important. The titles of two great medieval officers, the *constable* and the *marshal*, mean the same thing. *Constable*, Old Fr. *conestable* (*connétable*), is Lat. *comes stabuli*, stable fellow, and *marshal*, the first element of which is cognate with *mare*, while the second is modern Ger. *Schalk*, rascal, expresses the same idea in German. Both *constable* and *marshal* are now used of very high positions, but Policeman X. and the *farrier-marshal*, or shoeing-smith, of a troop of cavalry, remind them of the base degrees by which they did ascend. The *Marshalsea* where Little Dorrit lived is for *marshalsy*, marshals' office, etc. The *steward*, or *sty-ward*, looked after his master's pigs. He rose in importance until, by the marriage of Marjorie Bruce to Walter the *Stewart* of Scotland, he founded the most picturesque of royal houses. The *chamberlain*, as his name suggests, attended to the royal comforts long before he became a judge of wholesome literature.

All these names now stand for a great number of functions of varying importance. Other titles which are equally vague are *sergeant* (see p. 137) and *usher*, Old Fr. *uissier*[1] (*huissier*), lit. door-keeper, Lat. *ostiarius*, a porter. Another official was the *harbinger*, who survives only in poetry. He was a forerunner, or vauntcourier, who preceded the great man to secure him "harbourage" for the night, and his name comes from Old Fr. *herberger* (*héberger*), to shelter. As late as the reign of Charles II. we read that—

"On the removal of the court to pass the summer at Winchester, Bishop Ken's house, which he held in the right of his prebend, was marked by the *harbinger* for the use of Mrs Eleanor Gwyn ; but he refused to grant her admittance, and she was forced to seek for lodgings in another place."

(HAWKINS, *Life of Bishop Ken.*)

One of the most interesting branches of semantics, and the most useful to the etymologist, deals with the study of parallel metaphors in different languages. We have seen (p. 26) how, for instance, the names of flowers show that the same likeness has been observed by various races. The spice called *clove* and the *clove*-pink both belong to Lat. *clavus*, a nail. The German for pink is *Nelke*, a Low German diminutive, *nail-kin*, of

---

[1] As *huissier* has given *usher*, I would suggest that the family names *Lush* and *Lusher*, which Bardsley (*Dict. of English Surnames*) gives up, are for Fr. *l'uis* (cf. *Laporte*) and *l'uissier*. In modern French *Lhuissier* is not an uncommon name.

Nagel, nail. The spice, or *Gewürznelke*, is called in South Germany *Nägele*, little nail. A *clove* of garlic is quite a separate word; but, as it has some interesting cognates, it may be mentioned here. It is so called because the bulb *cleaves* naturally into segments.[1] The German name is *Knoblauch*, for Mid. High Ger. *klobelouch*, clove leek, by dissimilation of one *l*. The Dutch doublet is *kloof*, a chasm, gully, familiar in South Africa.

Ger. *Gift*, poison, lit. gift, and Fr. *poison*, Lat. *potio*, *potion-*, a drink, seem to date from treacherous times. On the other hand, Ger. *Geschenk*, a present, means something poured out (see *nuncheon*, p. 114), while a tip is in French *pourboire* and in German *Trinkgeld*, even when accepted by a lifelong abstainer. In English we "ride a *hobby*," *i.e.*, a hobby-horse, or wooden horse. German has the same metaphor, "ein *Steckenpferd* reiten," and French say "enfourcher un *dada*," *i.e.*, to bestride a gee-gee. *Hobby*, for Mid. Eng. *hobin*, a nag, was a proper name for a horse. Like *Dobbin* and *Robin*, it belongs to the numerous progeny of Robert.

In some cases the reason for a metaphor is not quite clear to the modern mind. The bloodthirsty weasel is called in French *belette*,[2] little beauty, in Italian *donnola*; and in Portuguese *doninha*, little lady, in Spanish *comadreja*, gossip (Fr. *commère*, Scot. *cummer*), in Bavarian *Schöntierlein*, beautiful little animal, in Danish *kjönne*, beautiful, and in older English *fairy*. From Lat. *medius* we get *mediastinus*, " a drugge (drudge) or lubber to doè all vile service in the house; a kitching slave" (Cooper). Why this drudge should have a name

---

[1] The *onion*, Fr. *oignon*, Lat. *unio*, *union-*, is so named because successive skins form an harmonious one-ness. It is a doublet of *union*.

[2] Perhaps a diminutive of Cymric *bele*, marten, but felt as from Fr. *belle*.

implying a middle position I cannot say; but to-day in Yorkshire a maid-of-all-work is called a *tweeny* (between maid).

A stock semantic parallel occurs in the relation between age and respectability. All of us, as soon as we get to reasonable maturity, lay great stress on the importance of deference to "elders." It follows naturally that many titles of more or less dignity should be evolved from this idea of seniority. The Eng. *alderman* is obvious. *Priest*, Old Fr. *prestre*[1] (*prêtre*), from Gk. πρεσβύτερος, comparative of πρέσβυς, old, is not so obvious. In the Romance languages we have a whole group of words, *e.g.*, Fr. *sire, sieur, seigneur*; Ital. *signor*, Span. *señor*, with their compounds *monsieur, messer*, etc., all representing either *senior* or *seniorem*. Ger. *Eltern*, parents, is the plural comparative of *alt*, old, and the first element of *seneschal* (see *marshal*, p. 82) is cognate with Lat. *senex*. From Fr. *sire* comes Eng. *sir*, and from this was formed the adjective *sirly*,[2] now spelt *surly*, which in Shakespeare still means haughty, arrogant—

"See how the *surly* Warwick mans the wall."
(3 *Henry* VI., v. i.)

A *list*, in the sense of enumeration, is a "strip." The cognate German word is *Leiste*, border. We have the original meaning in "*list* slippers." Fr. *bordereau*, a list, which became very familiar in connection with the Dreyfus case, is a diminutive of *bord*, edge. *Label* is the same word as Old Fr. *lambel* (*lambeau*), rag. *Scroll* is a diminutive of Old Fr. *escrou*,[3] rag, of German origin, and cognate with *shred* and *screed*. *Docket*,

---

[1] Cf. *Prester* John, the fabulous priest monarch of Ethiopia.
[2] Cf. *lordly, princely*, etc., and Ger. *herrisch*, imperious, from *Herr*, sir.
[3] Modern Fr. *écrou* is used only in the sense of prison register.

earlier *dogget*, is from an old Italian diminutive of *doga*, cask-stave, which meant a bendlet in heraldry. *Schedule* is a diminutive of Lat. *scheda*, "a scrowe" (Cooper), properly a strip of papyrus. Ger. *Zettel*, bill, ticket, is the same word. Thus all these words, more or less kindred in meaning, can be reduced to the primitive notion of strip or scrap.

Farce, from French, means stuffing. The verb to *farce*, which represents Lat. *farcire*, survives in the perverted *force* - meat. A parallel is *satire*, from Lat. *satura* (*lanx*), a full dish, hence a medley. Somewhat similar is the modern meaning of *magazine*, a "storehouse" of amusement or information.

The closest form of intimacy is represented by community of board and lodging, or, in older phraseology, "bed and board." *Companion*, with its numerous related words, belongs to Vulgar Lat. **companio*, *companion-*, bread-sharer. The same idea is represented by the pleonastic Eng. *messmate*, the second part of which, *mate*, is related to *meat*. *Mess*, food, Old Fr. *mes* (*mets*), Lat. *missum*, is in modern English only military or naval—

> "Herbs and other country *messes*
> Which the neat-handed Phillis dresses."
>
> (*Allegro*, 85.)

Another related word is Fr. *matelot*, earlier *matenot*, representing Du. *maat*, meat, and *genoot*, a companion. The latter word is cognate with Ger. *Genosse*, a companion, from *geniessen*, to enjoy or use together. In early Dutch we find also *mattegenoet*, through popular association with *matte*, hammock, one hammock serving, by a Box and Cox arrangement, for two sailors.

Comrade is from Fr. *camarade*, and this from Span. *camarada*, originally a "room-full," called in the French army *une chambrée*. This corresponds to Ger. *Geselle*, comrade, from *Saal*, room. The reduction of the collective to the individual is paralleled by Ger. *Bursche*, fellow, from Mid. High Ger. *burse*, college hostel ; cf. *Frauenzimmer*, wench, lit. women's room. It can hardly be doubted that *chum* is a corrupted clip from *chamber-fellow*.[1] It is thus explained in a Dictionary of the Canting Crew (1690), within a few years of its earliest recorded occurrence, and the reader will remember Mr Pickwick's introduction to the *chummage* system in the Fleet.

English *gossip*, earlier *god-sib*, related in God, a sponsor, soon developed the subsidiary meanings of boon companion, crony, tippler, babbler, etc., all of which are represented in Shakespeare. The case of Fr. *compère* and *commère*, godfather and godmother, is similar. Cotgrave explains *commérage* as " gossiping ; the acquaintance, affinity, or league that growes betweene women by christning a child together, or one for another." Ger. *Gevatter*, godfather, has also acquired the sense of Fr. *bonhomme*, Eng. *daddy*. From *commère* comes Scot. *cummer* or *kimmer*—

> " 'Tis merry, 'tis merry, *Cummers*, I trow,
>   To dance thus beneath the nightshade bough."
>   (INGOLDSBY, *The Witches' Frolic*.)

While christenings led to cheerful garrulity, the wilder fun of weddings has given the Fr. *faire la noce*, to go on

---

[1] The vowel is not so great a difficulty as it might appear. In the London pronunciation the *u* of such words as *but*, *cup*, *hurry*, etc., represents roughly a continental short *a*. This fact, familiar to phoneticians but disbelieved by others, is one of the first peculiarities noted by foreigners beginning to learn English. It is quite possible that *chum* is an accidental spelling for **cham*, just as we write *bungalow* for *bangla* (Bengal), *pundit* for *pandit*, and *Punjaub* for *Panjab*, five rivers, whence also probably the liquid called *punch*, from its five ingredients. *Cf.* also American to *slug*, *i.e.* to *slog*, which appears to represent Du. *slag*, blow—" That was for *slugging* the guard " (Kipling, An Error in the Fourth Dimension)—and the adjective *bluff*, from obsolete Du. *blaf*, broad-faced.

the spree. In Ger. *Hochzeit*, wedding, lit. high time, we have a converse development of meaning.

Parallel sense development in different languages sometimes gives us a glimpse of the life of our ancestors. Our verb to *curry* (leather) comes from Old Fr. *corréer*[1] (*courroyer*), to make ready, put in order, which represents a theoretical *con-red-are*, the root syllable of which is Germanic and cognate with our *ready*. Ger. *gerben*, to tan, Old High Ger. *garawen*, to make ready, is a derivative of *gar*, ready, complete, now used only as an adverb meaning "quite," but cognate with our *yare*—

> "Our ship—
> Which, but three glasses since, we gave out split—
> Is tight, and *yare*, and bravely rigg'd."
>
> (*Tempest*, v. i.)

Both words must have acquired their restricted meaning at a time when there was literally nothing like leather.

Even in slang we find the same parallelism exemplified. We call an old-fashioned watch a *turnip*. In German it is called *Zwiebel*, onion, and in Fr. *oignon*. Eng. *greenhorn* likens an inexperienced person to an animal whose horns have just begun to sprout. In Ger. *Gelbschnabel*, yellow bill, and Fr. *bec-jaune*, we have the metaphor of the fledgling. Ludwig explains *Gelbschnabel* by "chitty-face," *chit*, cognate with *kit*-ten, being a general term in Mid. English for a young animal. From *bec-jaune* we have Scot. *beejam*, freshman at the university. Cotgrave spells the French word *bejaune*, and gives, as he usually does for such words,[2]

---

[1] *Array*, Old Fr. *arréer*, is related.

[2] This is a characteristic of the old dictionary makers. The gem of my collection is Ludwig's gloss for *Lümmel*, "a long lubber, a lazy lubber, a slouch, a lordant, a lordane, a looby, a booby, a tony, a fop, a dunce, a simpleton, a wise-acre, a sot, a logger-head, a block-head, a nickampoop, a

a very full gloss, which happens, by exception, to be quotable—

"A novice ; a late prentice to, or young beginner in, a trade, or art ; also, a simple, ignorant, unexperienced, asse ; a rude, unfashioned, home-bred hoydon ; a sot, ninny, doult, noddy ; one that's blankt, and hath nought to say, when he hath most need to speake."

The Englishman intimates that a thing has ceased to please by saying that he is "fed up" with it. The Frenchman says "J'en ai soupé." Both these metaphors are quite modern, but they express in flippant form the same figure of physical satiety which is as old as language. *Padding* is a comparatively new word in connection with literary composition, but it reproduces, with a slightly different meaning, the figure expressed by *bombast*, lit. wadding, a derivative of Greco-Lat. *bombyx*, originally "silkworm," whence also *bombasine*. We may compare also "*fustian* eloquence"—

"And he, whose *fustian*'s so sublimely bad,
It is not poetry, but prose run mad."
(POPE, *Prologue to the Satires*, l. 187.)

And a very similar image is found in the Latin poet Ausonius—

"At nos illepidum, rudem libellum,
Burras, quisquilias ineptiasque
Credemus gremio cui fovendum ?"
(*Drepanio Filio.*)

Even to "take the cake" is paralleled by the Gk. λαβεῖν τὸν πυραμοῦντα, to be awarded the cake of roasted wheat and honey which was originally the prize of him who best kept awake during a night-watch.

lingerer, a drowsy or dreaming lusk, a pill-garlick, a slowback, a lathback, a pitiful sneaking fellow, a lungis, a tall slim fellow, a slim longback, a great he-fellow, a lubberly fellow, a lozel, an awkward fellow."

In the proverbial expressions which contain the concentrated wisdom of the ages we sometimes find exact correspondences. Thus "to look a gift-horse in the mouth" is literally reproduced in French and German. Sometimes the symbols vary, *e.g.*, the risk one is exposed to in acquiring goods without examination is called by us "buying a pig in a poke."[1] French and German substitute the cat. We say that "a cat may look at a king." The French *dramatis personæ* are a dog and a bishop, while German recognises no such subversive aphorism.

Every language has an immense number of metaphors to describe the various stages of intoxication. We, as a seafaring nation, have naturally a set of such metaphors taken from nautical English. In French and German the state of being "half-seas over" or "three sheets in the wind," and the action of "splicing the main brace" are expressed by various land metaphors. But the more obvious nautical figures are common property. We speak of being *stranded;* French says "*échouer* (to run ashore) dans une entreprise," and German uses *scheitern*, to strand, split on a rock, in the same way.

Finally, we observe the same principle in euphemism, or that form of speech which avoids calling things by their names. Euphemism is the result of various human instincts which range from religious reverence down to common decency. There is, however, a special type of euphemism which may be described as the delicacy of the partially educated. It is a matter of common observation that for educated people a spade is a spade, while the more outspoken class prefers to call it a decorated shovel. Between these

---

[1] *Poke*, sack, is still common in dialect, *e.g.* in the Kentish hop-fields. It is a doublet of *pouch*, and its diminutive is *pocket*.

two classes come those delicate beings whose work in
life is—

> "le retranchement de ces syllabes sales
> Qui dans les plus beaux mots produisent des scandales ;
> Ces jouets éternels des sots de tous les temps ;
> Ces fades lieux-communs de nos méchants plaisants ;
> Ces sources d'un amas d'équivoques infâmes,
> Dont on vient faire insulte à la pudeur des femmes."
>
> (MOLIÈRE, *Les Femmes savantes*, iii. 2.)

In the United States refined society has succeeded
in banning as improper the word *leg*, which must now
be replaced by *limb*, even when the possessor is a boiled
fowl,[1] and this refinement is not unknown in England.
This tendency shows itself especially in connection with
the more intimate garments and articles intended for
personal use. We have the absurd name *pocket
handkerchief*, *i.e.*, pocket hand cover-head, for a comparatively modern convenience, the earlier names of
which have more of the directness of the Artful Dodger's
"wipe." Ben Jonson calls it a *muckinder*. In 1829 the
use of the word *mouchoir* in a French adaptation of
Othello caused a riot at the Comédie Française. History
repeats itself, for, in 1907, a play by J. M. Synge was
produced in Dublin, but the "audience broke up in
disorder at the word *shift*" (*The Academy*, 14th Oct.
1911). This is all the more ludicrous when we reflect
that *shift*, *i.e.* change of raiment, is itself an early
euphemism for *smock ; cf.* Ital. *mutande*, "thinne under-
breeches" (Florio), from a country and century not
usually regarded as prudish. The fact is that, just
as the low word, when once accepted, loses its primitive

---

[1] The coloured ladies of Barbados appear to have been equally sensi-
tive.—"Fate had placed me opposite to a fine turkey. I asked my partner
if I should have the pleasure of helping her to a piece of the breast. She
looked at me indignantly, and said, 'Curse your impudence, sar ; I wonder
where you larn manners. Sar, I take a lilly turkey *bosom*, if you please.'"
(*Peter Simple*, Ch. 31.)

vigour (see *pluck*, p. 77), the euphemism is, by inevitable association, doomed from its very birth.

I will now give a few examples of the way in which the study of semantics helps the etymologist. The *antlers* of a deer are properly the lowest branches of the horns, what we now call brow-antlers. The word comes from Old Fr. *antoilliers*, which answers phonetically to a conjectured Lat. **ante-oculares*, from *oculus*, eye. This conjecture is confirmed by the Ger. *Augensprosse*, brow-antler, lit. eye-sprout.

Eng. *plover*, from Fr. *pluvier*, could come from a Vulgar Lat. **pluviarius*, belonging to rain. The German name *Regenpfeifer*, lit. rain-piper, shows this to be correct. It does not matter, etymologically, whether the bird really has any connection with rain, for rustic observation, interesting as it is, is essentially unscientific. The *honey*suckle is useless to the bee. The *slow-worm*, a corrupted form for *slayworm*, strike serpent,[1] is perfectly harmless, and the toad, though ugly, is not venomous, nor does he bear a jewel in his head.

Kestrel, a kind of hawk, represents Old Fr. *quercerelle* (*crécerelle*), "a kastrell" (Cotgrave). *Crécerelle* is a diminutive of *crécelle*, a rattle, used in Old French especially of the leper's rattle or clapper, with which he warned people away from his neighbourhood. It is connected with Lat. *crepare*, to resound. The Latin name for the kestrel is *tinnunculus*, lit. a little ringer, derived from the verb *tinnire*, to clink, jingle, "tintinnabulate." Cooper tells us that "they use to set them (kestrels) in pigeon houses, to make doves to love the place, bicause they feare away other haukes with their ringing voyce." This information is obtained from the Latin agriculturist

---

[1] The meaning of *worm* has degenerated since the days of the *Lindwurm*, the dragon slain by Siegfried. The Norse form survives in *Great Orme's Head*, the dragon's head.

Columella. This parallel makes it clear that Fr. *crécerelle*, kestrel, is a metaphorical application of the same word, meaning a leper's " clicket."

The curious word *akimbo* occurs first in Mid. English in the form *in kenebowe*. In half a dozen languages we find this attitude expressed by the figure of a jug-handle, or, as it used to be called, a pot-ear. The oldest equivalent is Lat. *ansatus*, used by Plautus, from *ansa*, a jug-handle. *Ansatus homo* is explained by Cooper as " a man with his arms on *kenbow*." The French for to stand with arms akimbo is " faire le pot a deux *anses*," and the same striking image occurs in German, Dutch, and Spanish. Hence it seems a plausible conjecture that *kenebowe* means " jug-handle." This is confirmed by the fact that Dryden translates *ansæ* by " kimbo handles," while Thomas' *Latin Dictionary* (1644) explains *ansatus homo* as " one that in bragging manner strowteth up and down with his armes *a-canne-bow*." Eng. *bow*, meaning anything bent, is used in many connections for handle. The first element may be *can*, applied to every description of vessel in earlier English, as it still is in Scottish, or it may be some Scandinavian word. In fact the whole compound may be Scandinavian.

Demure has been explained as from Mid. Eng. *mure*, ripe, mature, with prefixed *de*. But *demure* is the older word of the two, and while the loss of the atonic first syllable is normal in English (pp. 56-60), it would be hard to find a case in which a meaningless prefix has been added. Nor does the meaning of *demure* approximate very closely to that of ripe. It now has a suggestion of slyness, but in Milton's time meant sedate—

> " Come, pensive nun, devout and pure,
> Sober, stedfast, and *demure*." (*Penseroso*, l. 31.)

and its oldest meaning is calm, settled, used of the sea. When we consider that it is nearly equivalent to *staid*, earlier *stayed*, and compare the equivalent terms in other languages, *e.g.*, Lat. *sedatus*, Fr. *rassis*, Ger. *gesetzt*, etc., it seems likely that it is formed from the Old Norman *demurer* (*demeurer*), to stay, just as *stale* is formed from *estaler* (*étaler*), to display on a *stall*, or *trove*, in "treasure *trove*," from *trover* (*trouver*).

The origin of *lugger* is unknown, but the word is recorded a century later than *lugsail*, whence it is probably derived. The explanation of *lugsail* as a *sail* that is *lugged* seems to be a piece of folk-etymology. The French for *lugsail* is *voile de fortune*, and a still earlier name, which occurs in Tudor English, is *bona-venture*, *i.e.*, good luck. Hence it is not unreasonable to conjecture that *lugsail* stands for **luck-sail*, just as the name *Higson* stands for *Hickson* (see p. 160).

The *pips* on cards or dice have nothing to do with apple pips. The oldest spelling is *peeps*.[1] In the Germanic languages they are called "eyes," and in the Romance languages "points"; and the Romance derivatives of Lat. *punctus*, point, also mean "*peep* of day." Hence the *peeps* are connected with the verb to *peep*.

The game called *dominos* is French, and the name is taken from the phrase *faire domino*, to win the game. *Domino*, a hooded cloak worn by priests in winter, is an Italian word, obviously connected with Lat. *dominus*. French also has, in various games, the phrase *faire capot* with a meaning like that of *faire domino*. *Capot*, related to Eng. *cap* and Fr. *chapeau*, means properly a hooded cloak. The two metaphors are quite parallel, but it is impossible to say what was the original idea. Perhaps

[1] *Taming of the Shrew*, i. 2.

it was that of extinguishing the opponent by putting, as it were, his head in a bag.

The card game called *gleek* is often mentioned in Tudor literature. It is derived from Old Fr. *glic*, used by Rabelais, and the word is very common in the works of the more disreputable French poets of the 15th century. According to French archæologists it was also called *bonheur, chance, fortune,* and *hasard.* Hence it represents in all probability Ger. *Glück*, luck. The Old Fr. form *ghelicque* would correspond to Mid. High Ger. *gelücke.* The history of *tennis* (p. 9) and *trump* (p. 8) shows that it is not necessary to find the German word recorded in the same sense.

The word *sentry*, which occurs in English only, has no connection at all with *sentinel*, the earliest form of which is Ital. *sentinella*, of unknown origin. The older lexicographers obscured the etymology of *sentry*, which is really quite simple, by always attempting to treat it along with *sentinel*. It is a common phenomenon in military language that the abstract name of an action is applied to the building or station in which the action is performed, then to the group of men thus employed, and finally to the individual soldier. Thus Lat. *custodia* means (1) guardianship, (2) a ward-room, watch-tower, (3) the watch collectively, (4) a watchman. Fr. *vigie*, the look-out man on board ship, can be traced back in a similar series of meanings to Lat. *vigilia*, watching.[1] A *sentry*, now a single soldier, was formerly a band of soldiers—

> "What strength, what art can then
> Suffice, or what evasion bear him safe
> Through the strict *senteries* and stations thick
> Of angels watching round?"
> (*Paradise Lost*, ii. 410.)

[1] This is why so many French military terms are feminine, e.g., *recrue*, *sentinelle, vedette*, etc.

and earlier still a watch-tower, *e.g.*, Cotgrave explains Old Fr. *eschauguette* (*échauguette*) as "a *sentrie*, watch-tower, beacon." The purely abstract sense survives in the phrase "to keep *sentry*," *i.e.* guard—

> "Thou, when nature cannot sleep,
> O'er my temples *sentry* keep."
>
> (SIR T. BROWNE.)

It is a contracted form of *sanctuary*. In the 17th century it is a pretty familiar word in this sense.[1] The earliest example I have come across is in Nash—

> "He hath no way now to slyppe out of my hands, but to take *sentrie* in the Hospital of Warwick."
>
> (First Part of PASQUIL's *Apologie*, 1590.)

Fr. *guérite*, a sentry box, can be traced back in the same way to Old Fr. *garir* (*guérir*), to save. Cotgrave explains it as "a place of refuge, and of safe retyrall," also "a *sentrie*, or little lodge for a sentinell, built on high." It is to this latter sense that we owe Eng. *garret*. In medieval French it means refuge, sanctuary, *e.g.*, "Ceste roche est Ihesucrist meismes qui est li refuges et la *garite* aus humbles."[2] If French had not borrowed *sentinelle* from Italian, *guérite* would probably now mean "sentry"; *cf.* the history of *vigie* (p. 95), or of *vedette*, a cavalry sentry, but originally "a prying or peeping hole" (Florio), from Ital. *vedere*, to see.

---

[1] Skinner's *Etymologicon* (1671) has the two entries, *centry* pro *sanctuary* and *centry* v. *sentinel*.

[2] "This rock is Jesus Christ himself, who is the refuge and sanctuary of the humble."

CHAPTER VIII

METAPHOR

EVERY expression that we employ, apart from those that are connected with the most rudimentary objects and actions, is a metaphor, though the original meaning is dulled by constant use. Thus, in the above sentence, *expression* means what is " squeezed out," to *employ* is to "twine in" like a basket maker, to *connect* is to "weave together," *rudimentary* means "in the rough state," and an *object* is something "thrown in our way." A classification of the metaphors in use in the European languages would show that a large number of the most *obvious* kind, *i.e.* of those which "come to meet" one, are common property, while others would reflect the most striking habits and pursuits of the various races. It would probably be found that in the common stock of simple metaphor the most important contribution would come from agriculture, while in English the nautical element would occur to an extent quite unparalleled in other European languages. A curious agricultural metaphor which, though of Old French origin, now appears to be peculiar to English, is to *rehearse*, lit. to harrow over again (see *hearse*, p. 68).

Some metaphors are easy to track. It does not require much philological knowledge to see that *astonish*, *astound*, and *stun* all contain the idea of "thunder - striking," Vulgar Lat. *ex - tonare*. To *embarrass* is obviously connected with *bar*, and to *interfere* is to "strike between," Old Fr. *entreferir*. This word was especially used in the 16th century of a horse knocking its legs together in trotting, "to *interfeere*, as a horse" (Cotgrave). When we speak of a *prentice-hand*, sound *journeyman* work, and a *masterpiece*, we revive the medieval classification of artisans into learners, qualified workmen, and those who, by the presentation to their guild of a finished piece of work, were recognised as past (passed) masters.

But many of our metaphors are drawn from pursuits with which we are no longer familiar, or with arts and sciences no longer practised. *Disaster*, *ill-starred*, and such adjectives as *jovial*, *mercurial*, are reminiscent of astrology. To bring a thing to the *test* is to put it in the alchemist's or metallurgist's *test* or trying - pot (cf. *test*-tube), Old Fr. *test* (*têt*), which is related to Old Fr. *teste* (*tête*), head, from Lat. *testa*, tile, pot, etc., used in Roman slang for *caput*. Shakespeare has the complete metaphor—

> "Let there be some more *test* made of my metal,[1]
> Before so noble and so great a figure
> Be stamp'd upon it."
>
> *(Measure for Measure*, i. 1.)

The old butchers' shops which adjoin Nottingham Market Place are still called the *Shambles*. The word is similarly used at Carlisle, and probably elsewhere ; but to most people it is familiar only in the metaphorical sense of place of slaughter, generally regarded as a singular. Thus Denys of Burgundy says, "The beasts are in the *shambles*" (*Cloister and Hearth*, Ch. 33), really misusing the word, which does not mean slaughter-house, but the bench on which meat is exposed for sale. It is

[1] See *mettle*, p. 135.

a very early loan from Lat. *scamnum*, a bench or form ;
also explained by Cooper as "a step or grice (see
p. 109) to get up to bedde." The same diminutive
form occurs in Fr. *escabeau*, an office stool, and Ger.
Schemel, a stool. *Fusty*, earlier *foisty*, is no longer
used in its proper sense. It comes from Old Fr. *fusté*,
"*fusty ;* tasting of the caske, smelling of the vessell
wherein it hath been kept" (Cotgrave), a derivative of
Old Fr. *fust* (*fût*), a cask.[1]

The smith's art has given us *brand-new*, generally
corrupted into *bran-new*. Shakespeare uses *fire-new*—

> "You should then have accosted her ; and with some excellent
> jests, *fire-new* from the mint, you should have banged the youth
> into dumbness." (*Twelfth Night*, iii. 2.)

Modern German has *funkelnagelneu*, spark nail new ;
but in older German we find also *spanneu*, *splinterneu*,
chip new, splinter new ; which shows the origin of our
spick and span (new), *i.e.*, spike and chip new. French
has *tout battant neuf*, beating new, *i.e.*, fresh from the
anvil.

Many old hunting terms survive as metaphors. To
be *at bay*, Fr. *aux abois*, is to be facing the baying
hounds. The fundamental meaning of Old Fr. *abaier*
(*aboyer*), of obscure origin, is perhaps to gape at.[2] Thus
a right or estate which is in *abeyance* is one regarded
with open-mouthed expectancy. The *toils* are Fr.
toiles, lit. cloths, Lat. *tela*, the nets put round a thicket
to prevent the game from escaping. To "beat about
the bush" seems to be a mixture of two metaphors

---

[1] Lat. *fustis*, a staff, cudgel, gave also Old Fr. *fust*, a kind of boat,
whence obsolete Eng. *foist* in the same sense. Both meanings seem to go
back to a time when both casks and boats were "dug out" instead
of being built up.

[2] Related are *bouche béante*, or *bée*, mouth agape ; *bâiller*, to yawn ; and
badaud, "a gaping hoydon" (Cotgrave, *badault*).

which are quite unlike in meaning. To "beat the
bush" was the office of the beaters, who started the
game for others, hence an old proverb, "I will not beat
the bush that another may have the birds." "To go
about the bush" would seem to have been used
originally of a hesitating hound. The two expressions
have coalesced to express the idea for which French
says "y aller par quatre chemins." *Crestfallen* and
white feather belong to the old sport of cock-fighting.
Jeopardy is Old Fr. *jeu parti*, a divided game, hence an
equal encounter. To run full *tilt* is a jousting phrase.
To *pounce* upon is to seize in the *pounces*, the old word
for a hawk's claws. The ultimate source is Lat.
pungere, to prick, pierce. A goldsmith's *punch* was
also called a *pounce*, hence the verb to *pounce*, to make
patterns on metal. The northern past participle
pouncet[1] occurs in *pouncet-box*, a metal perforated globe
for scents—

> "And 'twixt his finger and his thumb he held
> A *pouncet-box*, which ever and anon
> He gave his nose, and took't away again."
>
> (1 *Henry IV.*, i. 3.)

To the language of hawking belongs also *haggard*.
Cotgrave defines *faulcon* (*faucon*) *hagard*, as "a faulcon
that preyed for her selfe long before she was taken."
Hence the sense wild, untameable. The original
meaning is hedge-hawk, the first syllable representing
Old High Ger. *hag*, hedge. *Hag*, a witch, is of cognate
origin.

The antiquity of dicing appears in the history of
Ger. *gefallen*, to please, originally used of the "fall" of
the dice. In Mid. High German it is always used
with *wohl*, well, or *übel*, ill; e.g., *es gefällt mir wohl*, it
"falls out" well for me. There can be no reasonable

---

[1] *Cf.* the *Stickit* Minister.

doubt that the *deuce !* is a dicer's exclamation at making
the lowest throw, two, Fr. *deux.* We still use *deuce* for
the two in cards, and German has *Daus* in both senses.
Tennis has given us *bandy,* Fr. *bander,* " to *bandie,* at
tennis " (Cotgrave). We now only bandy words or
reproaches, but Juliet understood the word in its literal
sense—

> " Had she affections and warm youthful blood,
>   She'd be as swift in motion as a ball ;
>   My words would *bandy* her to my sweet love,
>   And his to me."   (*Romeo and Juliet,* ii. 5.)

Fowling has given us *cajole, decoy,* and *trepan.* Fr.
cajoler, which formerly meant to chatter like a jay in a
cage, has in modern French assumed the meaning of
enjôler, earlier *engeoler,* " to incage, or ingaole "
(Cotgrave), hence to entice. Fr. *geôle* represents
Vulgar Lat. **caveola. Decoy,* earlier also *coy,* is Du.
kooi, cage. The later form is perhaps due to *duck-coy.*
Du. *kooi,* is also of Latin origin. It comes, like Fr.
cage, from Vulgar Lat. **cavea,* and has a doublet *kevie,*
whence Scot. *cavie,* a hen-coop. *Trepan* was formerly
trapan, and belongs to *trap*—

> " Some by the nose with fumes *trapan* 'em,
>   As Dunstan did the devil's grannam."
>   (*Hudibras,* ii. 3.)

It is now equivalent to *kidnap, i.e.* to *nab kids* (children),
once a lucrative pursuit. Charles Reade made use of
an authentic case in his *Wandering Heir.* The surgical
trepan is a different word altogether, and belongs to
Greco-Lat. *trypanon,* an auger, piercer. To *allure* is to
bring to the *lure,* or bait. To the same group of
metaphors belongs *inveigle,* which corresponds, with
altered prefix, to Fr. *aveugler,* to blind, Vulgar Lat.
* ab-oculare. A distant relative of this word is *ogle,*
probably Low German or Dutch ; *cf.* Ger. *liebäugeln*

"to ogle, to smicker, to look amorously, to cast sheeps-eyes, to cast amorous looks" (Ludwig). It is possible that *wheedle*, the origin of which is quite unknown, belongs here also. Ludwig explains *Schlinge*, properly a noose, as a "gin, snare, trap, train, or *wheedle*."

The synonymous *cozen* is a metaphor of quite another kind. Every young noble who did the grand tour in the 16th and 17th centuries spent some time at Naples, "where he may improve his knowledge in horsemanship" (Howell, *Instructions for Forreine Travell*, 1642). Now the Italian horse-dealers were so notorious that Dekker, writing about 1600, describes a swindling "horse-courser" as a "meere jadish Non-politane," a play on Neapolitan. The Italian name is *cozzone*, "a horse-courser, a horse-breaker, a craftie knave" (Florio), whence the verb *cozzonare*, "to have perfect skill in all *cosenages*" (Torriano). The essential idea of to *cozen* in the Elizabethans is that of selling faulty goods in a bad light, a device said to be practised by some horse-dealers. At any rate the words for horse-dealer in all languages, from the Lat. *mango* to the Amer. *horse-swapper*, mean swindler and worse things. *Cozen* is a favourite word with the Elizabethan dramatists, because it enables them to bring off one of those stock puns that make one feel "The less Shakespeare he"—

> "*Cousins*, indeed ; and by their uncle *cozen'd*
> Of comfort, kingdom, kindred, freedom, life."
> (*Richard III.*, iv. 4.)

In the *Merry Wives of Windsor* (iv. 5) there is a lot of word play on "cousins-german" and "German cozeners." An exact parallel to the history of *cozen* is furnished by the verb to *jockey*, from *jockey*, a horse-dealer, cheat, etc.

Scion is a metaphor from the garden. It is Fr. *scion*, " a scion ; a young and tender plant; a shoot, sprig, or twig " (Cotgrave). Ger. *Sprössling*, sprouting, is also used of an " offshoot " from a " stock." We have a similar metaphor in the word *imp*. We now *graft* trees, a misspelling of older *graffe*, Fr. *greffe*, Greco-Lat. *graphium*, a pencil, from the shape of the slip. The art of grafting was learnt from the Romans, who had a post-classical verb *imputare*,[1] to graft, which has given Eng. *imp*, Ger. *impfen*, Fr. *enter*, and is represented in most other European languages. *Imp* was used like *scion*, but degenerated in meaning. In Shakespeare it has already the somewhat contemptuous shade of meaning which we find in Ger. *Sprössling*, and is only used by comic characters; *e.g.*, Pistol calls Prince Hal " most royal *imp* of fame " (2 *Henry IV.*, v. 5); but Thomas Cromwell, in his last letter to Henry VIII., speaks of " that most noble *imp*, the prince's grace, your most dear son." The special sense of " young devil " appears to be due to the frequent occurrence of such phrases as " *imps* (children) of Satan," " the devil and his *imps*," etc. Ger. *impfen* also means to vaccinate. Our earlier term *inoculate* [2] originally meant to graft, and, in fact, *engraft* was also used in this sense. The latest development of the metaphor appears in skin grafting.

Zest is quite obsolete in its original meaning of a piece of orange peel used to give piquancy to wine. It is a French word of unknown origin, properly applied to the inner skin of fruit and nuts. Cotgrave explains it as " the thick skinne, or filme whereby the kernell of a wallnut is divided."

---

[1] Of uncertain origin. Lat. *putare*, to° cut (cf. *amputate*), or Gk. ἔμφυτος, implanted ?

[2] From *oculus*, eye, in the sense of bud.

CHAPTER IX

FOLK-ETYMOLOGY

THE sound, spelling, and even the meaning of a word are often perverted by influences to which the collective name of folk-etymology has been given. I here use the term to include all phenomena which are due to any kind of misunderstanding of a word. A word beginning with *n* sometimes loses this sound through its being confused with the *n* of the indefinite article *an*. Thus *an adder* and *an auger* are for *a nadder* (*cf.* Ger. *Natter*) and *a nauger*, Mid. Eng. *navegor*, properly an instrument for piercing the *nave* of a wheel. *Apron* was in Mid. English *naprun*, from Old Fr. *naperon*, a derivative of *nappe*, cloth. The *aitch-bone* was formerly the *nache-bone*, from Old Fr. *nache*, buttock, Vulgar Lat. *natica for *nates*. *Nache* is still used by French butchers. *Humble-pie* is a popular perversion of *umble-pie*, *i.e.*, a pie made from the *umbles*, or inferior parts of the stag. But *umble* is for earlier *numble*, Old Fr. *nomble*, formed, with dissimilation, from Lat. *lumbulus*, diminutive of *lumbus*, loin ; cf. *niveau* (p. 53). Thus *humble-pie* has etymologically no connection with humility. *Umpire* represents Old Fr. *non per* (*pair*), not equal, the *umpire* being a third person called in when two arbitrators could not agree. This appears clearly in the following extract from a letter written in

1431—

"And if so be that the said arbitrators may not accord before the said feast of Allhallows, then the said parties by the advice abovesaid are agreed to abide the award and ordinance of an *noumper* to be chosen by the said arbitrators."

For the sense we may compare Span. *tercero*, "the third, a broaker, a mediator" (Percyvall). *An eyas* falcon is for *a neyas* falcon, Fr. *niais*, foolish, lit. nestling, related to *nid*, nest. Rosenkrantz uses it in the literal sense—

"But there is, sir, an aiery of children, little *eyases*, that cry out on the top of question, and are most tyranically clapped for't." (*Hamlet*, ii. 2.)

Somewhat similar is the loss in French of initial *a* in *la boutique* for *l'aboutique*, Greco-Lat. *apotheca*, and *la Pouille* for *l'Apouille*, Apulia.

Ounce, a kind of tiger-cat, is from Fr. *once*, earlier *lonce*, "the *ounce*, a ravenous beast" (Cotgrave), taken as *l'once*. It is almost a doublet of *lynx*. The opposite has happened in the case of *a newt* for *an ewt* and *a nick-name* for *an eke-name*. *Eke*, also, occurs in the first stanza of John Gilpin. It is cognate with Ger. *auch*, also, and Lat. *augere*, to increase. *Nuncle*, the customary address of a court fool to his superiors—

"How now, *nuncle!* Would I had two coxcombs and two daughters." (*Lear*, i. 4.)

is for *mine uncle*. We also find *naunt*. *Nonce* occurs properly only in the phrase *for the nonce*, which is for earlier *for then ones*, where *then* is the dative of the definite article. Family names like *Nash*, *Nokes* are aphetic for *atten ash*, at the ash, *atten oakes*, at the oaks. The creation of such forms was perhaps helped by our tendency to use initial *n* in Christian names, e.g., *Ned* for *Edward*, *Noll* for *Oliver*, *Nell* for *Ellen*.

Agglutination of the definite article is common in French, e.g., *lingot*, ingot, *lierre*, ivy, for *l'ierre*, Lat. *hedera*, and the dialect *lévier*, sink, for *évier*, Lat. *aquarium*, whence Eng. *ewer*. The derivation of Fr. *landier*, andiron is unknown, but the *iron* of the English word is due to folk-etymology. Such agglutination occurs often in family names such as *Langlois*, lit. the Englishman, *Lhuissier*, the usher (see p. 83), and some of these have passed into English, e.g., *Levick* for *l'évêque*, the bishop. The two words *alarm* and *alert* include the Italian definite article. The first is Ital. *all'arme*, to arms, for *a le arme*, and the second is *all'erta* for *alla* (*a la*) *erta*, the last word representing Lat. *erecta*. With rolled *r*, *alarm* becomes *alarum*, whence the aphetic *larum*—

> "Then we shall hear their *larum*, and they ours."
> (*Coriolanus*, i. 4.)

Ger. *Lärm*, noise, is the same word. In Luther's time we also find *Allerm*.

We have the Arabic definite article in *alcalde*, or *alcade*, and *alguazil*, words of Spanish origin which are common in Elizabethan literature. They are two old friends from the *Arabian Nights*, the *cadi* and the *wazir* or *vizier*. The Arabic article also occurs in *acton*, Old Fr. *auqueton*, now *hoqueton*, for *al coton*, because originally used of a wadded coat—

> "But Cranstoun's lance, of more avail,
>   Pierced through, like silk, the Borderer's mail ;
> Through shield, and jack, and *acton* past,
>   Deep in his bosom broke at last."
> (SCOTT, *Lay*, iii. 6.)

In *alligator*, Span. *el lagarto*, the lizard, from Lat. *lacertus*, we have the Spanish definite article. See also *lariat*, p. 22.

Occasionally we have what is apparently the arbitrary prefixing of a consonant, e.g., *spruce* for *pruce* (p. 44). *Dapple gray* corresponds so exactly to Fr. *gris pommelé*, Mid. Eng. *pomeli gris*, Ger. *apfelgrau*, and Ital. *pomellato*, "spotted, bespeckled, pide, *dapple-graie*, or fleabitten, the colour of a horse" (Florio), that it is hard not to believe in an unrecorded *apple-gray*, especially as we have *daffodil* for earlier *affodil*, i.e., *asphodel*. Cotgrave has *asphodile* (*asphodèle*), "the *daffadill*, *affodill*, or *asphodill*, flower." The playful elaboration *daffadowndilly* is as old as Spenser.

A foreign word ending in a sibilant is sometimes mistaken for a plural. Thus Old Fr. *assetz* (*assez*), enough, Lat. *ad satis*, has given Eng. *assets*, plural, with a barbarous, but useful, singular *asset*. *Cherry* is for *cheris*, from a dialect form of Fr. *cerise*, and *sherry* for *sherris*, from *Xeres* in Spain (see p. 46). Falstaff opines that "a good *sherris*-sack [1] hath a twofold operation in it" (2 *Henry IV.*, iv. 3). *Pea* is a false singular from older *pease*, Lat. *pisum*. Perhaps the frequent occurrence of *pease-soup*, not to be distinguished from *pea-soup*, is partly responsible for this mistake. *Marquee*, a large tent, is from Fr. *marquise*. With this we may class the heathen *Chinee* and the *Portugee*. Milton wrote correctly of—

> "The barren plains
> Of Sericana, where *Chineses* drive
> With sails and wind their cany waggons light."
>
> (*Paradise Lost*, iii. 438.)

The vulgarism *shay* for *chaise* [2] is of similar formation.

---

[1] *Sack*, earlier also *seck*, is Fr. *sec*, dry, which, with spurious *t*, has also given Ger. *Sekt*, now used for champagne.

[2] Fr. *chaise*, chair, for older *chaire*, now used only of a pulpit or professorial chair, Lat. *cathedra*, is due to an affected pronunciation that prevailed in Paris in the 16th century.

Corp, for *corpse*, is also used provincially. *Kickshaws*
is really a singular from Fr. *quelque chose*—

> "Art thou good at these *kickshawses*, knight?"
> (*Twelfth Night*, i. 3.)

Cotgrave spells it *quelkchoses* (s.v. *fricandeau*).

Skate has a curious history. It is a false singular
from Du. *schaats*. This is from *escache*, an Old French
dialect form of *échasse*, stilt, which was used in the
Middle Ages for a wooden leg. It is of German origin,
and is related to *shank*. *Cf.*, for the sense development, Eng. *patten*, from Fr. *patin*, a derivative of *patte*,
foot, cognate with *paw*. *Skates* are still called *pattens*
by the fenmen of Cambridgeshire. We also had
formerly a doublet from Old Fr. *escache* directly, but
in the older sense, for Cotgrave has *eschasses* (*échasses*),
"stilts, or *scatches* to go on." *Row*, a disturbance,
belongs to *rouse*, a jollification—

> "The king doth wake to-night and takes his *rouse*."
> (*Hamlet*, i. 4.)

of uncertain origin, but probably felt as aphetic for
carouse. The bird called a *wheatear* was formerly
called *wheatears*, a corruption of a name best explained
by its French equivalent *cul blanc*, "the bird called
a *whittaile*" (Cotgrave). We may compare the bird-
name *redstart*, where *start* means rump.

Conversely a word used in the plural is sometimes
regarded as a singular, the result being a double
plural. Many Latin neuter plurals were adopted into
French as feminine singulars, e.g., *cornua*, *corne*, horn ;
labra, *lèvre*, lip ; *vela*, *voile*, sail. It is obvious that this
is most likely to occur in the case of plurals which are
used for a pair, or set, of things, and thus have a kind
of collective sense. *Breeches* or *breeks* is a double plural,

Anglo-Sax. *brēc* being already the plural of *brōc*. In Mid. English we still find *breche* or *breke* used of this garment. Scot. *trews*, trousers, is really a singular, from Fr. *trousse*. *Trousers* is for earlier *trouses*, at first used especially in speaking of the Irish. This is a special use of Fr. *trousse*, bundle, truss, from *trousser*, to tuck up. The very short knickerbockers of pages were called *trousses*, and when a page had completed his term of service, he was said to *quitter les trousses*. *Bodice* is for *bodies*, as *pence* is for *pennies*. Cotgrave explains *corset* by "a paire of *bodies* for a woman," and even Harrison Ainsworth speaks of "a pair of *bodice*" (*Jack Sheppard*, Ch. i.). *Trace*, of a horse, is the Old Fr. plural *trais* [1] (*traits*) of *trait*, "a teame-trace" (Cotgrave). *Apprentice* is the plural of Fr. *apprenti*, formerly *apprentif*, a derivative of *apprendre*, to learn, hence a disciple. *Invoice* is the plural of the obsolete *invoy*, from Fr. *envoi*, sending.

In the *Grecian steps*, at Lincoln, we have a popular corruption of the common Mid. Eng. and Tudor *grece*, *grese*, plural of Old Fr. *gré*, step, from Lat. *gradus*. Shakespeare spells it *grize*—

> "Let me speak like yourself; and lay a sentence,
> Which, as a *grize*, or step, may help these lovers
> Into your favour."
>
> (*Othello*, i. 3.)

Scot. *brose*, or *brewis*, was in Mid. Eng. *browes*, from Old Fr. *brouez*, plural of *brouet*, a word cognate with our *broth*. From this association comes perhaps the use of *broth* as a plural in some of our dialects. *Porridge*, not originally limited to oatmeal, seems to be a mixture of *pottage* and Mid. Eng. *porrets*, plural of *porret*, leek,

---

[1] The fact that in Old French the final consonant of the singular disappeared in the plural form helped to bring about such misunderstandings.

a diminutive from Lat. *porrum*. *Porridge* is still sometimes used as a plural in Scottish, *e.g.*, in Stevenson's
Kidnapped, Ch. iv., where David Balfour's uncle says,
" fine, halesome food, they're grand food, *parrich*," and
in the northern counties people speak of taking " a few
porridge, or broth." *Baize*, now generally green, is for
earlier *bayes*, the plural of the adjective *bay*, now used
only of horses ; *cf.* Du. *baai*, baize. The origin of the
adjective *bay*, Fr. *bai*, forms of which occur in all the
Romance languages, is Lat. *badius*, " of bay colour,
bayarde" (Cooper). Hence the name *Bayard*, applied
to FitzJames' horse in *The Lady of the Lake*, and earlier
to the steed that carried the four sons of Aymon.
Quince is the plural of *quin*, from the Norman form of
Old Fr. *coin* (*coing*). *Truce* is the plural of Mid. Eng.
trewe with the same meaning. It is related to Eng.
true, but, in this sense, probably comes to us from Old
Fr. *triue* (*trêve*), truce.

Earnest in the sense of " pledge "—

> " And, for an *earnest* of a greater honour,
> He bade me, from him, call thee Thane of Cawdor."
> (*Macbeth*, i. 3.)

has nothing to do with the adjective *earnest*. It is the
Mid. Eng. *ernes*, earlier *erles*, which survives as *arles*
in some of our dialects. The verb to *earl* is still
used in Cumberland of " enlisting " a servant with a
shilling in the open market. The Old French word
was *arres* or *erres*, now written learnedly *arrhes*, a
plural from Lat. *arrha*, " an *earnest* penny, *earnest*
money" (Cooper). The existence of Mid. Eng. *erles*
shows that there must have been also an Old French
diminutive form. For the apparently arbitrary change
of *l* to *n* we may compare *banister* for *baluster*
(see p. 55).

The *jesses* of a hawk—

> " If I do prove her haggard,[1]
> Though that her *jesses* were my dear heart-strings,
> I'd whistle her off, and let her down the wind,
> To prey at fortune."
>
> *(Othello*, iii. 3.)

were the thongs by which it was held or "thrown" into
the air. *Jess* is the Old Fr. *jes*, the plural of *jet*, from
jeter, to throw. In Colman's *Elder Brother* we read of
a gentleman who lounged and chatted, "not minding
time a *souse*," where *souse* is the plural of Fr. *sou*, halfpenny. From Fr. *muer*, to moult, Lat. *mutare*, we get
Fr. *mue*, moulting, later applied to the coop or pen in
which moulting falcons were confined, whence the phrase
"to *mew* (up)"—

> " More pity, that the eagles should be *mew'd*,
> While kites and buzzards prey at liberty."
>
> *(Richard III.*, i. 1.)

When, in 1534, the royal *mews*, or hawk-houses, near
Charing Cross were rebuilt as stables, the word acquired
its present meaning.

Chess, Old Fr. *esches* (*échecs*), is the plural of *check*,
Fr. *échec*, from Persian *shāh*, king. By analogy with
the "game of kings," the name *jeu des dames* was given
in French to draughts, still called *dams* in Scotland.
Draught, from *draw*, meant in Mid. English a "move"
at chess. The etymology of *tweezers* can best be
made clear by starting from French *étui*, a case, of
doubtful origin. This became in English *etwee*, or
twee, *e.g.*, Cotgrave explains *estui* (*étui*) as "a sheath,
case, or box to put things in ; and (more particularly)
a case of little instruments, as sizzars, bodkin, penknife,
etc., now commonly termed an *ettwee*." Such a case
generally opens book-fashion, each half being fitted

[1] *Haggard*, see p. 100.

with instruments. Accordingly we find it called a
surgeon's "pair of *twees*," or simply *tweese*, and later a
"pair of *tweeses*." The implement was named from
the case (*cf.* Fr. *boussole*, p. 117), and became *tweezers*
by association with *pincers* (Fr. *pinces*), *scissors*, etc.

The form of a word is often affected by association
with some other word with which it is instinctively
coupled. Thus *larboard*, for Mid. Eng. *ladeboard*, *i.e.*
loading side, is due to *starboard*, steering side. *Bridal*,
for *bride-ale*, from the liquid consumed at marriage
festivities, is due to analogy with *betrothal*, *espousal*,
etc. *Rampart* is from Old Fr. *rempar*, a verbal
noun from *remparer*, to repair; *cf.* Ital. *riparo*, "a
rampire, a fort, a banke" (Florio). By analogy with
boulevard, Old Fr. *boulevart*, of German origin and
identical with our *bulwark*, *rempar* became *rempart*.
The older form occurs under the forms *rampier*, *rampire*,
which survives in the dialect *ramper*, embankment,
causeway. For the spelling *rampire* we may compare
umpire (p. 105). The apple called a *jenneting*, sometimes
"explained" as for *June-eating*, was once spelt *geniton*,
no doubt for Fr. *jeanneton*, a diminutive of *Jean*. It
is called in French *pomme de Saint-Jean*, and in German
Johannisapfel, because ripe about St John's Day (June 21).
The modern form is due to such apple names as *golding*,
sweeting, *codlin*, *pippin*.

In the records of medieval London we frequently
come across the distinction made between people who
lived "in the city," Anglo-Fr. *deinz* (*dans*) *la cité*, and
"outside the city," Anglo-Fr. *fors* (*hors*) *la cité*. The
former were called *deinzein*, whence our *denizen*, and
the latter *forein*.[1] The Anglo-Norman form of modern

---

[1] An unoriginal *g* occurs in many English words derived from French,
e.g., *foreign*, *sovereign*, older *sovran*, *sprightly* for *spritely*, i.e., *sprite-like*,
delight, from Fr. *délit*, etc.

Fr. *citoyen* was *citein*, which became *citizen* by analogy
with the synonymous *denizen*. Even words which have
opposite meanings may affect each other by association.
Thus Lat. *reddere*, to give back, became Vulgar Lat.
*rendere by analogy with *prendere* (*prehendere*), to take
away; hence Fr. *rendre*. Our word *grief*, from Fr.
grief, is derived from a Vulgar Lat. *grĕvis, heavy (for
grăvis), which is due to *lĕvis*, light.

The plural of *titmouse* is now usually *titmice*, by
analogy with *mouse, mice*, with which it has no connection. The second part of the word is Anglo-Sax. *māse*,
used of several small birds. It is cognate with Ger.
Meise, titmouse, and Fr. *mésange*, "a titmouse, or
tittling" (Cotgrave). *Tit*, of Norse origin, is applied to
various small animals, and occurs also as a prefix in
titbit or *tidbit*. Cf. *tomtit* (p. 33).

The Spanish word *salva*, "a taste, a salutation"
(Percyvall), was used of the pregustation of a great
man's food or drink. We have given the name to the
tray or dish from which the "assay" was made, but, by
analogy with *platter, trencher*, we spell it *salver*. In
another sense, that of a "salutation" in the form of a
volley of shot, we have corrupted it into *salvo*. With
the use of Span. *salva* we may compare that of Ital.
credenza, lit. faith, "the taste or assaie of a princes
meate and drinke" (Florio); whence Fr. *crédence*, side-
board, used in English only in the ecclesiastical compound *credence table*, and Ger. *credenzen*, to pour out.

In spoken English the ending *-ew*, *-ue*, of French
origin, has been often changed to *-ee*, *-ey*. Thus *pedigree*
was formerly *pedigrew* (see p. 71). The fencing term
veney—

"I bruised my shin the other day with playing at sword and
dagger with a master of fence—three *veneys* for a dish of stewed
prunes." (*Merry Wives*, i. 1.)

also spelt *venew*, is from Fr. *venue*, " a *venny* in fencing "
(Cotgrave). *Carew* has become *Carey* and *Beaulieu*, in
Hampshire, is called *Bewley*. Under the influence of
these double forms we sometimes get the opposite
change, e.g., *purlieu*, now generally used of the outskirts
of a town, is for *purley*, a strip of disforested woodland.
This is a contraction of Anglo-Fr. *pour-allée*, used to
translate the legal Lat. *perambulatio*, a going through.
A change of *venue*[1] is sometimes made when it seems
likely that an accused person, or a football team, will
not get justice from a local jury. This *venue* is in law
Latin *vicinetum*, neighbourhood, which gave Anglo-Fr.
visné, and this, perhaps, by confusion with the *venire
facias*, or jury summons, became *venew*, *venue*.

In the preceding examples the form has been chiefly
affected. In the word *luncheon* both form and meaning
have been influenced by the obsolete *nuncheon*, a meal at
noon, Mid. Eng. *none-chenche*, for *none-schenche, noon
draught, from Anglo-Sax. *scencan*,[2] to pour. Drinking
seems to have been regarded as more important than
eating, for in some counties we find this *nuncheon*
replaced by *bever*, the Anglo-Fr. infinitive from Lat,
bibere, to drink. *Lunch*, a piece or hunk, especially of
bread, also used in the sense of a " snack " (*cf.* Scot.
" piece "), was extended to *luncheon* by analogy with
nuncheon, which it has now replaced—

> " So munch on, crunch on, take your *nuncheon*,
> Breakfast, supper, dinner, *luncheon*."
>   (BROWNING, *Pied Piper of Hamelin.*)

The term folk-etymology is often applied in a

---

[1] This word is getting overworked, *e.g.*, " The Derbyshire Golf Club links
were yesterday the *venue* of a 72-hole match " (*Nottingham Guardian*, 21st
Nov. 1911).

[2] *Cf.* Ger. *schenken*, to pour, and the Tudor word *skinker*, a drawer,
waiter (1 *Henry IV.*, ii. 4).

narrower sense to the corruption of words through a mistaken idea of their etymology or origin. The tendency of the uneducated is to distort an unfamiliar or unintelligible word into some form which suggests a meaning. In some cases we observe a kind of heavy jocularity, as in *sparrow-grass* for *asparagus*, or Rogue Riderhood's *Alfred David* for *affidavit*. In others there has been a wrong association of ideas, *e.g.*, the *primrose*, *rosemary*, and *tuberose* have none of them originally any connection with the *rose*. *Primrose* was earlier *primerole*, an Old French derivative of Latin *primula;* *rosemary*, French *romarin*, is from Lat. *ros marinum*, sea-dew; *tuberose* is the Latin adjective *tuberosus*, bulbous, tuberous. Or attempts are made at translation, such as Sam Weller's *Have his carcase* for *Habeas Corpus*, or the curious names which country folk give to such complaints as *bronchitis*, *erysipelas*, etc. Even Private Mulvaney's perversion of *locomotor ataxy*—" They call ut *Locomotus attacks us*," he sez, " bekaze," sez he, "it attacks us like a locomotive"—is probably genuine.

Our language is, owing to our borrowing habits, particularly rich in these gems. Examples familiar to everybody are *crayfish* from Fr. *écrevisse*, *gilly-flower* from Fr. *giroflée*, *shame-faced* for *shamefast*. Other words in which the second element has been altered are *causeway*, earlier *causey*, from the Picard form of Fr. *chaussée*, Lat. (*via*) *calciata*, *i.e.*, made with lime, *calx; penthouse*, for *pentice*, Fr. *appentis*, "the *penthouse* of a house" (Cotgrave), a derivative of Old Fr. *appendre*, to hang to. Fr. *hangar*, a shed, now introduced into English by aviators as unnecessarily as *garage* by motorists, probably contains the same idea of "hanging."

In *hiccough*, for earlier *hickup*, an onomatopœic word, the spelling, suggested by *cough*, has not affected the pronunciation. *Surcease* is Fr. *sursis*, past participle of *surseoir*, " to *surcease*, pawse, intermit, leave off, give over, delay or stay for a time," Lat. *supersedere*. *Taffrail* has been confused with *rail*, its more correct form being *tafferel*, from Du. *tafereel*, diminutive of *tafel*, picture, from Lat. *tabula*. It meant originally the flat part of the stern of a ship ornamented with carvings or pictures. This is called *tableau* in nautical French. Fr. *coutelas*, an augmentative of Old Fr. *coutel* (*couteau*), knife, gave Eng. *cutlass*, which has no more etymological connection with "cutting" than a *cutler*, Fr. *coutelier*, or a *cutlet*, Fr. *côtelette*, little rib, Lat. *costa*. *Cutlas* was popularly corrupted into *curtal-axe*, the form used by Rosalind—

> "A gallant *curtal-axe* upon my thigh,
>   A boar-spear in my hand."
>
> (*As You Like It*, i. 3.)

We may compare *pick-axe*, Mid. Eng. *pikeys*, Old Fr. *piquois*, *picquois*, " a pickax " (Cotgrave), from the verb *piquer*. The word *posthumous* has changed its meaning through folk - etymology. It represents the Lat. superlative *postumus*, latest born. By association with *humus*, ground, earth, it came to be used of a child born, or a work published, after its author's death, a meaning which the derivatives of *postumus* have in all the Romance languages.

The first part of the word has been distorted in *pursy*, short-winded—

> "And *pursy* insolence shall break his wind
>   With fear and horrid flight."
>
> (*Timon of Athens*, v. 5.)

Fr. *poussif*, from *pousser*, to push, Lat. *pulsus*, throbbing. It was formerly used also in connection with horses, *e.g.*, "You must warrant this horse clear of the glanders, and *pursyness*" (*The Gentleman's Dictionary*, 1705, s.v. *glanders*). *Arquebus*, Fr. *arquebuse*, is a doublet of *hackbut*, Old Fr. *haquebute*, "an *haquebut*, or *arquebuse*; a caliver" (Cotgrave). The corruption is due to *arcus*, bow. Both *arquebus* and *hackbut* are common in Scott—

> "With *hackbut* bent, my secret stand,
> Dark as the purposed deed, I chose."
> (*Cadyow Castle*.)

The origin is Du. *haakbus*, hook-gun, the second element of which appears in *blunderbuss*. The first part of this word has undergone so many popular transformations that it is difficult to say which was the original form. Ludwig has *Eine Donner-büchs*, *Blunder-büchs*, *oder Muszketon*, "a thunder-box; a blunder-buss; a musketoon; a wide-mouthed brass-gun, carrying about twenty pistol bullets at once." It was also called in German a *Plantier-büchs*, from *plantieren*, to plant, set up, because fired from a rest. Du. *bus*, like Ger. *Büchse*, means both "box" and "gun." In the *bushes*, or axle-boxes, of a cartwheel, we have the same word. The ultimate origin is Greek πύξος, the box-tree, whence also the learned word *pyx*. Fr. *boîte*, box, is cognate, and Fr. *boussole*, mariners' compass, is from the Italian diminutive *bossola*, "a boxe that mariners keepe their compasse in. Also taken for the compasse" (Florio).

Scissors were formerly *cizars* (*cf.* Fr. *ciseaux*), connected with Lat. *cædere*, to cut. The modern spelling is due to association with Lat. *scissor*, a cutter, tailor, from *scindere*, to cut. *Runagate* is well known to be a corrupt doublet of *renegade*, one who has "denied" his faith. *Recreant*, the present participle of Old Fr. *recreire*, Lat. *recredere*, contains very much the same idea; cf. *miscreant*, lit. unbeliever. *Jaunty*, *janty* in Wycherley and *genty* in Burns, is Fr. *gentil*, wrongly brought into connection with *jaunt*.

In some cases of folk-etymology it is difficult to see to what idea the corruption is due.[1] The mollusc called a *periwinkle* was in Anglo-Saxon *pinewincla*, which still survives in dialect as *pennywinkle*. It appears to have been influenced by the plant-name *periwinkle*, which is itself a corruption of Mid. Eng. *pervenke*, from Lat. *pervinca; cf.* Fr. *pervenche*. The material called *lutestring* was formerly *lustring*, Fr. *lustrine*, from its glossiness. A *wiseacre* is "one that knows or tells truth; we commonly use *in malam partem* for a fool" (Blount, *Glossographia*, 1674). This comes, through Dutch, from Ger. *Weissager*, commonly understood as *wise-sayer*, but really unconnected with *sagen*, to say. The Old High Ger. *wīzago*, prophet, is cognate with Eng. *witty*. The military and naval word *ensign* is in Shakespeare corrupted, in both its meanings, into *ancient*. Thus Falstaff describes his tatterdemalion recruits as "ten times more dishonourable ragged than an old-faced *ancient*," while *Ancient* Pistol is familiar to every reader. A *cordwainer*, from Old Fr. *cordouanier*, "a shoomaker, a *cordwainer*" (Cotgrave), worked with *cordouan*, "Cordovan leather; which is properly a goat's skin tanned." The modern French form *cordonnier* is due to association with *cordon*, a thong, bootlace, etc. *Witch-elm* has nothing to do with witches. It is for older *weech-elm*, *wiche-elm*, and belongs to Anglo-Sax. *wīcan*, to bend. *Service-tree* is a meaningless corruption of Mid. Eng. *serves*, an early loan word from Lat. *sorbus*.

In the case of a double-barrelled word, folk-

---

[1] Perhaps it is the mere instinct to make an unfamiliar word "look like something." Thus Fr. *beaupré*, from Eng. *bowsprit*, cannot conceivably have been associated with a fair meadow ; and *accomplice*, for *complice*, Lat. *complex, complic-*, can hardly have been confused with *accomplish*.

etymology usually affects one half only, e.g., *verdigris* is for Fr. *vert-de-gris*, for Old Fr. *vert de Grece*, Greek green. The reason for the name is unknown. Cotgrave calls it "Spanish green." Mid. English had the more correct *vertegresse* and *verte Grece* (Promptorium Parvulorum, 1440). The cavalry trumpet-call *boot and saddle* is for Fr. *boute-selle*, lit. "put saddle." *Court card* is for *coat card*, a name given to these cards from the dresses depicted on them. Florio has *carta di figura*, "a *cote* carde." The card game called *Pope Joan* would appear to be in some way corrupted from *nain jaune*, lit. "yellow dwarf," its French name.

But occasionally the results of folk-etymology are literally *preposterous*.[1] The Fr. *choucroute* is from *sūrkrūt*, a dialect pronunciation of Ger. *Sauer-kraut*, sour cabbage, so that the first syllable, meaning "sour," has actually been corrupted so as to mean "cabbage." Another example, which I have never seen quoted, is the name of a beech-wood near the little town of Remilly in Lorraine. The trees of this wood are very old and curiously twisted, and they are called in French *les jolis fous*, where *fou* (Lat. *fagus*) is the Old French for "beech" (*fouet*, whip, is its diminutive). This is rendered in German as *tolle Buchen*, mad beeches, the *fou* having been misunderstood as referring to the fantastic appearance of the trees.

Forlorn hope is sometimes used metaphorically as though the *hope* were of the kind that springs eternal in the human breast. In military language it now means the leaders of a storming party, but was earlier used of soldiers in any way exposed to special danger. Cotgrave has *enfans perdus*, "perdus; or the *forlorne hope* of a campe (are commonly gentlemen of companies)." It is from obsolete Du. *verloren hoop*,

---

[1] Lat. *præposterus*, from *præ*, before, and *posterus*, behind.

where *hoop*, cognate with Eng. *heap*, is used for a band or company. In 16th-century German we find *ein verlorener Haufe*. Both the Dutch and German words are obsolete in this sense.

The military phrase *to run the gauntlet* has no connection with *gauntlet*, glove. The older form is *gantlope*—

"Some said he ought to be tied neck and heels; others that he deserved to *run the gantlope*." (*Tom Jones*, vii. 1.)

It is a punishment of Swedish origin from the period of the Thirty Years' War. The Swedish form is *gat-lopp*, in which *gat* is cognate with Eng. *gate*, in its proper sense of "street," and *lopp* with Eng. *leap* and Ger. *laufen*, to run.

The *press-gang* had originally nothing to do with "pressing." When soldiers or seaman were engaged, they received earnest money called *prest*-money, *i.e.*, an advance on "loan," Old Fr. *prest* (*prêt*), and the engagement was called *presting* or *impresting*. Florio explains *soldato*, literally "paid," by "*prest* with paie as soldiers are." The popular corruption to *press* took place naturally as the method of enlistment became more pressing.

The *black art* is a translation of Old Fr. *nigromance*, "nigromancie, conjuring, the *black art*" (Cotgrave); but this is folk-etymology for *nécromantie*, Greco-Lat. *necromantia*, divination by means of the dead. The popular form *négromancie* still survives in French. To *curry favour* is a corruption of Mid. Eng. "to curry *favel*." The expression is translated from French. Palsgrave has *curryfavell*, a flatterer, "estrille faveau," *estriller* meaning "to curry (a horse)." *Faveau*, earlier *fauvel*, is the name of a horse in the famous *Roman de Fauvel*, a satirical Old French poem of the early 14th century. He symbolizes worldly vanity carefully tended by all classes of society. *Fauvel* is a diminutive of *fauve*, tawny, cognate with Eng. *fallow* (deer).

A very curious case of folk-etymology is seen in the old superstition of the *hand of glory*. This is understood to be a skeleton hand from the gallows which will point out hidden treasure—

> " Now mount who list,
> And close by the wrist
> Sever me quickly the Dead Man's fist."
> (INGOLDSBY, *The Hand of Glory*.)

It is simply a translation of Fr. *main de gloire*. But the French expression is a popular corruption of *mandragore*, from Lat. *mandragora*, the mandragore, or mandrake, to the forked roots of which a similar virtue was attributed, especially if the plant were obtained from the foot of the gallows.

Akin to folk-etymology is contamination, *i.e.*, the welding of two words into one. This can often be noticed in children, whose linguistic instincts are those of primitive races. I have heard a child, on her first visit to the Zoo, express great eagerness to see the *canimals* (*camels* × *animals*), which, by the way, turned out to be the giraffes. A small boy who learnt English and German simultaneously evolved, at the age of two, the word *spam* (*sponge* × Ger. *Schwamm*). In a college in the English midlands, a student named *Turpin*, who sat next to a student named *Constantine*, once heard himself startlingly addressed by a lecturer as *Turpentine*. People who inhabit the frontier of two languages, and in fact all who are in any degree bilingual, must inevitably form such composites occasionally. The *h* aspirate of Fr. *haut* can only be explained by the influence of Old High Ger. *hôh* (*hoch*). The poetic word *glaive* cannot be derived from Lat. *gladius*, sword, which has given Fr. *glai*, an archaic name for the gladiolus. We must invoke the help of a Gaulish word *cladebo*, sword, which is related to Gaelic *clay-more*, big sword. It has been said that in this word the swords of Cæsar and Vercingetorix still cross each other. In Old French we find *oreste*, a storm, combined from *orage* and *tempeste* (*tempête*). Fr. *orteil*, toe, represents the mixture of Lat. *articulus*, a little joint, with Gaulish *ordag*. A *battledore* was in Mid. English a washing beetle, which is in Provençal *batedor*, lit. beater. Hence it seems that this is one of the very few Provençal words which passed directly into English during the period of our occupation of Guienne. It has been contaminated by the cognate *beetle*. *Anecdotage* is a deliberate coinage.

In some cases it is impossible to estimate the different elements in a word. *Arbour* certainly owes its modern spelling to Lat. *arbor*, a tree, but it represents also Mid. Eng. *herbere*, *erbere*, which comes, through French, from Lat. * *herbarium*. But this can only mean herb-garden, so that the sense development of the word must have been affected by *harbour*, properly "army-shelter" (*cf.* Fr. *auberge*, p. 152). When Dryden wrote—

> "Tardy of aid, *unseal* thy heavy eyes,
> Awake, and with the dawning day arise."
> (*The Cock and the Fox*, 247.)

he was expressing a composite idea made up from the verb *seal*, Old Fr. *seeler* (*sceller*), Lat. *sigillare*, and *seel*, Old Fr. *ciller*, Vulgar Lat. * *ciliare*, from *cilium*, eye-brow. The latter verb, meaning to sew together the eyelids of a young falcon, was once a common word—

> "Come, *seeling* night,
> Scarf up the tender eye of pitiful day."
> (*Macbeth*, iii. 2.)

The verb *fret* is Anglo-Sax. *fretan*, to eat away (*cf.* Ger.

fressen). *Fret* is also used of interlaced bars in heraldry, in which sense it corresponds to Fr. *frette* with the same meaning; for this word, which also means ferrule, a Vulgar Lat. * *ferritta* (*ferrum*, iron) has been suggested. When Hamlet speaks of—

"This majestical roof *fretted* with golden fire,"

(ii. 3)

is he thinking of *frets* in heraldry, or of *fretwork*, or are these two of one origin? Why should *fret*, in this sense, not come from *fret*, to eat away, since *fretwork* may be described as the "eating away" of part of the material? Cf. *etch*, which comes, through Dutch, from Ger. *ätzen*, the factitive of *essen*, to eat. But the German for *fretwork* is *durchbrochene Arbeit*, "broken-through" work, and Old Fr. *fret* or *frait*, Lat. *fractus*, means "broken." Who shall decide how much our *fretwork* owes to each of these possible etymons?

That form of taxation called excise, which dates from the time of Charles I., has always been unpopular. Andrew Marvell says that *Excise*—

"With hundred rows of teeth the shark exceeds,
And on all trades like cassawar she feeds."

Dr Johnson defines it as "a hateful tax levied upon commodities, and adjudged not by the common judges of property, but wretches hired by those to whom excise is paid," an outburst which Lord Mansfield considered "actionable." The name, like the tax, came from the Netherlands,[1] where it was called *accijs*. In modern Dutch it has become *accijns*, through confusion with *cijns* tax (Lat. *census*; *cf.* Ger. *Zins*, interest). But the Dutch word is from Fr. *accise*, which appears in

[1] "'Twere cheap living here, were it not for the monstrous *excises* which are impos'd upon all sorts of commodities, both for belly and back."—James Howell, in a letter written from Amsterdam, 1619.

medieval Latin as *accisia*, as though connected with
" cutting " (cf. *tallage*, from Fr. *tailler*, to cut), or with the
" incidence " of the tax. It is perhaps a perversion of
Ital. *assisa*, " an imposition, or taxe, or assesment "
(Torriano); but there is also an Old Fr. *aceis* which
must be related to Latin *census*.

When folk-etymology and contamination work
together, the result is sometimes bewildering. Thus
equerry represents an older *querry* or *quirry*, still usual
in the 18th century. The modern spelling is due to
popular association with Lat. *equus*. But this *querry*
is identical with French *écurie*, stable, just as in Scottish
the *post* often means the *postman*. And *écurie*, older
escurie, is from Old High Ger. *sciura* (*Scheuer*, barn).
The word used in modern French in the sense of our
equerry is *écuyer*, older *escuier*, Lat. *scutarius*, shield-
bearer, whence our word *esquire*. This *écuyer* is in French
naturally confused with *écurie*, so that Cotgrave defines
escuyrie as " the stable of a prince, or nobleman ; also,
a *querry*-ship ; or the duties, or offices belonging thereto ;
also (in old authors) a *squire's* place ; or, the dignity, title,
estate of an esquire."

Cannibal is from Span. *canibal*, earlier *caribal*, i.e.
Carib, the *n* being due to contamination with Span.
canino, canine, voracious. It can hardly be doubted
that this word suggested Shakespeare's *Caliban*. *Seraglio*
is due to confusion between the Turkish word *serai*, a
palace, and Ital. *serraglio*, " an inclosure, a close, a padocke,
a parke, a cloister or secluse " (Florio), which belongs
to Lat. *sera*, a bolt or bar.

Ignorance of the true meaning of a word often leads
to pleonasm. Thus *greyhound* means *hound-hound*, the
first syllable representing Icel. *grey*, a dog. *Peajacket*
is explanatory of Du. *pij*, earlier *pye*, " py-gown, or
rough gown, as souldiers and seamen wear " (Hexham).

" On Greenhow Hill " means " on green hill hill," and
" Buckhurst Holt Wood " means " beech wood wood
wood," an explanatory word being added as its
predecessor became obsolete. The second part of
salt-cellar is not the ordinary word *cellar*, but Fr. *salière*,
" a salt-*seller* " (Cotgrave), so that the *salt* is unnecessary.
We speak pleonastically of " *dishevelled* hair," while
Old Fr. *deschevelé*, now replaced by *échevelé*, can only be
applied to a person, e.g., *une femme toute deschevelée*,
" discheveled, with all her haire disorderly falling about
her eares " (Cotgrave). The word *cheer* meant in
Mid. English " face." Its French original *chère* scarcely
survives except in the phrase *faire bonne chère*, lit.
" make a good face," a meaning preserved in " to be of
good *cheer*." In both languages the meaning has been
transferred to the more substantial blessings which the
pleasant countenance seems to promise, and also to the
felicity resulting from good treatment. The true
meaning of the word is so lost that we can speak of a
" *cheerful* face," *i.e.*, a face full of face.

But there are many words whose changes of form
cannot be altogether explained by any of the influences
that have been discussed in this and the preceding
chapters. Why should *cervelas*, " a large kind of
sausage, well season'd, and eaten cold in slices "
(Kersey's *Eng. Dict.*, 1720), now be *saveloy*? We
might invoke the initial letters of *sausage* to account for
part of the change, but the *oy* remains a mystery.
Cervelas, earlier *cervelat*, comes through French from Ital.
cervellato, " a kinde of dry sausage " (Florio), said to have
been originally made from pig's brains. *Hatchment* is
a corruption of *achievement*. It is now used of the
escutcheon of a deceased person displayed after his
death, but its earlier meaning was an addition to a coat
of arms granted for some achievement. We find the

natural contraction *achement* in the 16th century, but the *h* remains unexplained. French *omelette* has a bewildering history, but we can trace it almost to its present form. To begin with, an *omelet*, in spite of proverbs, is not necessarily associated with eggs. The origin is to be found in Lat. *lamella*, a thin plate,[1] which gave Old Fr. *lamelle*. Then *la lamelle* was taken as *l'alamelle*, and the new *alamelle* or *alemelle* became, with change of suffix, *alemette*. By metathesis (see p. 54) this gave *amelette*, still in dialect use, for which modern French has substituted *omelette*. The *o* then remains unexplained, unless we admit the influence of the old form *œuf-mollet*, a product of folk-etymology.

Counterpane represents Old Fr. *coute-pointe*, now corruptly *courte-pointe*, from Lat. *culcita puncta*, lit. "stitched quilt"; *cf.* Ger. *Steppdecke*, counterpane, from *steppen*, to stitch. In Old French we also find the corrupt form *contrepointe* which gave Eng. *counterpoint*—

> "In ivory coffers I have stuff'd my crowns;
> In cypress chests my arras, *counterpoints*,
> Costly apparel, tents and canopies."
>
> (*Taming of the Shrew*, ii. 1).

now unaccountably replaced by *counterpane*. In Mid. English we find also the correct form *quilt-point* from the Old Norman Fr. *cuilte* (*pur*)*pointe*, which occurs in a 12th-century poem on St Thomas of Canterbury. The hooped petticoat called a *farthingale* was spelt by Shakespeare *fardingale* and by Cotgrave *vardingall*.

---

[1] We have a parallel in Fr. *flan*, Eng. *flawn*—

> "The feast was over, the board was clear'd,
> The *flawns* and the custards had all disappear'd."
>
> (INGOLDSBY, *Jackdaw of Rheims*.)

Ger. *Fladen*, etc., a kind of omelet, ultimately related to Eng. *flat*. Cotgrave has *flans*, "flawnes, custards, eggepies; also, round planchets, or plates of metall."

This is Old Fr. *verdugalle*, of Spanish origin and derived from Span. *verdugo*, a (green) wand, because the circumference was stiffened with flexible switches before the application of whalebone or steel to this purpose. The *crinoline*, as its name implies, was originally strengthened with horse-hair, Lat. *crinis*, hair.   To return to the *farthingale*, the insertion of an *n* before *g* is common in English (see p. 77), but the change of the initial consonant is baffling.   The modern Fr. *vertugadin* is also a corrupt form.   *Isinglass* seems to be an arbitrary perversion of obsolete Du. *huyzenblas* (*huisblad*), sturgeon bladder ; *cf.* the cognate Ger. *Hausenblase*.

Few words have suffered so many distortions as *liquorice*.   The original is Greco-Lat. *glycyrrhiza*, literally "sweet root," corrupted into Latin *liquiritia*, whence Fr. *réglisse*, Ital. *legorizia*, *regolizia*, and Ger. *Lakritze*.   The Mid. English form *licoris* would appear to have been influenced by *orris*, a plant which also has a sweet root, while the modern spelling is perhaps due to *liquor*.

CHAPTER X

DOUBLETS

THE largest class of doublets is formed by those words of Latin origin which have been introduced into the language in two forms, the popular form through Anglo-Saxon or Old French, and the learned through modern French or directly from Latin. Obvious examples are *caitiff, captive; chieftain, captain; frail, fragile.* Lat. *discus*, a plate, quoit, gave Anglo-Sax. *disc*, whence Eng. *dish*. In Old French it became *deis*, Eng. *dais*, and in Ital. *desco*, "a deske, a table, a boord, a counting boord" (Florio), whence our *desk*. We have also the learned *disc* or *disk*, so that the one Latin word has supplied us with four vocables, differentiated in meaning, but each having the fundamental sense of a flat surface.

Dainty, from Old Fr. *deintié*, is a doublet of *dignity*. *Ague* is properly an adjective equivalent to *acute*, as in Fr. *fièvre aigue*. The *paladins* were the twelve peers of Charlemagne's *palace*, and a Count *Palatine* is a later name for something of the same kind. One of the most famous bearers of the title, Prince Rupert, is usually called in contemporary records the *Palsgrave*, from Ger. *Pfalzgraf*, lit. palace count. *Trivet*, Lat. *tripes*, *triped-*, dates back to Anglo-Saxon, though no one has satisfactorily explained why it should be taken as an emblem of "rightness." In the learned doublets *tripod* and *tripos* we have the Greek form. *Spice*, Old Fr. *espice* (*épice*), is a doublet of *species*. The medieval merchants recognised four "kinds" of spice, viz., saffron, cloves, cinnamon, nutmegs.

Coffin is the learned doublet of *coffer*, Fr. *coffre*, from Lat. *cophinus*. It was originally used of a basket or case of any kind, and even of a pie-crust—

> "Why, thou say'st true ; it is a paltry cap ;
> A custard-*coffin*, a bauble, a silken pie."
> (*Taming of the Shrew*, iv. 3.)

Its present meaning is an attempt at avoiding the mention of the inevitable, a natural human weakness which has popularised in America the horrible word *casket* in this sense. The Greeks, fearing death less than do the moderns, called a coffin plainly σαρκοφάγος, flesh-eater, whence indirectly Fr. *cercueil* and Ger. *Sarg*.

The homely *mangle*, which comes to us from Dutch, is a doublet of the warlike engine called a *mangonel*—

> "You may win the wall in spite both of bow and *mangonel*."
> (*Ivanhoe*, Ch. xxvii.)

which is Old French. The source is Greco-Lat. *manganum*, apparatus, whence Ital. *mangano*, with both meanings. The verb *mangle*, to mutilate, is unrelated.

Sullen, earlier *soleyn*, is a popular doublet of *solemn*, in its secondary meaning of glum or morose. In the early Latin - English dictionaries *solemn*, *soleyn*, and *sullen* are used indifferently to explain such words as *acerbus*, *agelastus*, *vultuosus*. Shakespeare speaks of "customary suits of *solemn* black" (*Hamlet*, i. 2), but makes Bolingbroke say—

> "Come, mourn with me for that I do lament,
> And put on *sullen* black incontinent."
> (*Richard II.*, v. 6.)

while the "*solemn* curfew (*Tempest*, v. 1) is described by
Milton as "swinging slow with *sullen* roar" (*Penseroso*,
l. 76). The meaning of *antic*, a doublet of *antique*, has
changed considerably, but the process is easy to follow.
From meaning simply ancient it acquired the sense of
quaint or odd, and was applied to grotesque[1] work in
art or to a fantastic disguise. Then it came to mean
buffoon, in which sense Shakespeare applies it to grim
death—

> "For within the hollow crown
> That rounds the mortal temples of a king,
> Keeps death his court ; and there the *antic* sits,
> Scoffing his state, and grinning at his pomp."
>
> (*Richard II.*, iii. 2.)

and lastly the meaning was transferred to the
capers of the buffoon. From Old High Ger. *faltan*
(*falten*), to fold, and *stuol* (*Stuhl*), chair, we get Fr.
fauteuil. Medieval Latin constructed the compound
faldestolium, whence our ecclesiastical *faldstool*, a litany
desk. *Revel* is from Old Fr. *reveler*, Lat. *rebellare*, so
that it is a doublet of *rebel*. Holyoak's *Latin Dictionary*
(1612) has *revells or routs*, "concursus populi illegitimus."
Its sense development, from a riotous concourse to a
festive gathering, has certainly been affected by Fr.
réveiller, to wake, whence *réveillon*, a Christmas Eve
supper, or "wake." Cf. Ital. *vegghia*, "a watch, a wake,
a *revelling* a nights" (Florio).

The very important word *money* has acquired its
meaning by one of those accidents which are so common
in word history. The Roman *mint* was attached to the
temple of Juno *Moneta, i.e.*, the admonisher, from *monēre*,
and this name was transferred to the building. The
Romans introduced *moneta*, in the course of their

---

[1] *I.e.*, grotto painting, Ital. *grottesca*, "a kinde of rugged unpolished
painters worke, anticke worke" (Florio).

conquests, into French (*monnaie*), German (*Münze*), and
English (*mint*). The French and German words still
have three meanings, viz., mint, coin, change. We have
borrowed the French word and given it the general
sense represented in French by *argent*, silver. The
Ger. *Geld*, money, has no connection with *gold*, but is
cognate with Eng. *yield*, as in "the *yield* of an invest-
ment," of which we preserve the old form in *wergild*,
payment for having killed a man (Anglo-Sax. *wer*). To
return to *moneta*, we have a third form of the word
in *moidore*—

> "And fair rose-nobles and broad *moidores*
> The waiter pulls out of their pockets by scores."
> (INGOLDSBY, *The Hand of Glory*.)

from Port. *moeda de ouro*, money of gold.

Sometimes the same word reaches us through
different languages. Thus *charge* is French and *cargo*
is Spanish, both belonging to a Vulgar Lat. *carricare,
from *carrus*, vehicle. In old commercial records we
often find the Anglo-Norman form *cark*, or *carke*, which
survives now only in a metaphorical sense, e.g. *carking*,
i.e. burdensome, care. Lat. *domina* has given us through
French both *dame* and *dam*,[1] and through Spanish
duenna; while Ital. *donna* occurs in the compound
madonna and the *donah* of the East End costermonger.
Lat. *datum*, given, becomes Fr. *dé* and Eng. *die*
(plural *dice*). Its Italian doublet is *dado*, now used in
English of a pattern which was originally cubical.
Scrimmage and *skirmish* are variant spellings of Fr.
escarmouche, from Ital. *scaramuccia*, of German origin
(see p. 59). But we have also, more immediately from
Italian, the form *scaramouch*. Blount's *Glossographia*
(1674) mentions *Scaramoche*, "a famous Italian Zani

---

[1] See p. 111. The aristocracy of the horse is still testified to by the use
of *sire* and *dam* for his parents.

(see p. 41), or mimick, who acted here in England, 1673." *Scaramouch* was one of the stock characters of the old Italian comedy, which still exists as the harlequinade of the Christmas pantomime, and of which some traces survive in the Punch and Judy show. He was represented as a cowardly braggart dressed in black. The golfer's *stance* is a doublet of the poet's *stanza*, both of them belonging to Lat. *stare*, to stand. *Stance* is Old French and *stanza* is Italian, "a *stance* or staffe of verses or songs" (Florio). A *stanza* is then properly a pause or resting place, just as a *verse*, Lat. *versus*, is a "turning" to the beginning of the next line.

Different French dialects have supplied us with many doublets. Old Fr. *chacier* (*chasser*), Vulgar Lat. *captiare*, for *captare*, a frequentative of *capere*, to take, was in Picard *cachier*, whence Eng. *catch*. In *cater* (see p. 58) we have the Picard form of Fr. *acheter*, but the true French form survives in the family name *Chater*.[1] In late Latin the neuter adjective *capitale*, capital, was used of property. This has given, through Old Fr. *chatel*, our *chattel*, while the doublet *catel* has given *cattle*, now limited to what was once the most important form of property. Fr. *cheptel* is still used of cattle farmed out on a kind of profit-sharing system. This restriction of the meaning of *cattle* is paralleled by Scot. *avers*, farm beasts, from Old Fr. *aver*[2] (*avoir*), property, goods. The history of the word *fee*, Anglo-Sax. *feoh*, cattle, cognate with Lat. *pecus*, whence *pecunia*, money, and Ger. *Vieh*, also takes us back to the times when a man's wealth was estimated by his flocks and herds; but, in this case, the sense development is exactly reversed.

Fr. *jumeau*, twin, was earlier *gemeau*, still used by

---

[1] Sometimes this name is for *cheater*, *escheatour* (p. 78).
[2] Cf. *avoirdupois*, earlier *avers de pois* (*poids*), goods sold by weight.

Corneille, and earlier still *gemel*, Lat. *gemellus*, diminutive of *geminus*, twin.   From one form we have the *gimbals*, or twin pivots, which keep the compass horizontal. Shakespeare uses it of clockwork—

> " I think, by some odd *gimmals*, or device,
>   Their arms are set like clocks, still to strike on."
>
> (1 *Henry VI.*, i. 2.)

and also speaks of a *gimmal* bit (*Henry V.*, iv. 2).   In the 17th century we find numerous allusions to *gimmal* rings (variously spelt).   The toothsome *jumble*, known to the Midlands as " brandy-snap," is the same word, this delicacy having apparently at one time been made in links.   We may compare the obsolete Ital. *stortelli*, literally " little twists," explained by Torriano (1659) as " winding simnels, wreathed *jumbals*."

A purely accidental difference in spelling may bring about a differentiation between two words which are identical in origin and meaning.   *Tret*, wrongly explained in all dictionaries that I have consulted, is Fr. *trait*, in Old French also *tret*, Lat. *tractus*, pull (of the scale).   It was an allowance of four pounds in a hundred, which was supposed to be equal to the sum of the " turns of the scale," which would be in the purchaser's favour if the goods were weighed in small quantities.   *Trait* is still so used in modern French.

Parson is a doublet of *person*, the priest perhaps being taken as " representing " the Church, for Lat. *persona*, an actor's mask, from *per*, through, and *sonare*, to sound, was also used of a costumed character or *dramatis persona*.   *Mask*, which ultimately belongs to an Arabic word meaning buffoon, has had a sense development exactly opposite to that of *person*, its modern meaning corresponding to the Lat. *persona* from which the latter started.   *Parson* shows the popular pronunciation of *er*, now modified by the influence of traditional spelling. We still have it in *Berkeley, clerk*,[1] *Derby, sergeant*, as we formerly did in *merchant*. Proper names, in which the orthography depends on the "taste and fancy of the speller," or the phonetic theories of the old parish clerk, often preserve the older pronunciation, *e.g.*, *Clark, Darbyshire, Marchant, Sargent.* *Posy*, in both its senses, is a contraction of *poesy*, the flowers of a nosegay expressing by their arrangement a sentiment like that engraved on a ring. The latter use is perhaps obsolete—

> "About a hoop of gold, a paltry ring
> That she did give me ; whose *posy* was
> For all the world like cutler's *poetry*
> Upon a knife : 'Love me and leave me not.'"
>
> (*Merchant of Venice*, v. 1.)

The poetic word *glamour* is the same as *grammar*, which had in the Middle Ages the sense of mysterious learning. From the same source we have the French corruption *grimoire*, "a booke of conjuring" (Cotgrave). *Glamour* and *gramarye* were both revived by Scott—

> "A moment then the volume spread,
> And one short spell therein he read ;
> It had much of *glamour* might."
>
> (*Lay*, iii. 9.)

> "And how he sought her castle high,
> That morn, by help of *gramarye*."
>
> (*Ibid.*, v. 27.)

For the change of *r* to *l* we have the parallel of *flounce* for older *frounce* (p. 55). *Quire* is the same word as *quair*, in the "King's *Quair*," *i.e.* book. Its Mid. English form is *quayer*, Old Fr. *quaer, caer* (*cahier*),

---

[1] Pronounced *clurk* by uneducated English people and educated Americans.

Lat. *quaternum* for *quaternio*, "a *quier* with foure sheetes" (Cooper).

A difference in spelling, originally accidental, but perpetuated by an apparent difference of meaning, is seen in *flour, flower; metal, mettle. Flour* is the *flower*, *i.e.* the finest part, of meal, Fr. *fleur de farine*, "*flower*, or the finest meale" (Cotgrave). In the *Nottingham Guardian* (29th Aug. 1911) I read that "Mrs Kernahan is among the increasing number of persons who do not discriminate between *metal* and *mettle*, and writes 'Margaret was on her *metal*.'" It might be added that this author is in the excellent company of Shakespeare—

> "See whe'r their basest *metal* be not mov'd."
>
> (*Julius Cæsar*, i. 1.)

There is no more etymological difference between *metal* and *mettle* than between the "temper" of a cook and that of a sword-blade.

Oriental words have sometimes come into the language by very diverse routes. *Sirup*, or *syrup*, *sherbet*, and (*rum*)-*shrub* are of identical origin, ultimately Arabic. *Sirup*, which comes through Spanish and French, was once used, like *treacle* (p. 69), of medicinal compounds—

> "Not poppy, nor mandragora,
> Nor all the drowsy *syrups* of the world,
> Shall ever medicine thee to that sweet sleep
> Which thou ow'dst yesterday."
>
> (*Othello*, iii. 3.)

Sherbet and *shrub* are directly borrowed through the medium of travellers—

> "'I smoke on *srub* and water, myself,' said Mr Omer."
> (*David Copperfield*, Ch. xxx.)

Sepoy, used of Indian soldiers in the English service, is

the same as *spahi*, the French name for the Algerian cavalry.

Tulip is from Fr. *tulipe*, formerly *tulipan*, "the delicate flower called a *tulipa, tulipie*, or Dalmatian cap" (Cotgrave). It is a doublet of *turban*. The German *Tulpe* was also earlier *Tulipan*.

The humblest of medieval coins was the *maravedi*, which came from Spain at an early date, though not early enough for Robin Hood to have said to Isaac of York, "I will strip thee of every *maravedi* thou hast in the world" (*Ivanhoe*, Ch. xxxiii.). The name is due to the Moorish dynasty of the *Al-moravides* or *Marabouts*. The Arab. *marabit* means hermit, and the name was given also to a kind of stork, the *marabout*, on account of the solitary and sober habits which have earned for him in India the name *adjutant* (p. 30).

Cipher and *zero* do not look like doublets, but both of them come from the same Arabic word. The medieval Lat. *zephyrum* connects the two forms. *Crimson* and *carmine*, the first French and the second Spanish, both belong to *kermes*, the cochineal insect, of Arabic origin.

The relationship between *cipher* and *zero* is perhaps better disguised than that between *furnish* and *veneer*, though this is by no means obvious. *Veneer*, spelt *fineer* by Smollett, is Ger. *fournieren*, borrowed from Fr. *fournir*[1] and specialised in meaning. Ebers' *German Dict.* (1796) has *furnieren*, "to inlay with several sorts of wood, to *veneer*."

The doublets selected for discussion among the hundreds which exist in the language reveal many etymological relationships which would hardly be suspected at first sight. Many other words might be

---

[1] Our verbs in *-ish* are from the *-iss-* stem of French verbs in *-ir*. This *-iss-*, as in *fournissant*, represents the *-isc* of Latin inchoative verbs.

quoted which are almost doublets. Thus *sergeant*, Fr. *sergent*, Lat. *serviens*, *servient-*, is almost a doublet of *servant*, the present participle of Fr. *servir*. The fabric called *drill* or *drilling* is from Ger. *Drillich*, "tick, linnen-cloth woven of three threads" (Ludwig). This is an adaptation of Lat. *trilix*, *trilic-*, which, through Fr. *treillis*, has given Eng. *trellis*. We may compare the older *twill*, of Anglo - Saxon origin, cognate with Ger. *Zwilch* or *Zwillich*, "linnen woven with a double thread" (Ludwig). *Robe*, from French, is cognate with *rob*, Ger. *Raub*, booty, the conqueror decking himself in the spoils of the conquered. *Musk* is a doublet of *meg* in *nutmeg*, Fr. *noix muscade*. In Mid. English we find *note-mugge*, and Cotgrave has the diminutive *muguette*, "a nutmeg"; *cf.* modern Fr. *muguet*, the lily of the valley. Fr. *dîner*, Old Fr. *disner*, and *déjeuner*, both represent Vulgar Lat. **dis-junare*, to break fast, from *jejunus*, fasting. The difference of form is due to the shifting of the accent in the Latin conjugation, e.g., *dis-junáre* gives *disner*, while *dis-júnat* gives Old Fr. *desjune*.

Admiral, earlier *amiral*, comes through French from the Arab. *amir*, an emir. Its Old French forms are numerous, and the one which has survived in English may be taken as an abbreviation of Arab. *amir al bahr*, emir on the sea. Greco-Lat. *pandura*, a stringed instrument, has produced an extraordinary number of corruptions, among which some philologists rank *mandoline*. Eng. *bandore*, now obsolete, was once a fairly common word, and from it, or from some cognate Romance form, comes the negro corruption *banjo*—

"'What is this, mamma? it is not a guitar, is it?' 'No, my dear, it is called a *banjore*; it is an African instrument, of which the negroes are particularly fond.'" (MISS EDGEWORTH, *Belinda*, Ch. xviii.)

Florio has *pandora, pandura,* "a musical instrument with three strings, a kit, a croude,[1] a rebecke." *Kit,* used by Dickens—

"He had a little fiddle, which at school we used to call a *kit,* under his left arm." (*Bleak House,* Ch. xiv.)

seems to be a clipped form from Old French dialect *quiterne,* for *guiterne,* Greco - Lat. *cithara.* Cotgrave explains *mandore* as a "*kitt,* small gitterne." The doublet *guitar* is from Spanish.

The two pretty words *dimity* and *samite* have been brought into connection by folk-etymology. *Dimity* is the plural *dimiti* of Ital. *dimito,* "a kind of course cotton or flanell" (Florio), from Greco - Lat. *dimitus,* double thread (cf. *twill*). *Samite,* Old Fr. *samit,* whence Ger. *Samt,* velvet, is in medieval Latin *hexamitus,* six-thread ; but this is a popular corruption of an Arabic original. The Italian form is *sciamito,* "a kind of sleave, feret, or filosello silke" (Florio). The word *feret* used here by Florio is from Ital. *fioretto,* little flower. It was also called *floret* silk. Florio explains the plural *fioretti* as "a kind of course silke called *f(l)oret* or *ferret* silke," and Cotgrave has *fleuret,* "course silke, *floret* silke." The word is not obsolete in the sense of tape—

"'Twas so fram'd and express'd no tribunal could shake it,
And firm as red wax and black *ferret* could make it."
(INGOLDSBY, *The Housewarming.*)

Parish and *diocese* are closely related, *parish,* Fr. *paroisse,* representing Greco - Lat. *par - oikia* (οἶκος, a house), and *diocese* coming through Old French from Greco-Lat. *di-oikesis.* *Skirt* is the Scandinavian doublet of *shirt,* from Vulgar Lat. *ex-curtus,* which has also given us *short.* The form without the prefix appears in Fr. *court,* Ger. *kurz,* and Eng. *kirtle*—"What stuff wilt have

1 See *Crowther,* p. 164.

a *kirtle* of?" (2 *Henry IV.*, ii. 4). These are all very early loan words.

A new drawing-room game for amateur philologists would be to trace relationships between words which have no apparent connection. In discussing, a few years ago, a lurid book on the "Mysteries of Modern London," *Punch* remarked that the existence of a *villa* seemed to be proof presumptive of that of a *villain*. This is etymologically true. An Old French *vilain*, "a villaine, slave, bondman, servile tenant" (Cotgrave), was a peasant attached to his lord's *ville* or domain, Lat. *villa*. For the degeneration in meaning we may compare Eng. *boor* and *churl*, and Fr. *manant*, a clod-hopper, lit. a dweller (see *manor*, p. 8). A *butcher*, Fr. *boucher*, must originally have dealt in goat's flesh, Fr. *bouc*, goat; *cf.* Ital. *beccaio*, butcher, and *becco*, goat. Hence *butcher* and *buck* are related. The extension of meaning of *broker*, an Anglo-French form of *brocheur*, shows the importance of the wine trade in the Middle Ages. A *broker* was at first one who "broached" casks with a *broche*, which means in modern French both brooch and spit. The essential part of a *brooch* is the pin or spike.

When Kent says that Cornwall and Regan "summon'd up their *meiny*, straight took horse" (*Lear*, ii. 4), he is using a common Mid. English and Tudor word which comes, through Old Fr. *maisniee*, from Vulgar Lat. **mansionata*, a houseful. A *menial* is a member of such a body. An Italian cognate is *masnadiere*, "a ruffler, a swashbuckler, a swaggerer, a high way theefe, a hackster" (Florio). Those inclined to moralise may see in these words a proof that the arrogance of the great man's flunkey was curbed in England earlier than in Italy. Old Fr. *maisniee* is now replaced by *ménage*, Vulgar Lat. **mansionaticum*. A derivative of this word is *ménagerie*, first applied to the collection of household animals, but now to a "wild beast show."

A *bonfire* was formerly a *bone-fire*. We find *bane-fire*, "ignis ossium," in a Latin dictionary of 1483, and Cooper explains *pyra* by "*bone-fire*, wherein men's bodyes were burned." Apparently the word is due to the practice of burning the dead after a victory. Hexham has *bone-fire*, "een *been-vier*, dat is, als men victorie brandt." *Walnut* is related to *Wal*es, Corn*wall*, the *Wall*oons, *Wall*achia and Sir William *Wall*ace. It means "foreign" nut. This very wide spread *wal* is supposed to represent the Celtic tribal name *Volcœ*. It was applied by the English to the Celts, and by the Germans to the French and Italians, especially the latter, whence the earlier Ger. *welsche Nuss*, for *Walnuss*. The German Swiss use it of the French Swiss, hence the canton *Wallis* or *Valais*. The Old French name for the *walnut* is *noix gauge*, Lat. *Gallica*. The relation of *umbrella* to *umber* is pretty obvious. The former is Italian, "a little shadow, a little round thing that women bare in their hands to shadow them. Also a broad brimd hat to keepe off heate and rayne. Also a kinde of round thing like a round skreene that gentlemen use in Italie in time of sommer or when it is very hote, to keepe the sunne from them when they are riding by the way (Florio)." *Umber* is Fr. *terre d'ombre*—

> "I'll put myself in poor and mean attire,
> And with a kind of *umber* smirch my face."
>
> (*As You Like It*, i. 3.)

Ballad, originally a dancing song, Prov. *ballada*, is a doublet of *ballet*, and thus related to *ball*. We find a late Lat. *ballare*, to dance, in Saint Augustine, but the history of this group of words is obscure. The sense development of *carol* is very like that of ballad. It is from Old Fr. *carolle*, "a kinde of dance wherein many

may dance together; also, a *carroll*, or Christmas song"
(Cotgrave). The form *corolla* is found in Provençal, and
carolle in Old French is commonly used, like Ger. *Kranz*,
garland, and Lat. *corona*, of a social or festive ring of
people. Hence there can be little doubt that the
origin of the word is Lat. *corolla*, a little garland.

Many "chapel" people would be shocked to know
that *chapel* means properly the sanctuary in which a
saint's relics are deposited. The name was first applied
to the chapel in which was preserved the *cape* or cloak
of St Martin of Tours. Ger. *Kapelle* also means
orchestra or military band. The doublet *capel* survives
in *Capel Court*, near the Exchange. *Tocsin* is literally
"touch sign." Fr. *toquer*, to tap, beat, cognate with
touch, survives in "*tuck* of drum" and *tucket*—

> "Then let the trumpets sound
> The *tucket* sonance and the note to mount."
>
> (*Henry V.*, iv. 2.)

while *sinet*, the diminutive of Old Fr. *sin*, sign, has given
sennet, common in the stage directions of Elizabethan
plays in a sense very similar to that of *tucket*.

Junket, Old Fr. *joncade*, "a certaine spoone-meat,
made of creame, rose-water, and sugar" (Cotgrave), Ital.
giuncata, "a kinde of fresh cheese and creame, so
called bicause it is brought to market upon rushes;
also a *junket*" (Florio), is related to *jonquil*, which
comes, through French, from Span. *junquillo*, a
diminutive from Lat. *juncus*, rush. The plant is
named from its rush-like leaves. *Ditto*, Italian, lit.
"said," and *ditty*, Old Fr. *dité*, are both past participles,
from the Latin verbs *dico* and *dicto* respectively. The
nave of a church is from Fr. *nef*, still occasionally used
in poetry in its original sense of ship, Lat. *navis*. It is
thus related to *navy*, Old Fr. *navie*, a derivative of

navis. Similarly Ger. *Schiff* is used in the sense of nave, though the metaphor is variously explained.

The old word *cole*, cabbage, its north country and Scottish equivalent *kail*, Fr. *chou* (Old Fr. *chol*), and Ger. *Kohl*, are all from Lat. *caulis*, cabbage; cf. *cauli*-flower. We have the Dutch form in *colza*, which comes, through French, from Du. *kool-zaad*, cabbage seed. *Cabbage* itself is Fr. *caboche*, a Picard derivative of Lat. *caput*, head. In modern French *caboche* corresponds to our vulgar "chump." A *goshawk* is a *goose hawk*, so called from its preying on poultry. *Merino* is related to *mayor*, which comes, through French, from Lat. *maior*, greater. Span. *merino*, Vulgar Lat. * *majorinus*, means both a magistrate and a superintendent of sheep-walks. From the latter meaning comes that of "sheepe driven from the winter pastures to the sommer pastures, or the wooll of those sheepe" (Percyvall). *Portcullis* is from Old Fr. *porte coulisse*, sliding door. Fr. *coulisse* is still used of many sliding contrivances, especially in connection with stage scenery, but in the portcullis sense it is replaced by *herse* (see p. 68), except in the language of heraldry. The masculine form *coulis* means a clear broth, or *cullis*, as it was called in English up to the 18th century. This suggests *colander*, which, like *portcullis*, belongs to Lat. *colare*, "to streine" (Cooper), whence Fr. *couler*, to flow.

Solder, formerly spelt *sowder* or *sodder*, and still so pronounced by the plumber, represents Fr. *soudure*, from the verb *souder;* cf. *batter*, from Old Fr. *batture*, and *fritter*, from Fr. *friture*. The French verb is from Lat. *solidare*, to consolidate. Fr. *sou*, formerly *sol*, a halfpenny, is said to come from Lat. *solidus*, the meaning of which appears also in the Italian participle *soldato*, a paid man. The Italian word has passed into French and German, displacing the older cognates *soudard* and *Söldner*, which now have a depreciatory sense. Eng. *soldier* is of Old French origin. It is represented in medieval Latin by *sol(i)darius*, glossed *sowdeor* in a vocabulary of the 15th century. As in *solder*, the *l* has been reintroduced by learned influence, but the vulgar *sodger* is nearer the original pronunciation.

CHAPTER XI

HOMONYMS

MODERN English contains some six or seven hundred pairs or sets of homonyms, *i.e.*, of words identical in sound and spelling but differing in meaning and origin. The *New English Dictionary* recognises provisionally nine separate nouns *rack*. The subject is a difficult one to deal with, because one word sometimes develops such apparently different meanings that the original identity becomes obscured, and even, as we have seen in the case of *flour* and *mettle* (p. 135), a difference of spelling may result. When Denys of Burgundy said to the physician, "Go to! He was no fool who first called you *leeches*," he was certainly unaware that the two *leeches* are identical, from Anglo-Sax. *læce*, healer. On the other hand, a resemblance of form may bring about a contamination of meaning. The verb to *gloss*, or *gloze*, means simply to explain or translate, Greco-Lat. *glossa*, tongue, etc.; but, under the influence of the unrelated *gloss*, superficial lustre, it has acquired the sense of specious interpretation.

That part of a helmet called the *beaver*—

> "I saw young Harry, with his *beaver* on,
> His cuisses on his thigh, gallantly arm'd,
> Rise from the ground like feather'd Mercury."
>
> (1 *Henry IV.*, iv. 1.)

has, of course, no connection with the animal whose fur has been used for some centuries for expensive hats. It comes from Old Fr. *bavière*, a child's bib, now replaced by *bavette*, from *baver*, to slobber.

It may be noted *en passant* that many of the revived medieval words which sound so picturesque in Scott are of very prosaic origin. Thus the *basnet*—

> "My *basnet* to a prentice cap,
> Lord Surrey's o'er the Till."
>
> (*Marmion*, vi. 21.)

or close-fitting steel cap worn under the ornamental helmet, is Fr. *bassinet*, a little basin. It was also called a *kettle hat*, or *pot*. Another obsolete name given to a steel cap was a privy *pallet*, from Fr. *palette*, a barber's bowl, a "helmet of Mambrino." To a brilliant living monarch we owe the phrase "mailed fist," a translation of Ger. *gepanzerte Faust*. *Panzer*, a cuirass, is etymologically a *pauncher*, or defence for the paunch. We may compare an article of female apparel, which took its name from a more polite name for this part of the anatomy, and which Shakespeare uses even in the sense of *Panzer*. Imogen, taking the papers from her bosom, says—

> "What is here?
> The scriptures of the loyal Leonatus,
> All turn'd to heresy? Away, away,
> Corrupters of my faith! You shall no more
> Be *stomachers* to my heart."
>
> (*Cymbeline*, iii. 4.)

Sometimes homonyms seem to be due to the lowest type of folk-etymology, the instinct for making an unfamiliar word "look like something" (see p. 118 footnote). To this instinct we owe the nautical *companion* (p. 153). *Trepan*, for *trapan*, to entrap, cannot have been confused with the surgical *trepan* (p. 101), although it has been assimilated to it. The *compound* in which the victims of "Chinese slavery" languished is the Malay *kampong*, an enclosure.

The scent called *bergamot* takes its name from *Bergamo*, in Italy, whence also Shakespeare's *bergomask* dance—

> "Will it please you to see the epilogue, or hear a *Bergomask* dance between two of our company?"
>
> (*Midsummer Night's Dream*, v. 1.)

but the *bergamot* pear is derived from Turkish *beg armudi*, prince's pear. With *beg*, prince, cf. *bey* and *begum*. The *burden* of a song is from Fr. *bourdon*, "a drone, or dorre-bee; also, the humming, or buzzing, of bees; also, the drone of a bag-pipe" (Cotgrave). It is of doubtful origin, but is not related to *burden*, a load, which is connected with the verb to *bear*.

To *cashier*, *i.e.*, break, a soldier, is from Du. *casseeren*, which is borrowed from Fr. *casser*, to break, Lat. *quassare*, frequentative of *quatere*, to shatter. In the 16th and 17th centuries we also find *cass* and *cash*, which are thus doublets of *quash*. Cotgrave has *casser*, "to *casse*, *cassere*, discharge." The past participle of the obsolete verb to *cass* is still in military use—

> "But the colonel said he must go, and he (the drum horse) was *cast* in due form and replaced by a washy, bay beast, as ugly as a mule." (KIPLING, *The Rout of the White Hussars*.)

The other *cashier* is of Italian origin. He takes charge of the *cash*, which formerly meant "counting-house," and earlier still "safe," from Ital. *cassa*, "a merchant's *cashe*, or counter" (Florio). This comes from Lat. *capsa*, a coffer, so that *cash* is a doublet of *case*, Fr. *caisse*. *Cf.* the goldsmith's term *chase*, for *enchase*, Fr. *enchâsser*, "to *enchace*, or set, in gold, etc." (Cotgrave). from *châsse*, coffer, shrine, also from Lat. *capsa*. From the same word comes (window) *sash*.

Gammon, from Mid. Eng. *gamen*, now reduced to *game*, survives as a slang word and also in the compound *backgammon*. In a *gammon* of bacon we have the Picard form of Fr. *jambon*, a ham, an augmentative of *jambe*, leg. Cotgrave has *jambon*, "a *gammon*." *Gambit* is related, from Ital. *gambetto*, "a tripping up of one's heels" (Torriano). A *game* leg is in dialect a *gammy* leg. This is Old Fr. *gambi*, "bent, crooked, bowed" (Cotgrave), which is still used in some French dialects in the sense of lame. It comes from the same Celtic root as *jambe*, etc.

Host, an army, now used only poetically or metaphorically, is from Old Fr. *ost*, army, Lat. *hostis*. The *host* who receives us is Old Fr. *oste* (*hôte*), Lat. *hospes*, *hospit-*, guest. These two *hosts* are, however, ultimately related. It is curious that, while modern Fr. *hôte* (*hospes*) means both "host" and "guest," the other *host* (*hostis*) is, very far back, a doublet of *guest*, the ground meaning of both being "stranger." "It is remarkable in what opposite directions the Germans and Romans have developed the meaning of the old hereditary name for 'stranger.' To the Roman the stranger becomes an enemy; among the Germans he enjoys the greatest privileges, a striking confirmation of what Tacitus tells us in his *Germania*." [1] In a dog *kennel* we have the Norman form of Fr. *chenil*, related to *chien*, but *kennel*, a gutter—

> "Go, hop me over every *kennel* home."
> (*Taming of the Shrew*, iv. 3.)

is a doublet of *channel* and *canal*.

"O villain! thou stolest a cup of sack eighteen years ago, and wert taken with the *manner*," says Prince Hal to Bardolph (1 *Henry IV.*, ii. 4). In the old editions this is spelt *manour* or *mainour* and means

---

[1] Kluge, *Etymologisches Wörterbuch*, Strassburg, 1899, s.v. *Gast*.

"in the act." It is an Anglo-French doublet of *manœuvre*, late Lat. *manu-opera*, handiwork, and is thus related to its homonym *manner*, Fr. *manière*, from *manier*, to handle. Another doublet of *manœuvre* is *manure*, now a euphemism for dung, but formerly used of the act of tillage—

"The *manuring* hand of the tiller shall root up all that burdens the soil." (MILTON, *Reason of Church Government.*)

Inure is similarly formed from Old French *enœuvrer*, literally "to work in," hence to accustom to toil.

John Gilpin's "good friend the *calender*" has nothing to do with the *calendar* which indicates the *calends* of the month, nor with the *calender*, or Persian monk, of the *Arabian Nights*, whom Mr Pecksniff described as a "one-eyed almanack." The verb to *calender*, to press and gloss cloth, etc., is from Old Fr. *calendrer* (*calandrer*), "to sleeke, smooth, plane, or polish, linnen cloth, etc." (Cotgrave). This word is generally considered to be related to *cylinder*, a conjecture which is supported by obsolete Fr. *calende*, used of the "rollers" by means of which heavy stones are moved.

A craft, or association of *masters*, was once called a *mistery* (for *mastery* or *maistrie*), usually misspelt *mystery* by association with a word of quite different origin and meaning. This accidental resemblance is often played on—

"Painting, sir, I have heard say, is a *mystery;* but what *mystery* there should be in hanging, if I should be hanged, I cannot imagine." (*Measure for Measure,* iv. 2.)

For the pronunciation, cf. *mister*, for *master*, and *mistress*.[1] The French for "mistery" is *métier*, earlier *mestier*, "a trade, occupation, *misterie*, handicraft"

---

[1] Now abbreviated to *miss* in a special sense.

(Cotgrave), from Old Fr. *maistier*, Lat. *magisterium*. In its other senses Fr. *métier* represents Lat. *ministerium*, service.

Pawn, a pledge, is from Old Fr. *pan*, with the same meaning. The origin of this word, cognates of which occur in the Germanic languages, is unknown. The *pawn* at chess is Fr. *pion*, a pawn, formerly also a foot-soldier, used contemptuously in modern French for a junior assistant master. This represents a Vulgar Lat. **pedo*, *pedon-*, from *pes*, foot; *cf.* Span. *peon*, " a footeman, a *pawne* at chesse, a pioner, or laborer " (Percyvall). In German the *pawn* is called *Bauer*, peasant, a name also given to the knave in the game of euchre, whence American *bower*[1]—

> " At last he put down a *right bower* (knave of trumps),
> Which the same Nye had dealt unto me."
> (BRET HARTE, *The Heathen Chinee*.)

When Jack Bunce says, " There will be the devil to *pay*, and no pitch hot " (Scott, *The Pirate*, Ch. xxxviii.), he is using a nautical term which has no connection with Fr. *payer*. To *pay*, *i.e.* to pitch, is from Old Fr. *peier* or *poier*, Lat. *picare*, from *pix*, pitch. Fr. *limon*, a lime, has given Eng. *lemon*,[2] but " *lemon* sole " is from Fr. *limande*, a flat-fish, dab. A *quarry* from which stone is obtained was formerly *quarrer*, Old Fr. *quarrière* (*carrière*), a derivative of Lat. *quadrus* ; cf. *quadratarius*, " a squarer of marble " (Cooper). The *quarry* of the hunter has changed its form and meaning. In Mid. English we find *quarré* and *quirré*, from Old Fr. *cuirée*, now *curée*, " a (dog's) reward ; the hounds' fees of, or part in, the game they have killed " (Cotgrave). The Old French form means " skinful " (cf. *poignée*, fistful), the hounds' reward being spread on the skin of the slain animal.

---

[1] The *Bowery* of New York was formerly a homestead.

[2] In modern French the lemon is called *citron* and the citron *cédrat*.

It is thus related to *cuirass*, originally used of leathern armour. In Shakespeare *quarry* usually means a heap of dead game—

> " Would the nobility lay aside their ruth,
>   And let me use my sword, I'd make a *quarry*
>   With thousands of these quarter'd slaves, as high
>   As I could pick my lance."
>
> <div align="right">(<i>Coriolanus</i>, i. 1.)</div>

In modern English it is applied rather to the animal pursued. Related to the first *quarry* is *quarrel*, the square-headed bolt shot from a crossbow, Old Fr. *carrel*. The modern Fr. *carreau* is used of many four-sided objects, *e.g.*, a square tile, the diamond at cards, a pane of glass. In the last sense both *quarrel* and *quarry* are still used by glaziers.

In a " *school* of porpoises " we have the Dutch doublet of *shoal*. The older spelling is *scull* (*Troilus and Cressida*, v. 5). A *sorrel* horse and the plant called *sorrel* are both French words of German origin. The adjective, used in venery of a buck of the third year, is a diminutive of Old Fr. *sor*, which survives in *hareng saur*, red herring, and is cognate with Eng. *sear*—

> " The *sear*, the yellow leaf."
>
> <div align="right">(<i>Macbeth</i>, v. 3.)</div>

The plant name is related to *sour*. Its modern French form *surelle* occurs now only in dialect, having been superseded by *oseille*, which appears to be due to the mixture of two words meaning sour, sharp, viz., Vulgar Lat. **acētula* and Greco-Lat. *oxalis*. The verb *tattoo*, to adorn the skin with patterns, is Polynesian. The military *tattoo* is Dutch. It was earlier *tap-to*, and was the signal for closing the " taps " or taverns. *Cf.* Ger. *Zapfenstreich*, lit. tap-stroke, the name of a play which was produced a few years ago in London under the title " Lights Out." Ludwig explains *Zapfenschlag* or

Zapfenstreich, as "die Zeit da die Soldaten aus den Schencken heimgehen müssen, the *taptow*."

Tassel, in "*tassel* gentle"—

> "O, for a falconer's voice,
> To lure this *tassel*-gentle back again."
>
> (*Romeo and Juliet*, ii. 2.)

is for *tercel* or *tiercel*, the male hawk, "so tearmed, because he is, commonly, a third part less than the female" (Cotgrave, s.v. *tiercelet*). The true reason for the name is doubtful. The pendent ornament called a *tassel* is a diminutive of Mid. Eng. *tasse*, a heap, bunch, Fr. *tas*. *Tent* wine is Span. *vino tinto, i.e.*, coloured—

> "Of this last there's little comes over right, therefore the vintners make *Tent* (which is a name for all wines in Spain, except white) to supply the place of it" (Howell, *Familiar Letters*, 1634).

The other *tent* is from the Old French past participle of *tendre*, to stretch.

The Shakesperian *utterance*—

> "Rather than so, come, fate, into the list,
> And champion me to the *utterance*."
>
> (*Macbeth*, iii. 1.)

is the Fr. *outrance*, in *combat à outrance, i.e.*, to the extreme, which belongs to Lat. *ultra*. It is quite unconnected with the verb to *utter*, from *out*.

We have seen how, in the case of some homonyms, confusion arises, and a popular connection is established, between words which are quite unrelated. The same sort of association often springs up between words which, without being homonyms, have some accidental resemblance in form or meaning, or in both. Such association may bring about curious changes in form and meaning. *Touchy*, which now conveys the idea of sensitiveness to *touch*, is corrupted from *tetchy*—

> "*Tetchy* and wayward was thy infancy." (*Richard III.*, iv. 4.)

The original meaning was something like "infected, tainted," from Old Fr. *teche* (*tache*), a spot. The word *surround* has completely changed its meaning through association with *round*. It comes from Old Fr. *suronder*, to overflow, Lat. *super-undare*, and its meaning and origin were quite clear to the 16th-century lexicographers. Thus Cooper has *inundo*, "to overflowe, to *surround*." A French bishop carries a *crosse*, and an archbishop a *croix*. These words are of separate origin. From *crosse*, which does not mean "cross," comes our derivative *crosier*, carried by both bishops and archbishops. It is etymologically identical, as its shape suggests, with the shepherd's *crook*, and the bat used in playing *lacrosse*.

The prophecy of the pessimistic *ostler* that, owing to motor-cars—

"*Osses* soon will all be in the circusses,
And if you want an *ostler*, try the work'uses." (E. V. LUCAS.)

shows by what association the meaning of *ostler*, Old Fr. *hostelier* (*hôtelier*) has changed. A *belfry* has nothing to do with *bells*. Old Fr. *berfroi* (*beffroi*) was a tower used in warfare. It comes from two German words represented by modern *bergen*, to hide, guard, and *Friede*, peace, so that it means "guard-peace." The triumph of the form *belfry* is due to association with *bell*, but the *l* is originally due to dissimilation, since we find *belfroi* also in Old French. The same dissimilation is seen in Fr. *auberge*, inn, Prov. *alberga* (cf. *harbinger*, p. 83), and in Old Fr. *escalberc*, *escauberc*, for *escarberc*, from Old High Ger. *scār*, a blade (*cf.* plough*share*), and *bergen*. Hence Eng. *scabbard*. Cf. *hauberk*, guard-neck, Ger. *Hals*,[1] neck.

The *buttery* is not so named from *butter*, but from

[1] Hence, or rather from Du. *hals*, the *hawse*-holes, the "throat" through which the cable runs.

bottles. It is for *butlery*, as *chancery* (see p. 80) is for *chancelry.* It is not, of course, now limited to bottles, any more than the *pantry* to bread or the *larder* to bacon, Fr. *lard*, Lat. *laridum.* The *spence*, aphetic for *dispense*, is now known only in Scotland, but has given us the name *Spencer.* The *still-room* maid is not extinct, but I doubt whether the *distilling* of strong waters is now carried on in the region over which she presides. A *journeyman* has nothing to do with *journeys* in the modern sense of the word, but works *à la journée*, by the day. *Cf.* Fr. *journalier*, " a *journey man ;* one that workes by the day " (Cotgrave), and German *Tagelöhner*, literally "day wager." On the other hand, a *day-woman* (*Love's Labour's Lost*, i. 2) is an explanatory pleonasm (cf. *greyhound*, p. 124) for the old word *day*, servant, milkmaid, etc., whence *dairy* and the common surname *Day.*

A *briar* pipe is made, not from *briar*, but from the root of heather, Fr. *bruyère*, of Celtic origin. A *catchpole* did not catch *polls, i.e.* heads, nor did he catch people with a *pole*, although a very ingenious implement, exhibited in the Tower of London Armoury, is catalogued as a *catchpole.* It corresponds to a French compound *chasse-poule*, catch-hen, in Picard *cache-pole*, the official's chief duty being to collect dues, or, in default, poultry. For *pole*, from Fr. *poule*, cf. *polecat*, also an enemy of fowls. The *companion*-ladder on shipboard is a product of folk-etymology. It leads to the *kampanje*, the Dutch for *cabin.* Both words belong to a late Lat. *capanna*, hut, which has a very numerous progeny. *Kajuit*, another Dutch word for cabin, earlier *kajute*, has given us *cuddy.*

A *carousal* is now regarded as a *carouse*, but the two are quite separate, or, rather, there are two distinct words *carousal.* One of them is from Fr. *carrousel*, a

word of Italian origin, meaning a pageant or carnival
with chariot races and tilting. This word, obsolete in
this sense, is sometimes spelt *el* and accented on the
last syllable—

> " Before the crystal palace, where he dwells,
>   The armed angels hold their *carousels*."
>   (ANDREW MARVELL, *Lachrymæ Musarum*.)

Ger. *Karussell* means a roundabout at a fair. Our
carousal, if it is the same word, has been affected in
sound and meaning by *carouse*. This comes, probably
through French, from Ger. *garaus*, quite out, in the
phrase *garaus trinken*, *i.e.*, to drink bumpers—

> " The queen *carouses* to thy fortune, Hamlet."
>   (*Hamlet*, v. 2.)

Rabelais says that he is not one of those who would
compel their companions to drink " *carous* et *alluz* (all-
aus) qui pis est" (*Pantagruel*, iii., Prologue). The
spelling *garous*, and even *garaus*, is found in 17th-
century English.

It is perhaps unnecessary to say that a *maul-stick*,
Dutch *maal-stok*, paint-stick, has nothing to do with the
verb to *maul*, formerly to *mall*,[1] *i.e.*, to hammer. Nor
is the painter's *lay-figure* connected with our verb to *lay*.
It is also, like so many art terms, of Dutch origin, the
lay representing Du. *lid*, limb, cognate with Ger.
Glied.[2] The German for lay-figure is *Gliederpuppe*,
joint-doll. Sewel's *Dutch Dict.* (1766) has *leeman*, or
ledeman, " a statue, with pliant limbs for the use of a
painter." A *footpad* is not a rubber-soled highwayman,
but a *pad*, or robber, who does his work on foot. He
was also called a *padder*—

---

[1] Hence the *Mall* and *Pall-Mall*, where games like croquet were played.
[2] The *g-* represents the Old High German prefix *gi-*, *ge-*. *Cf.* Eng.
luck and Ger. *Glück*.

"While Hudibras, with equal haste,
  On both sides laid about as fast,
  And spurr'd, as jockies use, to break,
  Or *padders*, to secure, a neck."

                    (BUTLER, *Hudibras*, iii. 1.)

i.e., one who takes to the "road," from Du. *pad*, path.
Pad, an ambling nag, a "roadster," is the same word.

Pen comes, through Old French, from Lat. *penna*, "a
penne, quil, or fether" (Cooper), while *pencil* is from
Old Fr. *pincel* (*pinceau*), a painter's brush, from Lat.
penicillus, a little tail. The modern meaning of *pencil*,
which still meant painter's brush in the 18th century, is
due to association with *pen*. The *ferrule* of a walking-
stick is a distinct word from *ferule*, an aid to education.
The latter is Lat. *ferula*, "an herbe like big fenell, and
maye be called fenell giant. Also a rodde, sticke, or
paulmer, wherewith children are striken and corrected
in schooles; a cane, a reede, a walking staffe" (Cooper).
Ferrule is a perversion of earlier *virrel*, *virrol*, Fr. *virole*,
"an iron ring put about the end of a staffe, etc., to
strengthen it, and keep it from riving" (Cotgrave).
The modern form is perhaps partly due to the preceding
word, the "staffe" acting as point of contact.

The modern meaning of *pester* is due to a wrong
association with *pest*. Its earlier meaning is to hamper
or entangle—

  "Confined and *pestered* in this pinfold here."

                    (*Comus*, l. 7.)

It was formerly *impester*, from Old Fr. *empestrer*
(*empêtrer*), "to *pester*, intricate, intangle, trouble,
incumber" (Cotgrave), originally to "hobble" a grazing
horse with *pasterns*, or shackles (see *pastern*, p. 69).

Mosaic work is not connected with *Moses*, but with
the *muses* and *museum*. *Sorrow* and *sorry* are quite
unrelated. *Sorrow* is from Anglo-Sax. *sorg*, *sorh*,

cognate with Ger. *Sorge*, anxiety. *Sorry*, Mid. Eng. *sori*, is a derivative of *sore*, cognate with Ger. *sehr*, very, lit. " painfully " ; *cf.* English " *sore* afraid," or the modern " *awfully* nice," which is in South Germany *arg nett*, " *vexatiously* nice."

It is probable that *vagabond*, Lat. *vagabundus*, has no etymological connection with *vagrant*, which appears to come from Old Fr. *waucrant*, present participle of *waucrer*, a common verb in the Picard dialect, probably related to Eng. *walk*. Cotgrave spells it *vaucrer*, " to range, roame, vagary, wander, idly (idle) it up and down." Cotgrave also attributes to it the special meaning of a ship sailing " whither wind and tide will carry it," the precise sense in which it is used in the 13th-century romance of *Aucassin et Nicolette*.

Other examples of mistaken associations are *scullion* and *scullery* (p. 39), and *sentry* and *sentinel* (p. 96). Many years ago *Punch* had a picture by Du Maurier called the " *Vikings* of Whitby," followed by a companion picture, the *Viqueens*. The word is not *vi-king* but *vik-ing*, the exact meaning of *vik* being doubtful.

CHAPTER XII

FAMILY NAMES

In the study of family names we come across very much the same phenomena as in dealing with other words. They are subject to the same phonetic accidents and to the distortions of folk-etymology, being "altered strangely to significative words by the common sort, who desire to make all to be significative" (Camden, *Remains concerning Britain*). Doublets and homonyms are of frequent occurrence, and the origin of some names is obscured by the well-meaning efforts of early philologists. It might be expected that a family name would by its very nature tend to preserve its original form. This is, however, not the case. In old parish registers one often finds on one page two or three different spellings for the same name, and there are said to be a hundred and thirty variants of *Mainwaring*.[1] The telescoped pronunciation of long names such as Cholmondeley, Daventry, Marjoribanks, Strachan, is a familiar phenomenon, and very often the telescoped form persists separately, *e.g.*, *Posnett* and *Poslett* occur often in Westmorland for *Postlethwaite*. *Beecham* exists by the side of *Beauchamp; Saint Clair* and *Saint Maur* are usually reduced to *Sinclair* and *Seymour;*

---

[1] This is probably the record for a proper name, but does not by any means equal that of the word *cushion*, of which about four hundred variants are found in old wills and inventories.

Boon[1] and *Moon* disguise the aristocratic *Bohun* and
Mohun. In a story by Mr Wells, *Miss Winchelsea's
Heart*, the name *Snooks* is gradually improved to
Sevenoaks, from which in all probability it originally
came, via *Senoaks*; cf. *sennight* for *seven-night*,
and such names as *Fiveash*, *Twelvetrees*, etc. Folk-
etymology converts *Arblaster*, the cross-bowman,
into *Alabaster*, *Fishwick* into *Physick*, and *Annabel* into
Hannibal and *Honeyball*. *Malthus* looks like Latin,
but is identical with *Malthouse*, just as *Bellows* is for
Bellhouse, *Loftus* for *Lofthouse*, and *Bacchus*, fined for
intoxication, Jan. 5, 1911, for *Bakehouse*. *Goodenough*
probably consists of *hough* or *haugh*, a hill, and the
name *Godwin*, while *Toogood*, *Thurgood*, and *Thoroughgood* are all corruptions of an old Saxon name *Thurgod*.
Godebert gives our *Godber*, but we have also the perversions *Godbehere*, *Goodbeer*, and *Gotobed*. Sometimes family vanity may have brought about a change.
Beaufoy is a grammatical monstrosity. Its older form
is *Beaufou*, fine beech (see p. 119), with an ambiguous
second syllable. Other examples of such corruptions
will be found in this chapter.

Family names fall into four great classes, which are,
in descending order of size, local, baptismal, functional,
and nicknames. But we have a great many homonyms,
names capable of two or more explanations. Thus
Bell may be for Fr. *le bel* or from a shop-sign, *Collet* a
diminutive of *Nicholas* or an aphetic form of *acolyte*.
Dennis is usually for *Dionysius*, but sometimes for
le Danois, the Dane; *Gillott*, and all family names
beginning with *Gill-*, may be from *Gillian* (see p. 42),
or from Fr. *Guillaume*. A famous member of the
latter family was *Guillotin*, the humanitarian doctor
who urged the abolition of clumsy methods of decapita-

---

[1] Another origin of this name is Fr. *le bon*.

tion. His name is a double diminutive, like Fr. *diablotin*, goblin. *Leggatt* is a variant of *Lidgate*, swing gate, and of *Legate*. *Lovell* is an affectionate diminutive or is for Old Fr. *louvel*, little wolf. It was also in Mid. English a dog's name, hence the force of the rime—

"The Rat (Ratcliffe), the Cat (Catesby), and *Lovell*, our dog,
Rule all England under the Hog." (1484.)

It has a doublet *Lowell*. The name *Turney*, well known in Nottingham, is from the town of *Tournay*, or is aphetic for *attorney*. In the following paragraphs I generally give only one source for each name, but it should be understood that in many cases two or more are possible. The forms also vary.

Baptismal names often give surnames without any suffix. Sometimes these are slightly disguised, e.g., *Cobbett* (Cuthbert), *Garrett* (Gerard), *Hammond*, Fr. *Hamon* (Hamo), *Hibbert* (Hubert), *Jessop* (Joseph), *Neil* (Nigel), *Custance* (Constance); or they preserve a name no longer given baptismally, e.g., *Aldridge* (Alderic), *Bardell* (Bardolph), *Goodeve* (Godiva), *Goodlake* (Guthlac), *Goodrich* (Goderic), *Harvey*[1] (Hervey, Fr. *Hervé*), *Mayhew* (Old Fr. *Mahieu*, Matthew). With the help of diminutive suffixes we get *Atkin* (Adam), *Bodkin* (Baldwin), *Larkin* (Lawrence), *Perkin*, *Parkin* (Peter), *Hackett* (Haco), *Huggin*, *Hutchin*, *Hewett*, *Hewlett*, *Howitt* (Hugh), *Philpot* (Philip), *Tibbet* (Theobald or Isabella), *Tillet* (Matilda), *Wilmot* (William), *Wyatt* (Guy), *Gibbon*,

[1] "The last two centuries have seen the practice made popular of using surnames for baptismal names. Thus the late Bishop of Carlisle was Harvey Goodwin, although for several centuries Harvey has been obsolete as a personal name" (Bardsley). Camden already complains that "surnames of honourable and worshipful families are given now to mean men's children for christian names." Forty years ago there was hardly a more popular name than *Percy*, while at the present day the admonition, "Be'ave yerself, '*Oward*," is familiar to the attentive ear.

Gilpin (Gilbert), etc., with numerous variants and further derivatives. The changes that can be rung on one favourite name are bewildering, *e.g.*, from *Robert* we have *Rob*, *Dob*, *Hob*, and *Bob ;* the first three with a numerous progeny, while *Bob*, now the favourite abbreviation, came into use too late to found a large dynasty. From *Richard* we have *Richards* and *Richardson*, and from its three abbreviations *Rick*, *Dick*, *Hick*, with their variants *Rich*, *Digg*, *Hig*, *Hitch*, probably the largest family of surnames in the language. As the preceding examples show, family names are frequently derived from the mother. Other examples, which are not quite obvious, are *Betts* (Beatrice), *Sisson* (Cecilia), *Moxon* and *Padgett* (Margaret, Moggy, Madge, Padge), *Parnell* (Petronilla), *Ibbotson* (Ib, Isabella), *Tillotson* (Matilda). One group of surnames is derived from baptismal names given according to the season of the Church. Such are *Pentecost*, *Pascal*, whence Cornish *Pascoe*, *Nowell*, and *Middlemas*, generally a corruption of *Michaelmas*. With these may be grouped *Loveday*, a day appointed for reconciliations.

Surnames derived from place of residence often contain a preposition, e.g., *Atwood*, *Underhill*, and sometimes the article as well, e.g., *Attenborough*, *Bythesea*. In *Surtees*, on the Tees, we have a French preposition and an English river name. Sometimes they preserve a word otherwise obsolete. *Barton*, a farmyard, originally a barley-field, has given its name to about thirty places in England, and thus, directly or indirectly, to many families. *Bristow* preserves what was once the regular pronunciation of *Bristol*. The famous north country name *Peel* means castle, as still in the Isle of Man. It is Old Fr. *pel* (*pal*), stake, and the name was originally given to a wooden hill-fort or stockade.

Many places which have given family names have

themselves disappeared from the map, while others, now of great importance, are of too recent growth to have been used in this way. Many of our family names are taken from those of continental towns, especially French and Flemish. Camden says, " Neither is there any village in Normandy that gave not denomination to some family in England." Such are *Bullen* or *Boleyn* (*Boulogne*), *Cullen* (*Cologne*), *Challis* (*Calais*), *Challen* (*Châlon*), *Chaworth* (*Cahors*), *Bridges* [1] (*Bruges*), *Druce* (*Dreux*), *Gaunt* (*Gand*, Ghent), *Lubbock* (*Lubeck*), *Luck* (*Luick*, Liège), *Mann* (*le Mans*), *Malins* (*Malines*, Mechlin), *Nugent* (*Nogent*), *Hawtrey* (*Hauterive*), and *Dampier* (*Dampierre*). To decide which is the particular *Hauterive* or *Dampierre* in question is the work of the genealogist. *Dampierre* (*Dominus Petrus*) means *Saint Peter*. In some cases these names have been simplified, *e.g.*, Camden notes that *Conyers*, from *Coigniers*, lit. quince-trees, becomes *Quince*.

French provinces have given us *Burgoyne*, *Champain*, *Gascoyne* or *Gaskin*, and *Mayne*, and adjectives formed from names of countries, provinces and towns survive in *Allman* (*Allemand*), *Brabazon* (*le Brabançon*, the Brabanter), *Brett* (*le Bret* or *le Breton* [2]), *Champneys* (*le Champenois*), with which we may compare *Cornwallis*, from the Old French adjective *cornwaleis*, man of Cornwall, *Pickard* (*le Picard*), *Poidevin* (*le Poitevin*), *Mansell*, Old Fr. *Mancel* (*le Manceau*), inhabitant of Maine or le Mans, *Hanway* and *Hannay* (*le Hannuyer*, the Hainaulter). To these may be added *Pollock*, the Pole, or *Polack*—

"Why then the *Polack* never will defend it."

(*Hamlet*, iv. 4.)

Loring (*le Lorrain*), assimilated to *Fleming*, *Janaway*,

---

[1] Of course also of English origin.
[2] Hence also the name *Britton*.

the Genoese, and *Hansard*, a member of the *Hanse* confederation. *Morris* means sometimes *Moorish* (see p. 45), and *Norris*, besides having the meaning seen in its contracted form *Nurse*, Fr. *nourrice*, may stand for *le Noreis*, the Northener. We still have a *Norroy* king-at-arms, who holds office north of the Trent.

In some cases the territorial *de* remains, e.g., *Dolman* is sometimes the same as *Dalmain*, *d'Allemagne*, *Daubeney* is *d'Aubigné*, *Danvers* is *d'Anvers* (Antwerp), *Devereux* is *d'Évreux*, a town which takes its name from the *Eboraci*, and *Disney* is *d'Isigny*. *Durrant* is the common French name *Durand*. With these may be mentioned *Dawnay*, from Old Fr. *aunai*,[1] a grove of alders. The last governor of the Bastille was the Marquis de *Launay* (*l'aunai*). There is a large group of such words in French, coming from Latin collectives in *-etum; d'Aubray* is from Lat. *arboretum*, and has given also the dissimilated form *Darblay*, famous in English literature. Other examples are *Chesney*, *Chaney*, etc., the oak-grove,[2] *Pomeroy*, the apple garden.

Names of French origin are particularly subject to corruption and folk-etymology. We have the classic example of Tess *Durbeyfield*.[3] Camden, in his *Remains concerning Britain*, gives, among other curious instances, *Troublefield* for *Turberville*. *Greenfield* is usually literal (cf. *Whitfield*, *Whittaker*, *Greenacre*, etc.), but occasionally for *Grenville*. *Summerfield* is for *Somerville*. The

---

[1] Old Fr. *vernai*, whence our *Verney*, *Varney*, has the same meaning; cf. *Duverney*, the name of a famous dancer. *Verne*, alder, is of Celtic origin.

[2] Cf. *Chenevix*, old oak, a name introduced by the Huguenots.

[3] Other examples quoted by Mr Hardy are *Priddle*, from *Paridelle*, and *Debbyhouse*—"The *Debbyhouses* who now be carters were once the *de Bayeux* family" (*Tess of the d'Urbervilles*, v. 35).

notorious *Dangerfield* was of Norman ancestry, from *Angerville*. *Mullins* looks a very English name, but it is from Fr. *moulin*, mill, as *Musters* is from Old Fr. *moustier*, monastery. *Phillimore* is a corruption of *Finnemore*, Fr. *fin amour*.

When we come to names which indicate office or trade, we have to distinguish between those that are practically nicknames, such as *King, Duke, Bishop, Cæsar*[1] (Julius Cæsar was a famous cricketer of the old school), and those that are to be taken literally. Many callings now obsolete have left traces in our surnames. The very common name *Chapman* reminds us that this was once the general term for a dealer (see p. 62), one who spends his time in *chaffering* or "*chopping* and changing." The *grocer*, or *engrosser, i.e.*, the man who bought wholesale, Fr. *en gros*,[2] came too late to supplant the family name *Spicer*. *Bailey*, Old Fr. *bailif* (*bailli*), represents all sorts of officials from a Scotch magistrate to a man in possession. *Bayliss* seems to be formed from it like Williams from William. *Chaucer*, Old Fr. *chaucier*, now replaced by *chaussetier*, " a hosier, or hose-maker" (Cotgrave), is probably obsolete as an English surname. Mr *Homer's* ancestors made helmets, Fr. *heaume*. *Jenner* is for *engenour*, engineer (see *gin*, p. 60). In *Ferrier* traditional spelling seems to have triumphed over popular pronunciation (*farrier*), but the latter appears in *Farrar*. Chaucer's *somonour* survives as *Sumner*. *Ark* was once a general name for a bin, hence

---

[1] These names are supposed to have been generally conferred in consequence of characters represented in public performances and processions. In some cases they imply that the bearer was in the employment of the dignitary. We find them in other languages, *e.g.*, Fr. *Leroy, Leduc, Lévêque ;* Ger. *König, Herzog, Bischof. Lévêque* has given Eng. *Levick, Vick*, and (Trotty) *Veck*.

[2] *Gross*, twelve dozen, seems to be of Germanic origin, the duodecimal hundred, Ger. *Grosshundert*, being Norse or Gothic. But Ger. *Grosshundert* means 120 only.

the name *Arkwright*. Nottingham still has a Fletcher Gate, Lister Gate, and Pilcher Gate. It is not surprising that the trade of the *fletcher*, Old Fr. *fleschier* (*Fléchier*), arrow-maker, should be obsolete. *Lister*, earlier *littester*, gave way to *dighester*, whence the name *Dexter*, well known in Nottingham, and this is now replaced by *dyer*. A *Pilcher* made *pilches*, or mantles; *cf.* the cognate Fr. name *Pélissier*, a maker of *pelisses*.[1] *Kiddier* was once equivalent to pedlar, from *kid*, a basket. Sailors still speak of the bread-*kid*. For the name *Wait*, see p. 70. The ancestor of the *Poyser* family made scales (*poises*), or was in charge of a public balance. *Faulkner*, falconer, *Foster*, *Forster*, forester, and *Warner*, warrener, go together. With the contraction of *Warner* we may compare *Marner*, mariner. *Crowther* means fiddler. The obsolete *crowd*, a fiddle, is of Celtic origin. It is a doublet of *rote*, the name of the instrument played by the medieval minstrels. Both words are used by Spenser.

Pinder, the man in charge of the pound or pinfold, was the name of a famous wicket-keeper of thirty years ago. The still more famous cricketing name of *Trumper* means one who blows the trump. Cf. *Horner* and *Corner*, which have, however, alternative origins, a maker of horn cups and a *coroner* respectively. A dealer in *shalloon* (see p. 43) was a *Chaloner* or *Chawner*. *Parminter*, a tailor, is as obsolete as its Old French original *parmentier*, a maker of *parements*, deckings, from *parer*, Lat. *parare*, to prepare. A member of the *Parmentier* family introduced the cultivation of the potato into France just before the Revolution, hence *potage Parmentier*, potato soup. The *white tawer* still plies his trade, but is hardly recognisable in *Whittier*. *Massinger* is a corruption of *messenger*. The *Todhunter*, or fox-

[1] *Surplice*, Old Fr. *surpelis*, is a compound of the same word. The original meaning is fur cloak.

hunter, used to get twelve pence per fox-head from the parish warden. *Coltman* is simple, but *Runciman*, the man in charge of the *runcies* or *rouncies*, is less obvious. *Rouncy*, a nag, is a common word in Mid. English. It comes from Old Fr. *roncin* (*roussin*), and is probably a derivative of Ger. *Ross*, horse. The Spanish form is *rocin*, "a horse or jade" (Minsheu, 1623), whence Don Quixote's charger *Rocin-ante*, "a jade formerly."

A park keeper is no longer called a *Parker*, nor a maker of palings and palissades a *Palliser*. An English sea-king has immortalised the trade of the *Frobisher*, or furbisher, and a famous bishop bore the appropriate name of *Latimer*, for *Latiner*. With this we may compare *Lorimer*, for *loriner*, harness-maker, a derivative, through Old French, of Lat. *lorum*, "a thong of leather; a coller or other thing, wherewith beastes are bounden or tyed; the reyne of a brydle" (Cooper). The *Loriners* still figure among the London City Livery Companies, as do also the *Bowyers*, *Broderers*, *Fletchers* (see p. 164), *Horners* (see p. 164), *Pattenmakers*, *Poulters* and *Upholders* (see p. 58). *Scriven*, Old Fr. *escrivain* (*écrivain*), is now usually extended to *Scrivener*. For *Cator* see p. 58. In some of the above cases the name may have descended from a female, as we have not usually a separate word for women carrying on trades generally practised by men. In French there is a feminine form for nearly every occupation, hence such names as *Labouchère*, the lady butcher, or the butcher's wife.

The meaning of occupative names is not always on the surface. It would, for instance, be rash to form hasty conclusions as to the pursuits of Richard *Kisser*, whose name occurs in medieval London records. He probably made *cuisses*,[1] thigh armour, Fr. *cuisse*, thigh, Lat. *coxa*. A *Barker* prepared bark for tanning pur-

---

[1] See quotation from *Henry IV.* (p. 145).

poses. *Booker* is a doublet of *Butcher*. A *Cleaver* was, in most cases, a mace-bearer, Old Fr. *clavier* (*Clavier* is a common family name in France) from Lat. *clava*, a club. He may, however, have sometimes been a porter, as Old Fr. *clavier* also means key-bearer, Lat. *clavis*, a key. A *Croker*, or *Crocker*, sold *crocks*, *i.e.*, pottery. A *Lander*, or *Launder*, was a washer-man, Fr. *lavandier*. A *Sloper* made " slops," *i.e.*, loose upper garments, overalls. A *Reeder* or *Reader* thatched with reeds. A *Walker* walked, but within a circumscribed space. He was also called a *Fuller*, Fr. *fouler*, to trample, or a *Tucker*, Old Fr. *touquer* (*toquer*), to beat, the Picard form of *toucher*. The fuller is still called *Walker* in Germany. *Kemp* is an Old English word for warrior, champion. It represents, like Ger. *kämpfen*, to fight, a very early loan from Lat. *campus*, in the sense of battle-field. *Banister* is a corruption of *balestier*, a cross-bow man ; cf. *banister* for *baluster* (p. 55).

Some of the occupative names in *-ward* and *-herd* are rather deceptive. *Hayward* means hedge[1] guard. *Howard* is a blend of *Hayward* and *Hereward*. The first source accounts for the frequent occurrence of this noble name. For the social elevation of the *sty-ward*, see p. 83. *Durward* is door-ward. The simple *Ward*, replaced in its general sense by *warden*, *warder*, etc., is one of our commonest surnames. Similarly *Herd*, replaced by *herdsman*, is borne as a surname by one who, if he attains not to the first three, is usually held more honourable than the thirty. *Hogarth* is for *Hoggart*, hog-herd ; *Seward* is sometimes for sow-herd ; *Calvert* represents calf-herd, and *Stoddart* stot[2]-herd, *i.e.*,

---

[1] The obsolete *hay*, hedge, is also a common surname, *Hay*, *Haig*, *Haigh*, etc.

[2] " 'Shentlemans !' cried Andie, 'Shentlemans, ye hielant *stot* ! If God would give ye the grace to see yersel' the way that ithers see ye, ye would throw your denner up'" (*Catriona*, Ch. XV.).

bullock-herd. *Lambert* is in some cases lamb-herd, and *Nutter* is in all probability a perversion of neat-herd, through the North Country and Scot. *nowt-herd*. It is a common surname in Lancashire, and Alice Nutter was one of the Lancashire Witches.

In a sense all personal names are nicknames, since they all give that additional information which enables us to distinguish one person from another. The practice of giving nicknames suggested by appearance, physique, or habits is common to the European languages; but, on the whole, our nicknames compare very unfavourably with those of savage nations. We cannot imagine an English swain calling his lady-love " Laughing Water." From Roman times onward, European nicknames are in their general character obvious and prosaic, and very many of them are the reverse of complimentary. The most objectionable have either disappeared,[1] or the original meaning has become so obscured as to cease to give offence to the possessor. When a man had any choice in the matter, he naturally preferred not to perpetuate a grotesque name conferred on some ancestor. Medieval names were conferred on the individual, and did not become definitely hereditary till the Reformation. In later times names could only be changed by form of law. It is thus that *Bugg* became *Norfolk Howard*, a considerable transformation inspired by a natural instinct to " avoid the opinion of baseness," as Camden puts it. We no longer connect *Gosse* with *goose*, nor *Pennefather*

---

[1] The following occur in the index to Bardsley's *English Surnames*:— Blackinthemouth, Blubber, Calvesmawe, Cleanhog, Crookbone, Damned-Barebones, Drunkard, Felon, Greenhorn, Halfpenny, Hatechrist, Hogsflesh, Killhog, Leper, Mad, Measle, Milksop, Outlaw, Peckcheese, Peppercorn, Poorfish, Pudding, Ragman, Scorchbeef, Sourale, Sparewater, Sweatinbed, Twopenny, Widehose.

with a miser.[1] In *Purcell* we lose Fr. *pourceau*, Old Fr. *pourcel*, little pig, *Fitch* no longer means a pole-cat, nor *Brock* a badger. On the other hand, we generally regard *Gosling* as a nickname, while it is more often a variant of *Jocelyn*.

Names descriptive of appearance or habits often correspond pretty closely with those that are found in French. In some cases they are probably mere translations. Examples are: *Merryweather* (*Bontemps*), *Drinkwater* (*Boileau*[2]), *Armstrong* (*Fortinbras*), *Lilywhite* (*Blanchefleur*). Among colour names we have *Black*, *Brown*, *White*, and *Grey*, but seem to miss *red*. The explanation is that for this colour we have adopted the Northern form *Reid* (*Read*, *Reed*), or such French names as *Rudge* (*rouge*), *Rouse* (*roux*), *Russell* (*Rousseau*). With the last of these, Old. Fr. *roussel*, cf. *Brunel* and *Morel*. Fr. *blond* has given *Blount*, *Blunt*, and the diminutive *Blundell*, which exist by the side of the fine old English name *Fairfax*, from Mid. Eng. *fax*, hair. Several other French adjectives have given us surnames, e.g., *Boon* (*bon*), *Bonner* (*débonnaire*), *Grant* (*grand*), *Curtis* (*courtois*), *Power* (*pauvre*), etc. *Payn* is the French adjective *païen*, pagan, properly a dweller in the country. For the meaning, cf. *heathen*.

But many apparent nicknames are products of folk-etymology. *Coward* is for *cowherd*, *Salmon* for *Salomon*, *Bone* for *Boon* (v.s.), *Dedman* is a corruption of *Debenham*. *Playfair* means play-fellow, from an old word connected with the verb to *fare*, to journey. *Patch* may sometimes have meant a jester, from his parti-coloured garments, but is more often a variant of *Pash*, *Pask*, a baptismal name given to children christened at Easter,

---

[1] *Pinse-maille* (*pince-maille*), " a pinch peny, scrape-good, nigard, miser, *penie-father*" (Cotgrave).

[2] Cf. also Ital. *Bevilacqua*.

Old Fr. *Pasque* (*Pâque*). Easter eggs are still called
pash, *pace*, or *paste* eggs in the north of England.
Blood is a Welsh name, son of *Lud*; cf. *Bevan*, *Bowen*,
etc. *Coffin* is Fr. *Chauvin*, a derivative of Lat. *calvus*,
bald. It has a variant *Caffyn*, the name of a famous
cricketer. *Dance*, for Dans, is related to Daniel as Wills
is to William. In the same way *Pearce* comes from
Peter or Pierre. The older form of the name Pearce
was borne by the most famous of ploughmen, as it still
is by the most famous of soapmakers. Names such
as *Bull*, *Peacock*, *Greenman*, are often from shop or
tavern signs. It is noteworthy that, as a surname, we
usually find the old form *Pocock*. The *Green Man*, still
a common tavern sign, represented a kind of savage;
cf. the Ger. *zum wilden Mann*.

In these remarks on surnames I have only tried to
show in general terms how they come into existence,
"hoping to incur no offence herein with any person,
when I protest in all sincerity, that I purpose nothing
less than to wrong any whosoever" (Camden). Many
names are susceptible of alternative explanations,
and it requires a genealogist, and generally some
imagination, to decide to which particular source a
given family can be traced. The two arguments sometimes drawn from armorial bearings and medieval Latin
forms are worthless. Names existed before escutcheons
and devices, and these are often mere puns, *e.g.*, the
Onslow family, of local origin, has adopted the excellent
motto *festina lente*, hurry slowly. The famous name
Sacheverell is latinised as *De Saltu Capellæ*, of the kid's
leap. This agrees with the oldest form *Sau-cheverell*,
which might conceivably stand for modern Fr. *saut du
chevreau*, but evidence is lacking. The fact that *Napier*
of Merchiston had for his device *n'a pier*, no equal, does
not make it any the less true that his ancestors were,

as the child said of Perkin Warbeck's parents, "really, respectable people" (see p. 52). Dr Brewer, in his *Dictionary of Phrase and Fable*, says of his own name, "This name, which exists in France as Bruhière and Brugière, is not derived from the Saxon *briwan* (to brew), but the French *bruyère* (heath), and is about tantamount to the German *Plantagenet* (broom plant)." A "German" Plantagenet should overawe even a Norfolk Howard. A more interesting identification, and a true one, is that of the name of the great engineer *Telford*, a corruption of *Telfer*, with *Taillefer*, the "iron cleaver."

A curious feature in nomenclature is the local character of some nicknames. A striking instance of this is the Notts name *Daft*.[1] "A Daft might have played in the Notts County Eleven in 1273 as well as in 1886" (Bardsley). The only occurrence of the name in the Hundred Rolls for the year 1273 is in the county of Notts.

---

[1] This word has degenerated. It is a doublet of *deft*.

CHAPTER XIII

ETYMOLOGICAL FACT AND FICTION

ROMANCE and Germanic etymology dates from the middle of the 19th century, and is associated especially with the names of two great Germans, Friedrich Diez, who published his *Wörterbuch der romanischen Sprachen* in 1853, and Jakob Grimm, whose *Deutsches Wörterbuch* dates from 1852. These two men applied in their respective fields of investigation the principles of comparative philology, and reduced to a science what had previously been an amusement for the learned or the ignorant.

Men have always been fascinated by word lore. The Greeks and Romans played with etymology in a somewhat metaphysical fashion, a famous example of which is the derivation of *lucus a non lucendo*. Medieval writers delight in giving amazing information as to the origin of the words they use. Their method, which may be called learned folk-etymology, consists in attempting to resolve an unfamiliar word into elements which give a possible interpretation of its meaning. Thus Philippe de Thaün, who wrote a kind of verse encyclopedia at the beginning of the 12th century, derives the French names of the days of the week as follows : *lundi*, day of light (*lumière*), *mardi*, day of toil or martyrdom (*martyre*), *mercredi*, day of market (*marché*), *jeudi*, day of joy (*joie*), *vendredi*, day of truth (*vérité*), *samedi*, day of sowing (*semence*).   Here we perhaps have, not so much complete ignorance, as the desire to be edifying, which is characteristic of the medieval etymologists.

Playful or punning etymology also appears very early.   Wace, whose *Roman de Rou* dates from about the middle of the 12th century, gives the correct origin of the word *Norman*—

> "Justez (*put*) ensemble *north* et *man*
> Et ensemble dites *northman*."

But he also records the libellous theory that *Normendie* comes from *north mendie* (begs).   We cannot always say whether an early etymology is serious or not, but many theories which were undoubtedly meant for jokes have been quite innocently accepted by comparatively modern writers.[1]

The philologists of the Renaissance period were often very learned men, but they had no knowledge of the phonetic laws by which sound change is governed. Nor were they aware of the existence of Vulgar Latin, which is, to a much greater extent than classical Latin, the parent of the Romance languages.   Sometimes a philologist had a pet theory which the facts were made to fit.   Hellenists like Henri Estienne believed in the

---

[1] The following "etymologies" occur, in the same list with a number which are quite correct, in a 16th-century French author, Tabourot des Accords :—

Bonnet, de *bon* et *net*, pource que l'ornement de la teste doit estre tel.

Chapeau, quasi, *eschappe eau ;* aussi anciennement ne le souloit on porter que par les champs en temps de pluye.

Chemise, quasi, sur *chair mise.*

Velours, quasi, *velu ours.*

Galant, quasi, *gay allant.*

Menestrier, quasi, *meine estrier* des espousées.

Orgueil, quasi, *orde gueule.*

Noise, vient de *nois* (*noix*), qui font noise et bruit portées ensemble.

Parlement, pource qu'on y *parle et ment !*

Greek origin of the French language, and derived *maison* from the Greek accusative δικον (δικος, a house) by the simple method of prefixing an *m.* At other periods there have been Celtomaniacs, *i.e.*, scholars who insisted on the Celtic origin of French.

The first English etymological dictionary which aims at something like completeness is the *Guide into the Tongues* of John Minsheu, published in 1617. This attempts to deal not only with English, but with ten other languages. It contains a great deal of learning, much valuable information for the student of Tudor literature, and some amazing etymologies. "To *purloine*,[1] or get privily away," is, says Minsheu, "a metaphor from those that picke the fat of the *loines*." *Parmaceti* (1 *Henry IV.*, i. 3), a corruption of *spermaceti*, he derives from Parma, which has given its name to *parmesan* cheese. On the word *cockney*[2] he waxes anecdotic, always a fatal thing in an etymologist. "*Cockney*, or *cockny*, applied only to one borne within the sound of Bow-bell, that is, within the City of London, which tearme came first out of this tale: That a cittizens sonne riding with his father out of London into the country, and being a novice and meerely ignorant how corne or cattell increased, asked, when he heard a horse *neigh*, what the horse did; his father answered, the horse doth *neigh*; riding farther he heard a *cocke* crow, and said, doth the *cocke* *neigh* too?"

Molière often makes fun of the etymologists of his time and has rather unfairly caricatured, as Vadius in

---

[1] Old Fr. *pourloignier*, to remove ; cf. *éloigner*.

[2] A very difficult word. Before it was applied to a Londoner it meant a milksop. It is thus used by Chaucer. Cooper renders *delicias facere*, "to play the wanton, to dally, to play the *cockney*." In this sense it corresponds to Fr. *acoquiné*, made into a *coquin*, "made tame, inward, familiar ; also, growne as lazy, sloathful, idle, as a beggar" (Cotgrave).

Les Femmes savantes, the great scholar Gilles Ménage, whose *Etymological Dictionary*, published in 1650, was long a standard work. Molière's mockery and the fantastic nature of some of Ménage's etymologies have combined to make him a butt for the ignorant, but it may be doubted whether any modern scholar, using the same implements, could have done better work. For Ménage the one source of the Romance languages was classical Latin, and every word had to be traced to a Latin word of suitable form or sense. Thus Fr. *haricot*[1] is connected by him with Lat. *faba*, a bean, *via* the conjectural "forms" *fabarius*, *fabaricus*, *fabaricotus*, *faricotus*, *haricotus*, a method to which no problem is insoluble.[2] He suggests that Fr. *geindre*, or *gindre*,[3] baker's man, comes from Lat. *gener*, son-in-law, because the baker's man always marries the baker's daughter; but this practice, common though it may be, is not of sufficiently unfailing regularity to constitute a philological law. Perhaps his greatest achievement was the derivation of Span. *alfana*,[4] a mare, from Lat. *equus*, a horse, which inspired a well-known epigram—

> "*Alfana* vient d'*equus*, sans doute,
> Mais il faut avouer aussi
> Qu'en venant de là jusqu'ici
> Il a bien changé sur la route."

These examples show that respect for Ménage need not prevent his work from being a source of innocent merriment. But the above epigram loses some of

---

[1] Origin quite unknown.

[2] "Sache que le mot *galant homme* vient d'*élégant*; prenant le *g* et l'*a* de la dernière syllabe, cela fait *ga*, et puis prenant *l*, ajoutant un *a* et les deux dernières lettres, cela fait *galant*, et puis ajoutant *homme*, cela fait *galant homme*." (Molière, *Jalousie du Barbouillé*, scène 2.)

[3] Old Fr. *joindre*, Lat. *iunior*.

[4] Of Arabic origin.

its point for modern philologists to whom equations
that look equally fantastic, *e.g.* Eng. *wheel* and Gk.
κύκλος,[1] are matters of elementary knowledge. On
the other hand, a close resemblance between words
of languages that are not nearly related is proof
presumptive, and almost positive, that the words
are quite unconnected. The resemblance between
English and German words is the resemblance of
first cousins, but the resemblance of Eng. *nut*, Ger.
Nuss to Lat. *nux* is accidental. Even in the case
of languages that are near akin, it is not safe to
jump to conclusions. The Greek cousin of Lat. *deus*
is not θεός, God, but Ζεύς, Jupiter.

An etymology that has anything to do with a person
or an anecdote is to be regarded with suspicion. For
both we want contemporary evidence, and, in the case
of an anecdote, we never, to the best of my knowledge,
get it. In Chapter III. are a number of instances of
words formed according to authentic evidence from
names of persons. But the old-fashioned etymologist
will not be denied his little story. Thus, in explanation
of *spencer* (p. 36), I find in an *Etymological Compendium*
of 1853 that " His Lordship, when Lord-lieutenant of
Ireland, being out a-hunting, had, in the act of leaping
a fence, the misfortune to have one of the skirts of his
coat torn off; upon which his lordship tore off the
other, observing, that to have but one left was like a
pig with one ear! Some inventive genius took the
hint, and having made some of these half-coats, out of
compliment to his lordship, gave them the significant
cognomen of Spencer!" This is what Pooh-Bah calls

---

[1] That is, they are both descended from the same Indo-Germanic
original. Voltaire was thus, superficially, right when he described
etymology as a science in which the vowels do not count at all and the
consonants very little.

"corroborative detail intended to give artistic veri-
similitude to a bald and unconvincing narrative."
From the same authority we learn that *hurly-burly*[1]
"is said to owe its origin to Hurleigh and Burleigh,
two neighbouring families, that filled the country around
them with contest and violence," and that the word
boh! "used to frighten children, was the name of Boh,
a great general, the son of Odin, whose very appellation
struck immediate panic in his enemies."[2]

The history of *chouse* exemplifies the same tendency.
There is no doubt that it comes from a Turkish word
meaning interpreter, spelt *chaus* in Hakluyt and *chiaus*
by Ben Jonson. The borrowing is parallel to that of
cozen (p. 142), interpreters having a reputation little
superior to that of horse-coursers. But a century and
a half after the introduction of the word we come
across a circumstantial story of a Turkish *chiaus* who
swindled some London merchants of a large sum in
1609, the year before Jonson used the word in the
Alchemist. "Corroborative detail" again. The story
may be true, but there is not an atom of evidence for
it, and Skinner, who suggests the correct derivation in
his *Etymologicon* (1671), does not mention it. Until
contemporary evidence is adduced, the story must be
regarded as one of those fables which have been
invented in dozens by early etymologists, and which
are perpetuated in popular works of reference. It is an
article of faith in Yorkshire that the coarse material
called *mungo* owes its name to the inventor of the

---

[1] *Cf.* Fr. *hurluberlu*, which occurs in Rabelais, and in Rostand's *Cyrano
de Bergerac.*

[2] I am tempted to quote further from this inexhaustible mine, e.g.,
lullaby from a fairy called *Ellaby Gathon*, whom nurses invited to watch
the sleeping babes. The title of this cherished volume is *Pulleyn's
Etymological Compendium*, 3rd ed., revised and improved by M. A. Thoms.
(Tegg & Co., 1853.)

machine used in its fabrication, who, when it stuck at a first trial, exclaimed with resolution, " It *mun go*."

Many stories have been composed *après coup* to explain the American *hoodlum* and the Australian *larrikin*, which are both older than our *hooligan* (see p. 10). The origin of *hoodlum* is quite obscure. The story believed in Australia with regard to *larrikin* is that an Irish policeman, giving evidence of the arrest of a rough, explained that the accused was *a-larrikin'* (larking) in the street, and this was misunderstood by a reporter. But there appears to be not the slightest foundation for this story. The word is perhaps a diminutive of the common Irish name *Larry*, also immortalised in the stirring ballad—

" The night before Larry was stretched."

As I write, there is a correspondence going on in the Nottingham papers as to the origin of the nickname *Bendigo*, borne by a local bruiser and evangelist, who gave his name to an Australian town and a fur cap. He was one of triplets, whom, according to one account, a jocular friend of the family nicknamed Shadrach, Meschach, and *Abed-Nego*, the last of which was the future celebrity. This is quite plausible, but there is no sound evidence. The rival theory is that when he was playing in the streets and his father appeared in the offing, his companions used to warn him by crying " *Bendy go !*" This theory disregards the assertion of the " oldest inhabitant " that the great man was never called *Bendy*, and the fact, familiar to any observer of the local dialect, that, even if he had been so called, the form of warning would have been, " Look aht, Bendy, yer daddy's a-coomen."

In the Supplement to Littré there is an article on *domino*, in which he points out that investigation must

start from the phrase *faire domino* (see p. 94). He
also quotes an absurd anecdote from a local magazine,
which professes to come from a "vieille chronique."
Littré naturally wants to know what chronicle. In
Scheler's Dictionary (Brussels, 1888), it is "proved"
by means of the same story elaborated, "que c'est là
la véritable origine du mot dont nous parlons."

In Brewer's *Dictionary of Phrase and Fable*, s.v.
sirloin, we read that "it is generally said that James I.
or Charles II. knighted the loin of beef, but Henry
VIII. had done so already." This sounds like a deter-
mination to get at the root of things, but does not go
far enough. The word is found in the 15th century,
and Fr. *surlonge*, from which it comes, in the 14th.
It is compounded of *sur*, over, and *longe*, a derivative
of Lat. *lumbus*, loin. The belief in the knightly origin
of *sirloin* was so strong that we find it playfully called
the *baronet* (*Tom Jones*, iv. 10). Hence, no doubt, the
name *baron* of beef for the double sirloin. *Tram* is per-
sistently connected with a Mr *Outram*, who flourished
about 1800. This is another case of intelligent anticipation, for the word is found in 1555. It means log or
beam, and was probably first applied to a log-road
laid across bad ground, what is called in America
a "corduroy" road. On the other hand, the obvious
and simple derivation of *beef-eater*, *i.e.* a man who is in
the enviable position of being sure of his daily allowance,[1] has been obscured by the invention of an
imaginary Fr. **beaufetier*, waiter at the side-board.
Professor Skeat attributes the success of this myth to

[1] The following explanation, given in Miège's *French Dictionary* (1688),
is perhaps not far wrong: "C'est ainsi qu'on appelle par dérision les
Yeomen of the Guard dans la cour d'Angleterre, qui sont des gardes à peu
près comme les cent Suisses en France. Et on leur donne ce nom-là, parce
qu' à la cour ils ne vivent que de bœuf : par opposition à ces collèges
d'Angleterre, où les Ecoliers ne mangent que du mouton."

its inclusion in Mrs Markham's *History of England*. But the most indestructible of all these superstitions is connected with the word *cabal*. It comes from a Hebrew word meaning hidden mystery, and is found in the chief Romance languages. The word is of frequent occurrence in English long before the date of Charles II.'s acrostic ministry,[1] though its modern meaning has naturally been affected by this historic connection.

Even anecdotic etymologies accepted by the most cautious modern authorities do not always inspire complete confidence. *Martinet* is supposed to come from the name of a well-known French officer who reorganised the French infantry about 1670. We find it used by Wycherley in 1676, forty years before Martinet's death. But this application of the name is unknown in French, which has, however, a word *martinet* meaning a kind of cat-o'-nine-tails. In English, *martinet* means the leech-line of a sail, hence, possibly, rope's end, and Wycherley applies the term to a brutal sea-captain. The most renowned of carriers is probably Hobson, of Cambridge. He was sung by Milton, and bequeathed to the town Hobson's conduit which cleanses the Cambridge gutters. To him is also ascribed the phrase *Hobson's choice*, from his custom of refusing to let out his horses except in strict rotation. But Richard Cocks, a merchant venturer living in Japan, uses "*Hodgson's* choice" in his diary for the year 1617, *i.e.*, fourteen years before the carrier left this world and became a legendary figure.

[1] An acrostic of this kind would have no point if it resulted in a meaningless word. In the same way the Old Fr. *Fauvel*, whence our *curry favour* (see p. 120), has medieval explanations of the acrostic kind, *e.g.*, as standing for the vices *Fainéantise, Avarice, Usure, Vanité, Envie, Luxure*. I am not sure about the exact vices, as I have lost the reference and quote from memory.

The most obvious etymology needs to be proved up to the hilt, and the process is rich in surprises. *Cambridge* appears to be the *bridge* over the *Cam*. But the river's older name, which it preserves above the town, is the *Granta*, and Bede calls the town itself *Grantacester*. Camden, in his *Britannia* (trad. Holland, 1637), notes that the county was called " in the English Saxon " *Grentbrigseyre*, and comments on the double name of the river. Nor can he "easily beleeve that *Grant* was turned into *Cam;* for this might seeme a deflexion some what too hardly streined, wherein all the letters but one are quite swallowed up." *Grantabrigge* became, by dissimilation (see p. 52), *Gantabrigge, Cantabrigge* (cf. *Cantab*), *Cantbrigge*, and, by assimilation (see p. 51), *Cambridge*, the river being rechristened from the name of the town. A *beggar* is not etymologically one who *begs*, or a *cadger* one who *cadges*. In each case the verb is evolved from the noun. About the year 1200 Lambert le *Bègue*, the Stammerer, is said to have founded a religious order in Belgium. The monks were called after him in medieval Latin *beghardi* and the nuns *beghinæ*. The Old Fr. *begard* passed into Anglo-French with the meaning of mendicant and gave our *beggar*. From *béguine* we get *biggin*, a sort of cap (2 *Henry IV.*, iv. 4). *Cadger*, or rather its Scot. form *cadgear*, a pedlar, occurs about one hundred and fifty years earlier than the verb to *cadge*. We find, noted as foreign words, in 16th-century Dutch, the words *cagie*, a basket carried on the back, and *cagiaerd*, one who carries such a basket. These must be of French origin, and come, like the obsolete Eng. *cadge*,[1] a panier, from *cage*, for the history of which

---

[1] There is also a word *cadge*, explained in the glossary to a book on falconry (1615) as a kind of frame on which an itinerant vendor of hawks carried his birds. But it is unrecorded in literature and labours under the

see p. 101. *Cadger* is used in Scottish of an itinerant
fish merchant with his goods carried in paniers by
a pony. *Tobacco* does not take its name from the
island of Tobago, but from the native name of the tube
through which the Caribs smoked it.

The traditional derivation of *vaunt* is from Fr.
vanter, and this from a late Lat. *vanitare*, to talk emptily,
used by St Augustine. This looks very simple, but
the real history of these words is most complicated.
In Mid. English we regularly find *avaunt*, which comes
from Old Fr. *avanter*, to put forward, from *avant*,
before. This gets mixed up during the Tudor period
with another *vaunt* from Fr. *vanter*, to extol, the
derivation of which can only be settled when its earliest
form is ascertained. At present we find *venter* as early
as *vanter*, and this would represent Lat. *venditare*
(frequentative of *vendere*, to sell), to push one's goods,
"to do anything before men to set forth himselfe and
have a prayse ; to *vaunt ;* to crake ; to brag" (Cooper).

A sound etymology must fulfil three conditions.
It must not violate the recognised laws of sound change.
The development of meaning must be clearly traced.
This must coincide with the earliest or fundamental sense
of the word. It goes without saying (see p. 125) that in
modern corruptions we are sometimes faced by cases
which it would be difficult to explain phonetically.
There are, in fact, besides the general phonetic and
semantic laws, a number of obscure and accidental
influences at work which are not yet codified. As
we have seen (p. 175), complete apparent dissimilarity
of sound and sense need not prevent two words from

---

suspicion of being a ghost-word. Its first occurrence, outside the dictionaries, is, I believe, in Mr Hewlett's *Song of Renny*, just published—"the
nominal service of a pair of gerfalcons yearly, in golden hoods, upon
a golden *cadge*" (Ch. i.).

being originally one ;[1] but we have to trace them both back until dissimilarity becomes first similarity and then identity.

The word *peruse* meant originally to wear out, Old Fr. *par-user*. In the 16th century it means to sort or sift, especially herbs, and hence to scrutinise a document, etc. But between the earliest meaning and that of sifting there is a gap which no ingenuity can bridge, and, until this is done, we are not justified in regarding the modern *peruse* as identical with the earlier.

The maxim of Jakob Grimm, " von den Wörtern zu den Sachen " is too often neglected. In dealing with the etymology of a word which is the name of an object or of an action, we must first find out exactly what the original object looked like or how the original action was performed. The etymologist must either be an antiquary or must know where to go for sound antiquarian information. I will illustrate this by three words denoting objects used by medieval or Elizabethan fighting men.

A fencing *foil* is sometimes vaguely referred to the verb *foil*, to baffle, with which it has no connection. The Fr. *feuille*, leaf, is also invoked, and compared with Fr. *fleuret*, a foil, the idea being that the name was given to the " button " at the point. Now the earliest *foils* and *fleurets* were not buttoned ; first, because they were pointless, and secondly, because the point was not used in early fencing. It was not until gunpowder began to bring about the disuse of heavy armour that anybody ever dreamt of thrusting. The earliest fencing was hacking with sword and buckler, and the early *foil*

---

[1] This seems to have been realised by the author of the *Etymological Compendium* (see p. 176, footnote), who tells us that the "term *swallow* is derived from the French *hirondelle*, signifying indiscriminately voracious, literally a marshy place, that absorbs or *swallows* what comes within its vortex."

was a rough sword-blade quite unlike the implement we now use. *Fleuret* meant in Old French a sword-blade not yet polished and hilted, and we find it used, as we do Eng. *foil*, of an apology for a sword carried by a gallant very much down at heel. As late as Cotgrave we find *floret*, " a foile ; a sword with the *edge* rebated." Therefore *foil* is the same as Fr. *feuille*,[1] which in Old French meant sword-blade, and is still used for the blade of a saw ; but the name has nothing to do with what did not adorn the tip. It is natural that Fr. *feuille* should be applied, like Eng. *leaf, blade*, to anything flat (*cf.* Ger. *Blatt*, leaf), and we find in 16th-century Dutch the borrowed word *folie*, used in the three senses of leaf, metal plate, broadsword, which is conclusive.

We find frequent allusions in the 16th and 17th centuries to a weapon called a *petronel*, a flint-lock firearm intermediate in size between an arquebus and a pistol. It occurs several times in Scott—

> " 'Twas then I fired my petronel,
>   And Mortham, steed and rider fell."
>   (*Rokeby*, i. 19.)

On the strength of a French form, *poitrinal*, it has been connected with Fr. *poitrine*, chest, and various explanations are given. The earliest is that of the famous Huguenot surgeon Ambroise Paré, who speaks of the " mousquets *poitrinals*, que l'on ne couche en joue, à cause de leur calibre gros et court, mais qui se tirent *de la poitrine*." I cannot help thinking that, if the learned author had attempted this method of discharging an early firearm, his anatomical experience, wide as it was, would have been considerably enlarged. Minsheu (1617) describes a *petronell* as " a horseman's peece first used in the Pyrenean mountaines, which hanged them

---

[1] And therefore identical with the *foil* of *tinfoil, counterfoil*, etc.

alwayes *at their breast*, readie to shoote, as they doe now at the horse's breast." This information is derived from Claude Fauchet, whose interesting *Antiquités françoises et gauloises* were published in 1579. Phillips, in his *New World of Words* (1678) tells us that this "kind of harquebuse, or horseman's piece, is so called, because it is to aim *at a horse's brest*, as it were *poictronel*." When we turn from fiction to fact, we find that the oldest French name was *pétrinal*, "a *petronell*, or horse-man's peece" (Cotgrave), occasionally corrupted, perhaps owing to the way in which the weapon was slung, into *poitrinal*. This corruption would be facilitated by the 16th-century pronunciation of *oi* (pei̯trine). The French word is borrowed either from Ital. *petronello, pietronello*, "a petronell" (Florio), or from Span. *pedreñal*, "a petronall, a horse-man's peece, ita dict. quod *silice petra* incenditur" (Minsheu, *Spanish Dictionary*, 1623). Thus Minsheu knew the origin of the word, though he had put the fiction in his earlier work. We find other forms in Italian and Spanish, but they all go back to Ital. *pietra, petra*, or Span. *piedra, pedra*, stone, flint. The usual Spanish word for flint is *pedernal*. Our word, as its form shows, came direct from Italian.[1] The new weapon was named from its chief feature; *cf.* Ger. *Flinte*, "a light gun, a hand-gun, pop-gun, arquebuss, fire-arm, fusil or fusee[2]" (Ludwig). The substitution of the flint-lock for the old match-lock brought about a re-naming of European fire-arms, and, as this substitution was first effected in the cavalry, *petronel* acquired the special meaning of horse-pistol. It is curious that,

---

[1] It is a diminutive of some word which appears to be unrecorded (*cf.* Fr. *pistolet* for the obsolete *pistole*). Charles Reade, whose archæology is very sound, makes Denys of Burgundy say, "*Petrone* nor harquebuss shall ever put down Sir Arbalest" (*Cloister and Hearth*, Ch. xxiv.); but I can find no other authority for the word.

[2] This word occurs in *Robinson Crusoe*.

while we find practically all the French and Italian fire-arm names in 17th-century German, a natural result of the Thirty Years' War, *petronel* does not appear to be recorded. The reason is probably that the Germans had their own name, viz., *Schnapphahn*, snap-cock, the English form of which, *snaphaunce*, seems also to have prevailed over *petronel*. Cotgrave has *arquebuse à fusil*, "a *snaphaunce*," and explains *fusil* as "a fire-steele for a tinder-box." This is medieval Lat. *focile*, from *focus*, fire, etc.

The most general name for a helmet up to about 1450 was *basnet*, or *bacinet*. This, as its name implies (see p. 145), was a basin-shaped steel cap worn by fighting men of all ranks. The knights and nobles wore it *under* their great ornamental helms.[1] The *basnet* itself was perfectly plain. About the end of the 16th century the usual English helmets were the *burgonet* and *morion*.[2] These were often very decorative, as may be seen by a visit to any collection of old armour. Spenser speaks of a "guilt engraven *morion*" (*Faerie Queene*, vii. 7). Between the basnet and these reigned the *salet* or *salade*, on which Jack Cade puns execrably—

"Wherefore, on a brick wall have I climbed into this garden, to see if I can eat grass, or pick a *sallet* another while, which is not amiss to cool a man's stomach this hot weather. And I think this word *sallet* was born to do me good, for many a time, but for a *sallet*, my brain-pan had been cleft with a brown-bill."

(*2 Henry VI.*, iv. 10.)

It comes, through Fr. *salade*, from Ital. *celata*, "a scull, a

[1] Over the tomb of the Black Prince in Canterbury Cathedral hangs his cumbrous tilting helmet. But the magnificent recumbent bronze effigy below represents him in his fighting kit, basnet on head.

[2] *Burgonet*, Fr. *bourguignotte*, is supposed to mean *Burgundian* helmet. The origin of *morion* is unknown, but its use by Scott in *Ivanhoe* is an anachronism by four centuries. Both words are used vaguely as general names for helmet.

helmet, a morion, a *sallat*, a headpiece" (Florio).   The
etymologists of the 17th century, familiar with the
appearance of "guilt engraven morions," connected it
with Lat. *cœlare*, to engrave, and this derivation has
been repeated ever since without examination.   Now
in the Tower of London Armoury is a large collection
of *salets*, and these, with the exception of one or two
late German specimens from the ornate period, are
plain steel caps of the simplest form and design.   The
salet was, in fact, the *basnet* slightly modified, worn by
the rank and file of 15th-century armies, and probably,
like the *basnet*, worn under the knight's tilting helm.
There is no Italian verb *celare*, to engrave, but there is
a very common verb *celare*, to conceal.   A steel cap was
also called in Italian *secreta*, "a thinne steele cap, or
close skull, worne under a hat" (Florio), and in Old Fr.
segrette, "an yron skull, or cap of fence" (Cotgrave).
Both words are confirmed by Duez, who, in his *Italian-
French Dictionary* (1660), has *secreta*, "une secrette, ou
segrette, un morion, une bourguignotte, armure de teste
pour les picquiers."   Ergo, the *salet* belongs to Lat.
celare, to hide, secrete.

   We now *caulk* a ship by forcing oakum into the
seams.   Hence the verb to *caulk* is explained as coming
from Mid. Eng. *cauken*, to tread, Old Fr. *cauquer*,
caucher, Lat. *calcare*, from *calx*, heel.   This makes the
process somewhat acrobatic, although this is not,
philologically, a very serious objection.   But we *caulk*
the ship or the seams, not the oakum.   Primitive
caulking consisted in plastering a wicker coracle with
clay.   The earliest *caulker* on record is Noah, who
pitched[1] his ark within and without with pitch.   In the
Vulgate (*Genesis*, vi. 14), the *pitch* is called *bitumen* and

---

[1] See *pay* (p. 149).   It will be found that all verbs of this nature are
formed from the name of the substance applied.

the verb is *linere*, "to daub, besmear, etc." Next in chronological order comes the mother of Moses, who "took for him an ark of bulrushes, and daubed it with slime and with pitch" (*Exodus*, ii. 3), *bitumine ac pice* in the Vulgate. Bitumen, or mineral pitch, was regularly applied to this purpose, even by Elizabethan seamen. Failing this, anything sticky and unctuous was used, *e.g.*, clay or lime. *Lime* now means usually oxide calcium, but its original sense is anything viscous; *cf.* Ger. *Leim*, glue, and our bird-*lime*. Our *caulk* is in medieval Latin *calcare*, and this represents a rare Latin verb *calicare*, to plaster with lime, from *calx*, lime. The oldest example of the verb to *caulk* is about 1500. In Mid. English we find to *lime* used instead, *e.g.*, in reference to the ark, "set and *limed* agen the flood" (c. 1250), and "*lyme* it with cleye and pitche within and without" (Caxton, 1483). Almost every language which has a nautical vocabulary uses for our *caulk* a verb related to Fr. *calfater*. This is of Spanish or Portuguese origin. The Portuguese word is *calafetar*, from *cal*, lime, and *afeitar*, to put in order, trim, etc.

The readiness of lexicographers to copy from each other sometimes leads to ludicrous results. The origin of the word *curmudgeon* is quite unknown; but, when Dr Johnson was at work on his dictionary, he received from an unknown correspondent the suggestion that it was a corruption of Fr. *cœur méchant*, wicked heart. Accordingly we find in his dictionary, "It is a vitious manner of pronouncing *cœur méchant*, Fr. an unknown correspondent." John Ash, LL.D., who published a very complete dictionary in 1775, gives the derivation "from the French *cœur*, unknown, and *méchant*, a correspondent," an achievement which, says Todd, "will always excite both in foreigners and natives a harmless smile!"

It is thus that "ghost-words" come into existence. Every considerable English dictionary, from Spelman's *Glossarium* (1664) onward, has the entry *abacot*, "a cap of state, wrought up into the shape of two crowns, worn formerly by English kings." For the history of this "word" see the *New English Dictionary*, the editor of which has laid this particular ghost.[1] *Abacot* seems to be a misprint or misunderstanding of *a bicocket*, a kind of horned head-dress. It corresponds to an Old Fr. *bicoquet* and Span. *bicoquete*, cap, the derivation of which is uncertain. Of somewhat later date is *brooch*, "a painting all in one colour," which likewise occurs in all dictionaries of the 18th and 19th centuries. This is due to Miège (*French Dict.* 1688) misunderstanding Cotgrave. There is a Fr. *camaïeu*, a derivative of *cameo*, which has two meanings, viz., a cameo *brooch* and a monochrome painting with a cameo effect. Miège appears to have taken the second meaning to be explanatory of the first, hence his entry—*brooch*, "camayeu, ouvrage de peinture qui n'est que d'une couleur." In Manwayring's *Seaman's Dictionary* (1644), the old word *carvel*, applied to a special build of ship, is misprinted *carnell*, and this we find persisting, not only in the compilations of such writers as Bailey, Ash, etc., but even in technical dictionaries of the 18th century "by officers who serv'd several years at sea and land." The Anglo-Saxon name for the kestrel (see p. 92) was *stangella*, stone-yeller (*cf.* nightin*gale*), which appears later as *stonegall* and *staniel*. In the 16th century we find the curious spelling *steingall*, *e.g.*, Cooper explains *tinnunculus* as "a kistrel, or a kastrell; a *steyngall*." In Cotgrave we find it printed *fleingall*, a form which recurs in several later dictionaries of the 17th century.

[1] See letter by Dr Murray, now Sir James Murray, in the *Athenæum*, Feb. 4, 1884.

Hence, somewhere between Cooper and Cotgrave, an ornithologist or lexicographer must have misprinted *fleingall* for *steingall* by the common mistake of *fl* for *ſt*, and the ghost-word persists into the 18th century.

The difficulty of the etymologist's task is exemplified by the complete mystery which often enshrouds a word of comparatively recent appearance. A well-known example is the word *Huguenot*, for which fifteen different etymologies have been proposed. We first find the word used in 1550, and by 1572 the French word-hunter Tabourot, generally known as des Accords, has quite a number of theories on the subject. He is worth quoting in full—

"De nostre temps ce mot de *Huguenots*, ou *Hucnots* s'est ainsi intronisé : quelque chose qu'ayent escrit quelques-uns, que ce mot vient *Gnosticis hæreticis qui luminibus extinctis sacra faciebant*, selon Crinit : ou bien du Roy Hugues Capet, ou de la porte de Hugon à Tours par laquelle ils sortoient pour aller à leur presche. Lors que les pretendus Reformez implorerent l'ayde des voix des Allemans, aussi bien que de leurs armees : les Protestans estans venus parler en leur faveur, devant Monsieur le Chancelier, en grande assemblee, le premier mot que profera celuy qui portoit le propos, fut, *Huc nos venimus :* Et apres estant pressé d'un reuthme (*rhume*, cold) il ne peut passer outre ; tellement que le second dit le mesme, *Huc nos venimus.* Et les courtisans presents qui n'entendoient pas telle prolation ; car selon la nostre ils prononcent *Houc nos venimous*, estimerent que ce fussent quelques gens ainsi nommez : et depuis surnommerent ceux de la Religion pretenduë reformee, *Hucnos :* en apres changeant *C* en *G*, *Hugnots*, et avec le temps on a allongé ce mot, et dit *Huguenots.* Et voylà la vraye source du mot, s'il n'y en a autre meilleure." [1]

The only serious etymology is Ger. *Eidgenoss*, oath companion, which agrees pretty well with the earliest

---

[1] The *Encyclopædia Britannica* does not imitate the wise reticence of Tabourot's saving clause, but pronounces authoritatively for the *porte de Hugon* fable.

recorded Swiss - French form, *eiguenot*, in Bonivard's *Chronicle of Geneva*.

The engineering term *culvert* first appears about 1800, and there is not the slightest clue to its origin. *Swank* is only a year or two old. Is it evolved from *swagger*? If so, how? Or is it the Scot. *swank*, limber, tall, agile; *swankie*, a strapping youth? If so, who brought it suddenly to England? The word *ogre*, first used by Perrault in his *Contes de Fées* (1697), has occasioned much grave and learned speculation. Perhaps the philologists of the future may theorise as sapiently as to the origin of *jabberwock* and *bandersnatch*.

INDEX

ABACOT, 118
abet, 70 n.
abeyance, 99
abominate, 3
abracadabra, 13 n.
accomplice, 118 n.
acquaint, 72
acton, 116
adder, 104
adjutant, 30, 136
admiral, 137
affidavit, 4
ague, 128
aitch-bone, 104
akimbo, 93
Alabaster, 158
alarm, 106
alarum, 106
albert chain, 35
alcade, 106
alderman, 85
Aldridge, 159
Alec, 64
alert, 106
alguazil, 106
alibi, 4
alley, 63
alligator, 106
Allman, 161
allure, 101
alone, 57
A.M., 3
ampersand, 52
analysis, 6
ancient, 118
andiron, 106
Andrea Ferrara, 46
anecdotage, 122
animal, 4

anlace, 54
Annabel, 53
ansatus, 93
antic, 130
antlers, 92
ant-lion, 29
apache, 11
Apfelsine, 28
appeach, 57
appendicitis, 10
apprentice, 109
apricot, 18
Aprikose, 18
apron, 52, 104
Arabella, 53
arbour, 122
arch, 76
argosy, 46
aringo, 21
arles, 110
armada, 2
armée, 2
Armitage, 50
Armstrong, 168
aroma, 6
arquebus, 117
arrant, 76
arras, 43
array, 88, n. 1
arrière-ban, 67
assassin, 20
assegai, 23
asset, 107
assize, 57
assoil, 9
assoilzie, 9
astonish, 97
astound, 97
atlas, 6

atomy, 57
atout, 8
Atkin, 159
Attenborough, 160
Atwood, 160
auberge, 152
Aubray, 162
Augensprosse, 92
auger, 104
avers, 132
avoirdupois, 132
ayah, 24

BACCHUS, 158
'baccy, 60
bacinet, 185
bachelor's buttons, 27
backgammon, 147
badaud, 99, *n.* 2
Bailey, 163
bâiller, 99, *n.* 2
bait, 70 *n.*
baize, 110
Bakerloo, 61
bald, 34
bald-faced stag, 34
ball, 34
ballad, 140
ballet, 140
balusters, 55
ban, 66
banal, 67
bandy, 101
Banister, 166
banister, 55
banlieue, 67
banjo, 137
bannal, 67 *n.*
Bardell, 159
Barker, 165
baron, 178
barracking, 12
bartisan, 13
Barton, 160
Bart's, 61
basilisk, 34
basnet, 145, 185
bastinado, 23, *n.* 1
battant neuf, 91
batter, 142
battledore, 122
bay, 99, 110
Bayard, 110

Bayliss, 163
bead, 68
beadroll, 68
beadsman, 68
béant, 99, *n.* 2
beat the bush, 99
Beaufoy, 158
Beaulieu, 114
beaupré, 118 *n.*
beaver, 144
bec-jaune, 88
bedlam, 56
Beecham, 157
beef-eater, 178
beejam, 88
beg, 180
begum, 146
belcher, 78
beldam, 78
belette, 84
belfry, 152
Bell, 158
Bella, 64
belladonna, 78
Bellows, 158
Bendigo, 177
benêt, 41
bergamot, 146
bergeronnette, 30
bergomask, 146
Bert, 64
bess, 38
bet, 70 *n.*
bête à bon Dieu, 32
Betts, 160
betty, 38
bever, 114
beverage, 54
bey, 146
bezant, 45
bible, 79
bike, 61
bilbo, 46
billiments, 60
Billingsgate, 44
billy-cock, 36
binnacle, 58
Bishop, 163
biz, 61
black art, 120
blackguard, 77
bland, 74
Blood, 169

Blount, 168
bluff, 87 *n.*
Blundell, 168
blunderbuss, 117
Blunt, 168
Bob, 160
bobby, 41
bodice, 109
Bodkin, 159
boîte, 117
Boleyn, 161
bombasine, 89
bombast, 89
bona-fide, 3
bonfire, 140
bonhomme, 74
bonne femme, 74
Bonner, 168
bonus, 4
boojum, 14
book, 79
Booker, 165
boom, 15
Boon, 158, 168
boor, 77
boot and saddle, 119
bordereau, 85
borel, 67
boss, 18
boulevard, 112
boussole, 117
boutique, 105
bouvreuil, 30
bovril, 14
bowdlerise, 37
bower, 149
Bowery, 149, *n.* 1
bowie, 36
bowyer, 165
boycott, 37
Brabazon, 161
brand new, 99
brandy, 63
branks, 7
brasse, 80
brazil, 47
breeches, 108
breeks, 108
Brett, 161
Brewer, 170
briar, 153
bridal, 112
Bridges, 161

brig, 61
brigantine, 61
brisk, 58, *n.* 2
Bristow, 160
Britton, 161 *n.*
Brock, 168
broderer, 165
broker, 139
bronze, 44
brooch, 139, 188
brose, 109
brougham, 35
Bruin, 32
Brunel, 168
buccaneer, 56 *n.*
Büchse, 117
Buchstabe, 79
buck, 139
Buckhurst Holt, 125
budget, 80
bugle, 63
Bull, 169
Bullen, 161
bulwark, 112
buncombe, 44
bungalow, 87 *n.*
bunkum, 44
burden, 146
bureau, 67
burgonet, 185
Burgoyne, 161
burke, 37
Bursche, 87
bus, 63
bushes, 117
butcher, 139
buttery, 152
buxom, 75
Bythesea, 160

CAB, 61
cabal, 179
cabbage, 142
caboche, 142
cad, 61
caddie, 61
cadge, 180
Cæsar, 163
Caffyn, 169
cage, 101
cahier, 155
caitiff, 128
cajole, 101

calculation, 80
calendar, 148
calender, 148
Caliban, 124
callant, 61
calumet, 22
Calvert, 166
cambric, 43
Cambridge, 180
camomile, 29
canary, 47
cancel, 80
cancer, 31
canif, 50
canker, 31
cannibal, 124
canter, 61
canvass, 66
cape, 24
Capel Court, 141
capestro, 61
capot, 94
captain, 128
captive, 128
carat, 18
Carew, 114
cargo, 131
cark, 131
carmine, 136
carnell, 188
carol, 140
carousal, 153
carouse, 153
cartridge, 56
case, 146
cashier, 16, 146
cashmere, 43
casket, 129
cass, 146
cast, 146
caste, 24
catch, 131
catchpole, 153
cate, 57
caterpillar, 29
catkin, 30
Catonet, 38
Cator, 58, 132
cattle, 132
caucus, 12
caudle, 7
cauliflower, 142
caulk, 186

causeway, 115
caveat, 4
cavestrolo, 61
cavie, 101
celandine, 27
cercueil, 129
cerf-volant, 34
cervelas, 125
chabouk, 23
chaise, 107, n. 2
Challen, 161
Challis, 161
Chaloner, 164
chamberlain, 83
chambrée, 86
chameleon, 29
Champain, 161
Champneys, 161
chancel, 80
chancellor, 80
chancery, 153
Chaney, 162
Chantecler, 32
chap, 61
chapeau, 24
chapel, 24, 141
chaperon, 24
chaplet, 24
Chapman, 163
chapman, 61
chare, 2
charge, 131
charwoman, 2
chase, 146
Chater, 132
chaton, 30
chattel, 132
Chaucer, 163
chauvin, 12
chawbuck, 23
Chawner, 164
Chaworth, 161
cheat, 78, 132 n.
check, 80, 111
cheer, 125
chelidonium, 27
chenapan, 50
Chenevix, 16, n. 2
chenille, 30
cheptel, 132
cheque, 81
chequer, 80
cherry, 107

Chesney, 162
chess, 111
chesterfield, 36
cheval-de-frise, 43, *n*. 1
chevalet, 35
chevaucher, 60
chewet, 34
chieftain, 128
chime, 8
Chinee, 107
chippendale, 36
chit, 88
chore, 2
chortle, 14
chou, 142
choucroute, 119
chouse, 136
chuet, 34
chum, 87
churl, 77
cinch, 21
cinematograph, 10
cipher, 136
cit, 61
citizen, 113
Clark, 134
Claude, 41
claymore, 122
Cleaver, 165
clerk, 134
clothes-horse, 35
clove, 83
club, 71
cobalt, 40
Cobbett, 159
cobra, 24
cockney, 173
cocoa-nut, 20
coffer, 129
Coffin, 169
coffin, 129
cognovit, 4
colander, 142
Colas, 91
cole, 142
Collet, 158
colon, 6
colonel, 53
Coltman, 165
colza, 142
comadreja, 84
comma, 6
commère, 84

companion, 86, 153
compassion, 2
complex, 4
compound, 146
comptroller, 81
comrade, 86
connect, 97
constable, 82
contrôle, 81
controller, 81
Conyers, 161
coon, 59
cooper, 74 *n.*
coopering, 61
cordonnier, 118
cordwainer, 118
corne, 108
Corner, 164
Cornwallis, 161
corp, 108
corsair, 20
costermonger, 58, *n.* 1
counterpane, 126
counterpoint, 126
court-card, 119
Coward, 168
coward, 33
cowslip, 27
cozen, 102
crack, 61
cracovienne, 46
crane, 34
crane's bill, 26
cratch, 7
cravat, 44
crayfish, 115
credence table, 113
crestfallen, 100
crétin, 41
crew, 59
Cri, 61
crimson, 136
crinoline, 127
Crocker, 165
Croker, 165
crowfoot, 26
Crowther, 164
crozier, 152
cubit, 80
Cuddy, 33
cuddy, 153
cuirass, 150
cuisse, 165

Cullen, 161
cullis, 142
culverin, 7, 34
culvert, 190
cummer, 84, 87
curée, 149
curmudgeon, 187
currant, 45
curry, 88
curry favour, 120
curtal axe, 116
Curtis, 168
cushion, 157 *n.*
cuss, 61
Custance, 159
custodia, 95
cutlass, 54, 116
cutler, 116
cutlet, 116

Dada, 84
dado, 131
daffadowndilly, 107
daffodil, 107
Daft, 170
Dago, 41
dahlia, 28
dainty, 128
dairy, 153
dais, 128
daisy, 26
Dalmain, 162
dam, 111, 131
damask, 43
dame, 131
dame-jeanne, 40
Dampier, 161
damson, 45
Dance, 169
dandelion, 26
dandy, 42
Dangerfield, 163
Danvers, 162
dapper, 74
dapple-gray, 167
darbies, 37
Darblay, 162
Darbyshire, 134
Daubeney, 162
dauphin, 31
Daus, 101
davier, 38
davit, 38

Dawnay, 162
Day, 153
day-woman, 153
dé, 56, 131
dead men's fingers, 27
Debbyhouse, 162, *n.* 3
debenture, 5
decoy, 101
Dedman, 168
déjeuner, 137
delf, 44
deliberate, 3
delight, 112 *n.*
demijohn, 40
demure, 93
denizen, 112
Dennis, 158
Denry, 64
Depew, 8
dérive, 50
derrick, 36
derring-do, 13
derringer, 35
desk, 128
deuce, 101
Deus, 175
Devereux, 162
Dexter, 164
dexterity, 3
di, 8
diablotin, 159
diane, 9
diaper, 48
Dick, 160
dickens, 40
die, 131
Dietrich, 38
Digg, 160
digit, 80
dimity, 138
dinde, 48
dindon, 48
dîner, 137
diocese, 138
dirge, 4
dirk, 17
dirk, 38
Dirne, 75
disaster, 98
disc, 128
dish, 128
dishevelled, 125
disk, 128

dismal, 8
Disney, 162
ditto, 141
ditty, 141
Dob, 160
Dobbin, 84
docket, 85
dodo, 30
dogma, 6
doily, 36
Dolman, 162
doll, 39
dollar, 45
dominie, 5
domino, 94
Dompfaffe, 30
donah, 131
doninha, 84
donkey engine, 34
donnola, 84
do re me fa sol la si, 6
dornick, 43
dotterel, 30
dowlas, 44
Drachen, 34
dragon, 35
Drakenberg, 27
dram, 80
drat, 60
draught, 111
drawing-room, 60
drill, 137
drilling, 137
Drinkwater, 168
dropsy, 56
drub, 23, *n.* 1
Druce, 161
drugget, 48
ducat, 43
duenna, 131
duffel, 44
Duke, 163
dummer Peter, 41
dunce, 41
Dupuy, 7
Durbeyfield, 162
Durrant, 162
Durward, 166
duty, 10
Duverney, 162, *n.* 1
dyrk, 38

EAGER, 73

earnest, 110
easel, 16, 35
échouer, 90
écouvillon, 39
écrou, 85, *n.* 3
écurie, 124
écuyer, 124
effendi, 19
Eisenhut, 26
eke, 105
elbow, 80
ell, 80
Emmot, 33
embarrass, 98
emir, 137
émouchet, 35
employ, 97
ensign, 118
epitome, 6
equerry, 124
'Erb, 64
ermine, 44
errant, 76
escabeau, 99
escheat, 78
eschew, 59
esquire, 59, 124
etch, 16, 123
étincelle, 54
ewer, 106
example, 59
exchequer, 80
excise, 123
exeat, 4
exit, 4
expression, 97
eyas, 105
eyre, 76

Faire la noce, 87
Fairfax, 168
fairy, 71, 84
falconet, 34
faldstool, 130
fane, 53
farce, 86
Farrar, 163
farrier, 82
farthingale, 126
Fata Morgana, 71
Faulkner, 164
fauteuil, 130
Fauvel, 121, 179 *n.*

fay, 71
feckless, 11
fed up, 89
fee, 132
feeble, 53
fellow-feeling, 2
felon, 22
fence, 59
fender, 59
ferret, 30, 138
Ferrier, 163
ferrule, 155
ferule, 155
fetish, 23
fever-few, 27
fiat, 4
filbert, 32
filibuster, 55
fille, 75
fire-new, 99
firkin, 19 *n.*
Fitch, 168
fives, 9
flail, 53
flawn, 126 *n.*
Fletcher, 164
floret, 138
florin, 45
flounce, 55
flour, 135
flower, 135
foil, 182
foist, 99 *n.*
folio, 5
fond, 73
foot, 79
footpad, 154
force-meat, 86
foreign, 112
forget-me-not, 29
forlorn hope, 16, 119
Forster, 164
Foster, 164
fou, 73
fouet, 119
Frauenzimmer, 87
fragile, 128
frail, 53, 128
freebooter, 56
fret, 122
fretwork, 123
frieze, 43
fritter, 142

Frobisher, 165
froncle, 22
frontispiece, 75, *n.* 1
frounce, 55
fuchsia, 28
fugleman, 53
Fuller, 166
funkelnagelneu, 99
furlong, 80
furlough, 16
furoncle, 22
fusee, 184
fusil, 185
fustian, 43, 89
fustian-anapes, 41
fusty, 99

GALVANISM, 36
gambit, 147
gamboge, 46
game, 147
gammon, 147
gammy, 147
gamut, 6
gantlope, 120
garage, 115
garble, 19, 66
garce, 75
garibaldi, 35
garret, 96
Garrett, 159
gas, 14
Gascoyne, 161
Gaskin, 161
gauge, 140
Gaunt, 161
gauntlet, 120
geezer, 11
gefallen, 100
geindre, 174
Gelbschnabel, 88
Geld, 131
generous, 3
genius, 4
gent, 61
geranium, 27
gerben, 88
Geschenk, 84
Geselle, 86
Gevatter, 87
Gewehr, 59 *n.*
Gibbon, 159
Gift, 84

gift horse, 90
Gillott, 158
gilly-flower, 115
Gilpin, 160
gimbals, 133
gimmal, 133
gin, 60, 62
gindre, 174
gingham, 48
gist, 9
glai, 121
glaive, 121
glamour, 11, 55, 134
gleek, 95
gloss, 144
gloze, 144
Godbehere, 158
goffer, 72
Gogs, 60
gonfalon, 52
Goodbeer, 158
Goodenough, 158
Gooddeve, 159
Goodlake, 159·
Goodrich, 159
gorilla, 24
goshawk, 142
Gosling, 168
Gosse, 167
gossip, 87
Gotobed, 158
goupil, 32
graft, 103
grail, 11
grain, 80
gramarye, 134
grampus, 29
Grant, 168
Great Orme, 92
Grecian steps, 104
Greenfield, 162
greengage, 29
greenhorn, 88
Greenhow, 125
Greenman, 169
greyhound, 124
grief, 113
grimaldello, 38
grimalkin, 39
grimoire, 134
grize, 109
grocer, 163
grog, 62

grogram, 51
gross, 163
grotesque, 130 *n.*
guérite, 96
guinea, 47
guinea-fowl, 47
guinea-pig, 29, 47
guillotine, 158
guitar, 138
guts, 77
guy, 41

HABEAS CORPUS, 115
hack, 61
hackbut, 117
Hackett, 159
hag, 100
haggard, 100
Hahnenfuss, 26
Haig, 166 *n.*
half a mo', 61
halibut, 32
Hammond, 159
hand, 80
hand of glory, 121
hangar, 115
Hannay, 161
Hannibal, 158
Hansard, 162
Hansom, 51 *n.*
Hanway, 161
harangue, 21, 50
harbinger, 2, 83
harbour, 2
harry, 2
Harvey, 159
hatchell, 11
hatchment, 125
hauberk, 152
haut, 121
'haviour, 60
hawse, 152 *n.*
Hawtrey, 161
Hay, 166 *n.*
Hayward, 166
hearse, 68
heart's ease, 27
heckle, 11
hempie, 61
Herd, 166
Hereford, 2
hermitage, 50
herrisch, 85, *n.* 2

Hewett, 159
Hewlett, 159
Hibbert, 159
hiccough, 115
Hick, 160
Hig, 160
hinterland, 12
hippopotamus, 29
Hitch, 160
Hob, 160
hobby, 84
hobgoblin, 33
Hobson's choice, 179
Hochzeit, 88
hock, 62
Hogarth, 166
holland, 43
hollyhock, 32
homely, 74
Homer, 163
homme, 50
Honeyball, 158
honte, 50
hooligan, 10
Horner, 164
host, 2, 147
Howard, 166
Howitt, 159
Huggin, 159
huguenot, 189
humble pie, 104
hunks, 75
hurly-burly, 64, 176
hussar, 19
hussy, 75
Hutchin, 159

IB, 64
Ibbotson, 160
ill-starred, 98
imp, 103
indenture, 82
index, 4
Indian corn, 47
Indian ink, 47
indigo, 46
infantry, 69
innuendo, 3
inoculate, 103
insult, 3
interfere, 98
inure, 148
inveigle, 101

invoice, 109
Irrgarten, 58
isinglass, 127
item, 4

JACK, 38, 40
jackanapes, 41
jackass, 33
jackdaw, 33
jacket, 40
Janaway, 161
jaquette, 34
jarvey, 37
jaunty, 117
jean, 43
jemmy, 38
Jenner, 163
jenneting, 112
Jenny wren, 33
jeopardy, 100
jesses, 111
Jessop, 159
jest, 68
jilt, 42
jingo, 11
jockey, 41, 102
Johannisapfel, 112
jolis fous, 119
jonquil, 141
joss, 24
journeyman, 98, 153
jovial, 98
jug, 39
Juggins, 40 *n.*
Juliet, 42
jumble, 113
junket, 141

KAFIR, 23, *n.* 2
kail, 142
Kanzel, 80
Kemp, 166
kennel, 147
kerseymere, 43
kestrel, 92
kickshaws, 108
Kiddier, 164
kidnap, 101
kilderkin, 19
kilt, 17
kimmer, 87
King, 163
kirtle, 138

Kisser, 165
kit, 138
kitcat, 38
kite, 34
kittle, 54
kjönne, 84
Klaus, 38
kloof, 84
knapsack, 16
knave, 50
Knecht, 77
knickerbockers, 40
knight, 77
Knoblauch, 84
Kohl, 142
kooi, 101

LAAGER, 16
label, 85
Labouchère, 165
lace, 22
lacrosse, 152
lady-bird, 32
lady's bedstraw, 32
lady's garter, 32
lady's slipper, 32
Lambert, 167
Lambertsnuss, 32
lampoon, 8
lancegay, 23
Lander, 166
landier, 106
landscape, 16
Langlois, 106
larboard, 112
larder, 153
lariat, 22, 106
Larkin, 159
larkspur, 26
Lärm, 106
larrikin, 10, 177
larum, 106
lasso, 22
lateen, 47
Latimer, 165
Launay, 162
Launder, 166
lavandière, 30
lawn, 46
lay-figure, 16, 154
leaguer, 16
leg, 91
legend, 3

Leggatt, 159
lemon, 149
lemon sole, 149
level, 53
lévier, 106
Levick, 106
lèvre, 108
Lhuissier, 83 *n.*
libel, 38
liber, 79
liebäugeln, 101
lierre, 106
Lilywhite, 168
limbeck, 58
limbo, 5
lime, 51
Limehouse, 44
limner, 58
Lindwurm, 92 *n.*
lingot, 106
liquorice, 127
list, 85
Lister, 164
little Mary, 39
livery, 70
lobelia, 28
locomotor ataxy, 115
lockram, 44
Loftus, 158
Lombard, 57
lone, 57
'longing, 60
loo, 63
lords and ladies, 27
Lorimer, 165
Loring, 161
Loveday, 160
Lovell, 159
love in a mist, 27
Lowell, 159
Löwenmaul, 26
Löwenzahn, 26
Lubbock, 161
lucifer, 4
Luck, 161
lucus, 171
lugger, 94
lugsail, 94
lumber-room, 70
luncheon, 114
lupus, 31
Lush, 83 *n.*
Lusher, 83 *n.*

MABEL, 53
macadamise, 37
mackintosh, 35
Macnab, 17 *n.*
Macpherson, 17 *n.*
Madeira, 47
madge owlet, 33
madonna, 131
magazine, 86
magenta, 35 *n.*
maggot, 54
magnet, 44
magnolia, 38
magpie, 33
Mahomet, 42
mailed fist, 145
main de gloire, 121
Mainwaring, 157
majolica, 44
Malins, 161
malkin, 38
Mall, 154
malmsey, 46
Malthus, 158
malvoisie, 46
mammet, 39
manant, 139
mandarin, 24
mandoline, 137
mangle, 129
mangonel, 129
Mann, 161
manner, 147
manœuvre, 148
manor, 8
Mansell, 161
mansworn, 13 *n.*
manual, 3
manure, 148
marabout, 136
maravedi, 136
marble, 63
Marchant, 134
Marienkäfer, 32
marionnette, 39
marmalade, 28
Marner, 164
marquee, 107
Marriot, 33
marshal, 82
Marshalsea, 82
martello, 54
martin, 33

martinet, 179
martin-pêcheur, 33
mascot, 11
mask, 133
masnadiere, 139
Massinger, 164
masterpiece, 98
match, 7
mate, 86
matelot, 86
Maud, 64
maudlin, 56
maul, 154
Maulbeere, 53
maul-stick, 154
maxim, 35
maximum, 4
Mayhew, 159
Mayne, 161
mayor, 142
maze, 58
mazurka, 45
mediastinus, 84
Meerschweinchen, 47
megrims, 31
meiny, 139
melon, 28
ménage, 139
menagerie, 139
mend, 57
ménétrier, 70
menial, 139
merchant, 62
mercurial, 98
merino, 142
Merryweather, 168
mesmerism, 36
mess, 86
messmate, 86
metal, 135
métier, 148
mettle, 98 *n.*, 135
mews, 111
miasma, 6
Middlemass, 160
milliner, 44
miniature, 74
minstrel, 70
mint, 131
minx, 75
miscreant, 117
miser, 4
misnomer, 8

miss, 148 *n.*
mistery, 148
mizen, 8
mob, 61
Mohock, 11
moidore, 131
moineau, 30
money, 130
monkey, 32
monkey-wrench, 34
monk's hood, 26
monnaie, 131
Moon, 158
Morel, 168
morion, 185
Morris, 162
morris dance, 45
morris pike, 45
mosaic, 155
mosquito, 35
Mother Carey's chicken, 33
mouchoir, 91
moustique, 54
Moxon, 160
muckinder, 91
muguet, 137
mulberry, 53
mulligrubs, 31
Mullins, 163
mungo, 176
Münze, 131
mûre, 53
mushroom, 51
musk, 137
musket, 35
muslin, 43
mustang, 21
Musters, 163
mutande, 91
mystery, 148

Nägele, 84
namby-pamby, 64
Napier, 52, 169
napkin, 52
nappe, 52
Nash, 105
naunt, 105
nausea, 6
nave, 141
navvy, 63
navy, 141
nectar, 6

nectarine, 6
Ned, 105
Neddy, 33
négromancie, 120
negus, 36
Neil, 159
Nelke, 83
Nell, 105
news, 105
nice, 78
nickel, 40
nickname, 105
nickum, 41
nickumpoop, 41
Nicodème, 41
nicotine, 36
niddering, 13
nincompoop, 41
ninny, 41
ninnyhammer, 41
niveau, 53
noddy, 41
noddypeak, 41
Nokes, 105
Noll, 105
nonce, 105
Norfolk Howard, 167
Norman, 172
Norris, 162
Norroy, 162
nostrum, 4
Nowell, 160
Nugent, 161
nuncheon, 114
nuncle, 105
Nurse, 162
nut, 175
nutmeg, 137
Nutter, 167
nux, 175

OBJECT, 97
obligation, 3
obvious, 97
odium, 4
odsbodikins, 60
ogle, 101
ogre, 190
oignon, 88
oiseau de Saint Martin, 33
Old Nick, 40
omelet, 126
omen, 4

omnibus, 5
onion, 84, *n.* 1
Onslow, 169
orange, 28
oreste, 122
oriel, 53
orlop, 16
orrery, 36
orteil, 122
ortolan, 30
oseille, 150
ostler, 50, 152
ounce, 105

PAD, 154
padder, 154
padding, 89
Padgett, 160
padrastro, 22
paj, 61
paladin, 128
Palatine, 128
palaver, 24
pallet, 145
Palliser, 165
Pall Mall, 154
palmer, 30
Palsgrave, 128
palsy, 56
pamphlet, 38
pandy, 5
pantaloons, 40
pantry, 153
Panzer, 145
paper, 79
parable, 24
parbleu, 60
parchment, 45, 79 *n.*
parish, 56, 138
Parker, 165
Parkin, 159
parley, 24
parmaçeti, 173
parmesan, 173
Parminter, 164
Parnell, 160
parole, 24
parrot, 33
parson, 133
Partlet, 32
partridge, 56
Pascal, 160
Pascoe, 160

pasquinade, 37
pastern, 69
past master, 98
Patch, 168
patch, 7
pathos, 6
patten, 108
patter, 63
paume, 9
pauper, 4
Pav, 61
pawn, 149
pay, 149
Payne, 168
paynim, 71
pea, 107
peach, 45, 57
peajacket, 124
peal, 57
Pearce, 169
pecunia, 132
pedigree, 71, 113
Peel, 160
pelargonium, 27
pèlerin, 53
Pélissier, 164
pen, 155
pencil, 155
Pennefather, 167
Pentecost, 160
penthouse, 115
peon, 149
perch, 80
periwig, 58, *n.* 2
periwinkle, 118
Perkin, 159
Perrot, 33
person, 133
pert, 74
peruse, 182
pester, 69, 155
Peterchen, 38
petrel, 33
petronel, 183
Pettifer, 71
Pettigrew, 71
petty, 73
pew, 7
Phillimore, 163
Philpot, 159
Physick, 158
pickaback, 65
pick-axe, 116

Pickard, 151
pie, 34
piebald, 34
pierrot, 33
pig-iron, 34
Pilcher, 164
pilgrim, 53
pinchbeck, 36
Pinder, 164
pine-apple, 28
pion, 149
pips, 94
plain, 74
plaudit, 5
plover, 92
pluck, 77
pocket, 90 *n.*
pocket-handkerchief, 91
Pocock, 169
Poidevin, 61
pointe, 61
poison, 84
poke, 90
polecat, 153
polka, 45
Pollock, 161
Poll parrot, 33
polonaise, 46
polony, 45
pomander, 52
pomcitron, 29
pomegranate, 29
Pomeranze, 28
Pomeroy, 162
pomme de pin, 28
ponder, 1
Pope Joan, 119
porcelain, 35
porcupine, 29
porpoise, 29
porridge, 109
port, 46
portcullis, 142
porter, 74
Portugee, 107
Poslett, 157
Posnett, 157
possum, 59
posthumous, 116
post-mortem, 3
posy, 134
potence, 36
Potz, 60

pouce, 80
Pouille, 105
poulterer, 58
pounce, 100
pouncet-box, 100
pourboire, 84
Power, 168
power, 8
pow-wow, 12
Poyser, 164
prayer, 68
premises, 5
premisses, 5
premium, 4
prentice, 58, 98
prepense, 1
preposterous, 119 *n.*
press-gang, 120
Prester John, 85, *n.* 2
Priddle, 163, *n.* 3
priest, 85
primrose, 115
proctor, 56
pub, 61
pudding, 68
puisne, 73
pun, 61
punch, 87 *n.*
pundigrion, 61
Punjaub, 87 *n.*
puny, 73
Purcell, 168
purlieu, 114
purley, 114
pursy, 116
purview, 4
Puy de Dôme, 7
puzzle, 59
python, 6
pyx, 6, 117

QUAINT, 72
quair, 134
quarrel, 150
quarry, 149
quarto, 5
quean, 75
querry, 124
query, 5
quilt, 126
quince, 110
quintal, 19
quire, 134

quirry, 124
quirt, 21
quorum, 5

RACK, 144
radius, 4
raiment, 56
rampart, 112
ramper, 112
ranch, 21
rappee, 8
Read, 168
Reader, 166
reasty, 72
reata, 21
rebus, 4
recreant, 117
recruit, 59
redstart, 108
Reed, 168
Reeder, 166
Regenpfeifer, 92
Regenschirm, 59 *n.*
Reginald, 32
rehearse, 97
Reid, 168
reine Claude, 29
relent, 3
remainder, 8
remnant, 8
Renard, 32
rendre, 113
renegade, 117
requiem, 4
restive, 72
revel, 130
revelly, 9
Reynold, 32
Rich, 160
Rick, 160
Rittersporn, 26
rival, 3
Rob, 160
rob, 137
robe, 137
Robin, 84
robin, 33
Rocinante, 165
romance, 67
Ronald, 32
rosemary, 115
rossignol, 38
roster, 16

rouncy, 165
Rouse, 160
rouse, 108
row, 108
Rudge, 168
rudimentary, 79
rum, 62
rummage, 70
runagate, 117
Runciman, 165
Russell, 168
rusty, 72

SABOTAGE, 10
Sacheverell, 169
sack, 107 *n.*
sake, 1
saker, 34
salade, 185
salet, 185
salary, 3
salt-cellar, 125
Salmon, 168
salver, 113
salvo, 113
samite, 138
samphire, 32
sample, 58
Samt, 138
sandwich, 36
Sandy, 64
Sankt Peters Vogel, 33
Saragossa, 46
sarcenet, 43
sardine, 44
Sargent, 137
sash, 146
sassafras, 27
satire, 86
saveloy, 125
saxifrage, 27
scabbard, 152
scallion, 74
scaramouch, 59 *n.*
scavenger, 77
schedule, 86
scheitern, 90
Schemel, 99
schirmen, 59 *n.*
school, 51, 150
Schöntierlein, 84
scintilla, 4
scion, 103

scissors, 117
score, 82
screed, 85
scrimer, 59 *n.*
scrimmage, 59 *n.*
Scriven, 165
scroll, 85
scruple, 80
scullery, 39
scullion, 39
'sdeath, 60
seal, 122
sea-lion, 29
sear, 150
search, 52
secretary, 30
sedan, 48
seel, 122
seesaw, 64
sehr, 156
seigneur, 85
Sekt, 107 *n.*
selig, 41
sendal, 43
seneschal, 85
senior, 4
señor, 85
sentinel, 95
sentry, 95
sepoy, 135
seraglio, 124
serge, 25
sergeant, 137
serpent, 34
servant, 137
service-tree, 118
Seward, 166
sexton, 56
Seymour, 157
shalloon, 43
shallop, 50
shallot, 44
shambles, 98
shame-faced, 115
shark, 30
shawm, 22
shay, 107
Sheepshanks, 71
sherbet, 135
sherry, 46, 107
shift, 91
shilly-shally, 64
shirk, 30

shirt, 138
short, 138
shrapnel, 35
shred, 85
shrew, 31
shrewd, 31
shrive, 68
shrub, 135
sieur, 85
signor, 85
silhouette, 36
silk, 25
silly, 41
silly Johnny, 41
Sinclair, 157
sinister, 3
sir, 85
sirloin, 178
sire, 85, 131 *n.*
sirup, 69, 135
Sisson, 160
sizar, 57
size, 57
sjambok, 23
skate, 108
skeeter, 59
sketch, 16, 20
skew, 58
skinker, 114 *n.*
skipper, 15
skirmish, 56, 59 *n.*, 131
skirt, 138
slave, 20
slim, 18
slogan, 13
slow-worm, 92
slug, 87 *n.*
slug-horn, 13
smock, 91
smug, 74
snap, 16
snapdragon, 26
snaphaunce, 185
snapsack, 16
snark, 14
snickersnee, 64
Snooks, 158
soccer, 61
solder, 142
Söldner, 143
solemn, 129
sorrel, 150
sorrow, 155

sorry, 155
soudard, 143
souillon, 39
souse, 111
sovereign, 112 *n.*
spade, 71
spahi, 136
span, 80
spaniel, 45
sparrow-grass, 115
spatula, 71
spec', 61
spence, 153
Spencer, 60, 153
spencer, 36, 115
spice, 59, 129
Spicer, 163
spick and span, 99
spinning-jenny, 38
Spitalfields, 59
spite, 60
Spittlegate, 59
splay, 60
sponge, 51
Spoonerism, 55
sport, 60
sprightly, 112 *n.*
sprite, 59
Sprössling, 103
spruce, 44
squarson, 61
squire, 58
stable, 51
stage, 59
staid, 94
stain, 60
stale, 94
stance, 132
staniel, 188
stank, 24
stanza, 132
starboard, 112
stationer, 58, *n.* 1
Steckenpferd, 89
Steinbrech, 27
steingall, 188
sterling, 73
stevedore, 70 *n.*
steward, 83
Stewart, 83
stickler, 69
still-room, 153
stimulus, 4

Stoddart, 166
stomacher, 145
stone, 80
stonegall, 188
Storchschnabel, 26
stortelli, 133
stout, 74
stranded, 90
stun, 97
sullen, 129
Summerfield, 162
Sumner, 163
supercilious, 3
surcease, 116
surly, 85
surplice, 164 *n.*
surround, 151
Surtees, 160
swank, 190
sward, 77
sweet William, 27
sympathy, 2
synopsis, 6

TABBY, 43
taffrail, 116
taint, 59
talisman, 19
tallage, 124
tally, 81
talon, 8
Tammany, 12
tandem, 4
tank, 24
tankard, 54
tansy, 27
tantalise, 37
tante, 64
tarantella, 46
tarantula, 46
tartan, 17, 43
tassel, 151
'tater, 60
tattoo, 16, 150
tawdry, 60
tease, 11
teasel, 11
'tec, 60
teetotaller, 6
teetotum, 5
Telford, 170
'tench, 60
tender, 59

tenet, 4
tennis, 9
tent, 151
termagant, 42
test, 98
testy, 72
tetchy, 151
thimble, 56
Thoroughgood, 158
Tibbet, 159
Tibert, 32
tick, 61
tidbit, 113
'Tilda, 64
Tillet, 159
Tillotson, 160
tilt, 100
tinnunculus, 92
tinsel, 54
tire, 58
tit, 113
titbit, 113
titmouse, 113
tittle-tattle, 64
'Tizer, 64
tobacco, 181
toby jug, 40
tocsin, 140
Todhunter, 164
toils, 99
tolle Buchen, 119
tomtit, 33, 113
Tono-Bungay, 14
Toogood, 158
Tooley St., 60
touchy, 151
tousle, 11
Towser, 11
toy, 16
Tozer, 11
trace, 109
tram, 178
traveller's joy, 27
treacle, 69
trellis, 137
trepan, 101
tret, 113
trews, 17, 109
tribunal, 4
tripod, 129
tripos, 129
trivet, 128
trivial, 3

trouble, 54
Troublefield, 162
trousers, 109
trove, 56, 94
troy, 46
truce, 110
trump, 8
Trumper, 164
tuberose, 115
Tucker, 166
tulip, 136
turban, 136
turkey, 47
Turney, 159
turnip, 88
tweeny, 85
tweezers, 111
twill, 137

UMBER, 140
umbrella, 140
umpire, 104
uncouth, 2
Underhill, 160
undertaker, 58, *n.* 1
unkempt, 2
unseal, 122
upholder, 165
upholsterer, 58
usher, 83
usquebaugh, 63
utterance, 151

VAGABOND, 156
vagrant, 156
vambrace, 56
vamoose, 9
vamp, 56
van, 56, 63
vane, 53
vanguard, 56
varech, 50
Varney, 162, *n.* 1
'varsity, 64
varsovienne, 46
vaunt, 181
vauntcourier, 57
Veck, 163
vedette, 96
vellum, 51
veneer, 136
venew, 114
veney, 113

venom, 5
venue, 114
verdigris, 119
verheeren, 2
Verney, 162, *n.* 1
verse, 132
vertugadin, 127
vet, 61
veto, 4
Vick, 163
victoria, 35
videlicet, 4
vie, 60
vigie, 95
vignette, 75
viking, 156
villa, 139
villain, 139
vinegar, 73
viva-voce, 3
viz., 4
voile, 108
voltaism, 36

WAFER, 71
wag, 61
Wait, 164
waits, 70
Walker, 166
wallet, 54
walnut, 140
Ward, 166
warison, 13
Warner, 164
Wat, 33
wattle, 54
weed, 2
week-end, 11
Weenen, 28
weir, 59 *n.*
wellington, 35

wench, 75
wergild, 131
wheatear, 108
wheedle, 102
wheel, 175
whisky, 58, *n.* 2, 63
white feather, 100
Whittaker, 162
Whittier, 164
wig, 63
Wilmot, 159
wipe, 61
wire, 61
wiseacre, 118
wisteria, 28
witch-elm, 118
worsted, 44
worthy, 74
write, 79
Wyatt, 159

XERES, 46

YACHT, 16
yard, 80
yare, 88
Ysopet, 38

ZANY, 41
Zentner, 19
zero, 136
zest, 103
Zeitel, 86
zigzag, 64
zijde, 25
Zins, 123
Zoo, 61
zounds, 60
Zwiebel, 88
Zwilch, 137

Catalog
of
DOVER BOOKS

BOOKS EXPLAINING SCIENCE

(Note: The books listed under this category are general introductions, surveys, reviews, and non-technical expositions of science for the interested layman or scientist who wishes to brush up. Dover also publishes the largest list of inexpensive reprints of books on intermediate and higher mathematics, mathematical physics, engineering, chemistry, astronomy, etc., for the professional mathematician or scientist. For our complete Science Catalog, write Dept. catrr., Dover Publications, Inc., 180 Varick Street, New York 14, N. Y.)

CONCERNING THE NATURE OF THINGS, Sir William· Bragg. Royal Institute Christmas Lectures by Nobel Laureate. Excellent plain-language introduction to gases, molecules, crystal structure, etc. explains "building blocks" of universe, basic properties of matter, with simplest, clearest examples, demonstrations. 32pp. of photos; 57 figures. 244pp. 5⅜ x 8.
T31 Paperbound **$1.35**

MATTER AND LIGHT, THE NEW PHYSICS, Louis de Broglie. Non-technical explanations by a Nobel Laureate of electro-magnetic theory, relativity, wave mechanics, quantum physics, philosophies of science, etc. Simple, yet accurate introduction to work of Planck, Bohr, Einstein, other modern physicists. Only 2 of 12 chapters require mathematics. 300pp. 5⅜ x 8.
T35 Paperbound **$1.60**

THE COMMON SENSE OF THE EXACT SCIENCES, W. K. Clifford. For 70 years, Clifford's work has been acclaimed as one of the clearest, yet most precise introductions to mathematical symbolism, measurement, surface boundaries, position, space, motion, mass and force, etc. Prefaces by Bertrand Russell and Karl Pearson. Introduction by James Newman. 130 figures. 249pp. 5⅜ x 8.
T61 Paperbound **$1.60**

THE NATURE OF LIGHT AND COLOUR IN THE OPEN AIR, M. Minnaert. What causes mirages? haloes? "multiple" suns and moons? Professor Minnaert explains these and hundreds of other fascinating natural optical phenomena in simple terms, tells how to observe them, suggests hundreds of experiments. 200 illus; 42 photos. xvi + 362pp.
T196 Paperbound **$1·95**

SPINNING TOPS AND GYROSCOPIC MOTION, John Perry. Classic elementary text on dynamics of rotation treats gyroscopes, tops, how quasi-rigidity is induced in paper disks, smoke rings, chains, etc, by rapid motion, precession, earth's motion, etc. Contains many easy-to-perform experiments. Appendix on practical uses of gyroscopes. 62 figures. 128pp.
T416 Paperbound **$1.00**

A CONCISE HISTORY OF MATHEMATICS, D. Struik. This lucid, easily followed history of mathematics from the Ancient Near East to modern times requires no mathematical background itself, yet introduces both mathematicians and laymen to basic concepts and discoveries and the men who made them. Contains a collection of 31 portraits of eminent mathematicians. Bibliography. xix + 299pp. 5⅜ x 8.
T255 Paperbound **$1.75**

THE RESTLESS UNIVERSE, Max Born. A remarkably clear, thorough exposition of gases, electrons, ions, waves and particles, electronic structure of the atom, nuclear physics, written for the layman by a Nobel Laureate. "Much ·more thorough and deep than most attempts . . . easy and delightful," CHEMICAL AND ENGINEERING NEWS. Includes 7 animated sequences showing motion of molecules, alpha particles, etc. 11 full-page plates of photographs. Total of nearly 600 illus. 315pp. 6⅛ x 9¼.
T412 Paperbound **$2.00**

WHAT IS SCIENCE?, N. Campbell. The role of experiment, the function of mathematics, the nature of scientific laws, the limitations of science, and many other provocative topics are explored without technicalities by an eminent scientist. "Still an excellent introduction to scientific philosophy," H. Margenau in PHYSICS TODAY. 192pp. 5⅜ x 8.
S43 Paperbound **$1.25**

FADS AND FALLACIES IN THE NAME OF SCIENCE, Martin Gardner. The standard account of the various cults, quack systems and delusions which have recently masqueraded as science: hollow earth theory, Atlantis, dianetics, Reich's orgone theory, flying saucers, Bridey Murphy, psionics, irridiagnosis, many other fascinating fallacies that deluded tens of thousands. "Should be read by everyone, scientist and non-scientist alike," R. T. Birge, Prof. Emeritus, Univ. of California; Former President, American Physical Society. Formerly titled, "In the Name of Science." Revised and enlarged edition. x + 365pp. 5⅜ x 8.

T394 Paperbound **$1.50**

THE STUDY OF THE HISTORY OF MATHEMATICS, THE STUDY OF THE HISTORY OF SCIENCE, G. Sarton. Two books bound as one. Both volumes are standard introductions to their fields by an eminent science historian. They discuss problems of historical research, teaching, pitfalls, other matters of interest to the historically oriented writer, teacher, or student. Both have extensive bibliographies. 10 illustrations. 188pp. 5⅜ x 8.   T240 Paperbound **$1.25**

THE PRINCIPLES OF SCIENCE, W. S. Jevons. Unabridged reprinting of a milestone in the development of symbolic logic and other subjects concerning scientific methodology, probability, inferential validity, etc. Also describes Jevons' "logic machine," an early precursor of modern electronic calculators. Preface by E. Nagel. 839pp. 5⅜ x 8.   S446 Paperbound **$2.98**

SCIENCE THEORY AND MAN, Erwin Schroedinger. Complete, unabridged reprinting of "Science and the Human Temperament" plus an additional essay "What is an Elementary Particle?" Nobel Laureate Schroedinger discusses many aspects of modern physics from novel points of view which provide unusual insights for both laymen and physicists. 192 pp. 5⅜ x 8.

T428 Paperbound **$1.35**

BRIDGES AND THEIR BUILDERS, D. B. Steinman & S. R. Watson. Information about ancient, medieval, modern bridges; how they were built; who built them; the structural principles employed; the materials they are built of; etc. Written by one of the world's leading authorities on bridge design and construction. New, revised, expanded edition. 23 photos; 26 line drawings, xvii + 401pp. 5⅜ x 8.   T431 Paperbound **$1.95**

HISTORY OF MATHEMATICS, D. E. Smith. Most comprehensive non-technical history of math in English. In two volumes. Vol. I: A chronological examination of the growth of mathematics from primitive concepts up to 1900. Vol. II: The development of ideas in specific fields and areas, up through elementary calculus. The lives and works of over a thousand mathematicians are covered; thousands of specific historical problems and their solutions are clearly explained. Total of 510 illustrations, 1355pp. 5⅜ x 8. Set boxed in attractive container.   T429, T430 Paperbound, the set **$5.00**

PHILOSOPHY AND THE PHYSICISTS, L. S. Stebbing. A philosopher examines the philosophical implications of modern science by posing a lively critical attack on the popular science expositions of Sir James Jeans and Arthur Eddington. xvi + 295pp. 5⅜ x 8.

T480 Paperbound **$1.65**

ON MATHEMATICS AND MATHEMATICIANS, R. E. Moritz. The first collection of quotations by and about mathematicians in English. 1140 anecdotes, aphorisms, definitions, speculations, etc. give both mathematicians and layman stimulating new insights into what mathematics is, and into the personalities of the great mathematicians from Archimedes to Euler, Gauss, Klein, Weierstrass. Invaluable to teachers, writers. Extensive cross index. 410pp. 5⅜ x 8.

T489 Paperbound **$1.95**

NATURAL SCIENCE, BIOLOGY, GEOLOGY, TRAVEL

A SHORT HISTORY OF ANATOMY AND PHYSIOLOGY FROM THE GREEKS TO HARVEY, C. Singer. A great medical historian's fascinating intermediate account of the slow advance of anatomical and physiological knowledge from pre-scientific times to Vesalius, Harvey. 139 unusually interesting illustrations. 221pp. 5⅜ x 8.   T389 Paperbound **$1.75**

THE BEHAVIOUR AND SOCIAL LIFE OF HONEYBEES, Ronald Ribbands. The most comprehensive, lucid and authoritative book on bee habits, communication, duties, cell life, motivations, etc. "A MUST for every scientist, experimenter, and educator, and a happy and valuable selection for all interested in the honeybee," AMERICAN BEE JOURNAL. 690-item bibliography. 127 illus.; 11 photographic plates. 352pp. 5⅜ x 8⅜.   S410 Clothbound **$4.50**

TRAVELS OF WILLIAM BARTRAM, edited by Mark Van Doren. One of the 18th century's most delightful books, and one of the few first-hand sources of information about American geography, natural history, and anthropology of American Indian tribes of the time. "The mind of a scientist with the soul of a poet," John Livingston Lowes. 13 original illustrations, maps. Introduction by Mark Van Doren. 448pp. 5⅜ x 8.   T326 Paperbound **$2.00**

STUDIES ON THE STRUCTURE AND DEVELOPMENT OF VERTEBRATES, Edwin Goodrich. The definitive study of the skeleton, fins and limbs, head region, divisions of the body cavity, vascular, respiratory, excretory systems, etc., of vertebrates from fish to higher mammals, by the greatest comparative anatomist of recent times. "The standard textbook," JOURNAL OF ANATOMY. 754 illus. 69-page biographical study. 1186-item bibliography. 2 vols. Total of 906pp. 5⅜ x 8.   Vol. I: S449 Paperbound **$2.50**
      Vol. II: S450 Paperbound **$2.50**

THE BIRTH AND DEVELOPMENT OF THE GEOLOGICAL SCIENCES, F. D. Adams. The most complete and thorough history of the earth sciences in print. Covers over 300 geological thinkers and systems; treats fossils, theories of stone growth, paleontology, earthquakes, vulcanists vs. neptunists, odd theories, etc. 91 illustrations, including medieval, Renaissance wood cuts, etc. 632 footnotes and bibliographic notes. 511pp. 308pp. 5⅜ x 8.   T5 Paperbound **$2.00**

FROM MAGIC TO SCIENCE, Charles Singer. A close study of aspects of medical science from the Roman Empire through the Renaissance. The sections on early herbals, and "The Visions of Hildegarde of Bingen," are probably the best studies of these subjects available. 158 unusual classic and medieval illustrations. xxvii + 365pp. 5⅜ x 8.   T390 Paperbound **$2.00**

SAILING ALONE AROUND THE WORLD, Captain Joshua Slocum. Captain Slocum's personal account of his single-handed voyage around the world in a 34-foot boat he rebuilt himself. A classic of both seamanship and descriptive writing. "A nautical equivalent of Thoreau's account," Van Wyck Brooks. 67 illus. 308pp. 5⅜ x 8.   T326 Paperbound **$1.00**

TREES OF THE EASTERN AND CENTRAL UNITED STATES AND CANADA, W. M. Harlow. Standard middle-level guide designed to help you know the characteristics of Eastern trees and identify them at sight by means of an 8-page synoptic key. More than 600 drawings and photographs of twigs, leaves, fruit, other features. xiii + 288pp. 4⅝ x 6½.
T395 Paperbound **$1.35**

FRUIT KEY AND TWIG KEY ("Fruit Key to Northeastern Trees," "Twig Key to Deciduous Woody Plants of Eastern North America"), **W. M. Harlow.** Identify trees in fall, winter, spring. Easy-to-use, synoptic keys, with photographs of every twig and fruit identified. Covers 120 different fruits, 160 different twigs. Over 350 photos. Bibliographies. Glossaries. Total of 143pp. 5⅝ x 8⅜.   T511 Paperbound **$1.25**

INTRODUCTION TO THE STUDY OF EXPERIMENTAL MEDICINE, Claude Bernard. This classic records Bernard's far-reaching efforts to transform physiology into an exact science. It covers problems of vivisection, the limits of physiological experiment, hypotheses in medical experimentation, hundreds of others. Many of his own famous experiments on the liver, the pancreas, etc., are used as examples. Foreword by I. B. Cohen. xxv + 266pp. 5⅜ x 8.
T400 Paperbound **$1.50**

THE ORIGIN OF LIFE, A. I. Oparin. The first modern statement that life evolved from complex nitro-carbon compounds, carefully presented according to modern biochemical knowledge of primary colloids, organic molecules, etc. Begins with historical introduction to the problem of the origin of life. Bibliography. xxv + 270pp. 5⅜ x 8.   S213 Paperbound **$1.75**

A HISTORY OF ASTRONOMY FROM THALES TO KEPLER, J. L. E. Dreyer. The only work in English which provides a detailed picture of man's cosmological views from Egypt, Babylonia, Greece, and Alexandria to Copernicus, Tycho Brahe and Kepler. "Standard reference on Greek astronomy and the Copernican revolution," SKY AND TELESCOPE. Formerly called "A History of Planetary Systems From Thales to Kepler." Bibliography. 21 diagrams. xvii + 430pp. 5⅜ x 8.
S79 Paperbound **$1.98**

URANIUM PROSPECTING, H. L. Barnes. A professional geologist tells you what you need to know. Hundreds of facts about minerals, tests, detectors, sampling, assays, claiming, developing, government regulations, etc. Glossary of technical terms. Annotated bibliography. x + 117pp. 5⅜ x 8.   T309 Paperbound **$1.00**

DE RE METALLICA, Georgius Agricola. All 12 books of this 400 year old classic on metals and metal production, fully annotated, and containing all 289 of the 16th century woodcuts which made the original an artistic masterpiece. A superb gift for geologists, engineers, libraries, artists, historians. Translated by Herbert Hoover & L. H. Hoover. Bibliography, survey of ancient authors. 289 illustrations of the excavating, assaying, smelting, refining, and countless other metal production operations described in the text. 672pp. 6¾ x 10¾. Deluxe library edition.   S6 Clothbound **$10.00**

DE MAGNETE, William Gilbert. A landmark of science by the man who first used the word "electricity," distinguished between static electricity and magnetism, and founded a new science. P. F. Mottelay translation. 90 figures. lix + 368pp. 5⅜ x 8.   S470 Paperbound **$2.00**

THE AUTOBIOGRAPHY OF CHARLES DARWIN AND SELECTED LETTERS, Francis Darwin, ed. Fascinating documents on Darwin's early life, the voyage of the "Beagle," the discovery of evolution, Darwin's thought on mimicry, plant development, vivisection, evolution, many other subjects Letters to Henslow, Lyell, Hooker, Wallace, Kingsley, etc. Appendix. 365pp. 5⅜ x 8.   T479 Paperbound **$1.65**

A WAY OF LIFE AND OTHER SELECTED WRITINGS OF SIR WILLIAM OSLER. 16 of the great physician, teacher and humanist's most inspiring writings on a practical philosophy of life, science and the humanities, and the history of medicine. 5 photographs. Introduction by G. L. Keynes, M.D., F.R.C.S. xx + 278pp. 5⅜ x 8.   T488 Paperbound **$1.50**

LITERATURE

WORLD DRAMA, B. H. Clark. 46 plays from Ancient Greece, Rome, to India, China, Japan. Plays by Aeschylus, Sophocles, Euripides, Aristophanes, Plautus, Marlowe, Jonson, Farquhar, Goldsmith, Cervantes, Molière, Dumas, Goethe, Schiller, Ibsen, many others. One of the most comprehensive collections of important plays from all literature available in English. Over ⅓ of this material is unavailable in any other current edition. Reading lists. 2 volumes. Total of 1364pp. 5⅜ x 8.　　　　　　　　　　　　　Vol. I, T57 Paperbound **$2.00**
　　　　　　　　　　　　　　　　　　　　　　　　　　　　Vol. II, T59 Paperbound **$2.00**

MASTERS OF THE DRAMA, John Gassner. The most comprehensive history of the drama in print. Covers more than 800 dramatists and over 2000 plays from the Greeks to modern Western, Near Eastern, Oriental drama. Plot summaries, theatre history, etc. "Best of its kind in English," NEW REPUBLIC. 35 pages of bibliography. 77 photos and drawings. Deluxe edition. xxii + 890pp. 5⅜ x 8.　　　　　　　　　　　　　　　T100 Clothbound **$5.95**

THE DRAMA OF LUIGI PIRANDELLO, D. Vittorini. All 38 of Pirandello's plays (to 1935) summarized and analyzed in terms of symbolic techniques, plot structure, etc. The only authorized work. Foreword by Pirandello. Biography. Bibliography. xiii + 350pp. 5⅜ x 8.
　　　　　　　　　　　　　　　　　　　　　　　　　　　T435 Paperbound **$1.98**

ARISTOTLE'S THEORY OF POETRY AND THE FINE ARTS, S. H. Butcher, ed. The celebrated "Butcher translation" faced page by page with the Greek text; Butcher's 300-page introduction to Greek poetic, dramatic thought. Modern Aristotelian criticism discussed by John Gassner. lxxvi + 421pp. 5⅜ x 8.

　　　　　　　　　　　　　　　　　　　　　　　　　　　T42 Paperbound **$2.00**

EUGENE O'NEILL: THE MAN AND HIS PLAYS, B. H. Clark. The first published source-book on O'Neill's life and work. Analyzes each play from the early THE WEB up to THE ICEMAN COMETH. Supplies much information about environmental and dramatic influences. ix + 182pp. 5⅜ x 8.　　　　　　　　　　　　　　　　　　　　　　　T379 Paperbound **$1.25**

INTRODUCTION TO ENGLISH LITERATURE, B. Dobrée, ed. Most compendious literary aid in its price range. Extensive, categorized bibliography (with entries up to 1949) of more than 5,000 poets, dramatists, novelists, as well as historians, philosophers, economists, religious writers, travellers, and scientists of literary stature. Information about manuscripts, important biographical data. Critical, historical, background works not simply listed, but evaluated. Each volume also contains a long introduction to the period it covers.

Vol. I: **THE BEGINNINGS OF ENGLISH LITERATURE TO SKELTON, 1509, W. L. Renwick. H. Orton.** 450pp. 5⅛ x 7⅛.　　　　　　　　　　　　　　　　　T75 Clothbound **$3.50**

Vol. II: **THE ENGLISH RENAISSANCE, 1510-1688, V. de Sola Pinto.** 381pp. 5⅛ x 7⅛.
　　　　　　　　　　　　　　　　　　　　　　　　　　　T76 Clothbound **$3.50**

Vol. III: **THE AUGUSTANS AND ROMANTICS, 1689-1830, H. Dyson, J. Butt.** 320pp. 5⅛ x⸳7⅛.
　　　　　　　　　　　　　　　　　　　　　　　　　　　T77 Clothbound **$3.50**

Vol. IV: **THE VICTORIANS AND AFTER, 1830-1914, E. Batho, B. Dobrée.** 360pp. 5⅛ x 7⅛.
　　　　　　　　　　　　　　　　　　　　　　　　　　　T78 Clothbound **$3.50**

EPIC AND ROMANCE, W. P. Ker. The standard survey of Medieval epic and romance by a foremost authority on Medieval literature. Covers historical background, plot, literary analysis, significance of Teutonic epics, Icelandic sagas, Beowulf, French chansons de geste, the Niebelungenlied, Arthurian romances, much more. 422pp. 5⅜ x 8.　　　T355 Paperbound **$1.95**

THE HEART OF EMERSON'S JOURNALS, Bliss Perry, ed. Emerson's most intimate thoughts, impressions, records of conversations with Channing, Hawthorne, Thoreau, etc., carefully chosen from the 10 volumes of The Journals. "The essays do not reveal the power of Emerson's mind . . .as do these hasty and informal writings," N. Y. TIMES. Preface by B. Perry. 370pp. 5⅜ x 8.　　　　　　　　　　　　　　　T447 Paperbound **$1.85**

A SOURCE BOOK IN THEATRICAL HISTORY, A. M. Nagler. (Formerly, "Sources of Theatrical History.") Over 300 selected passages by contemporary observers tell about styles of acting, direction, make-up, scene designing, etc., in the theatre's great periods from ancient Greece to the Théâtre Libre. "Indispensable complement to the study of drama," EDUCATIONAL THEATRE JOURNAL. Prof. Nagler, Yale Univ. School of Drama, also supplies notes, references. 85 illustrations. 611pp. 5⅜ x 8.　　　　　　　　　　　　　T515 Paperbound **$2.75**

THE ART OF THE STORY-TELLER, M. L. Shedlock. Regarded as the finest, most helpful book on telling stories to children, by a great story-teller. How to catch, hold, recapture attention; how to choose material; many other aspects. Also includes: a 99-page selection of Miss Shedlock's most successful stories; extensive bibliography of other stories. xxi + 320pp. 5⅜ x 8.　　　　　　　　　　　　　　　　　　　　　　　T245 Clothbound **$3.50**

THE DEVIL'S DICTIONARY, Ambrose Bierce. Over 1000 short, ironic definitions in alphabetical order, by America's greatest satirist in the classical tradition. "Some of the most gorgeous witticisms in the English language," H. L. Mencken. 144pp. 5⅜ x 8.　　T487 Paperbound **$1.00**

MUSIC

A DICTIONARY OF HYMNOLOGY, John Julian. More than 30,000 entries on individual hymns, their authorship, textual variations, location of texts, dates and circumstances of composition, denominational and ritual usages, the biographies of more than 9,000 hymn writers, essays on important topics such as children's hymns and Christmas carols, and hundreds of thousands of other important facts about hymns which are virtually impossible to find anywhere else. Convenient alphabetical listing, and a 200-page double-columned index of first lines enable you to track down virtually any hymn ever written. Total of 1786pp. 6¼ x 9¼. 2 volumes.   T133. The Set, Clothbound **$15.00**

STRUCTURAL HEARING, TONAL COHERENCE IN MUSIC, Felix Salzer. Extends the well-known Schenker approach to include modern music, music of the middle ages, and Renaissance music. Explores the phenomenon of tonal organization by discussing more than 500 compositions, and offers unusual new insights into the theory of composition and musical relationships. "The foundation on which all teaching in music theory has been based at this college," Leopold Mannes, President, The Mannes College of Music. Total of 658pp. 6½ x 9¼. 2 volumes.   S418 The set, Clothbound **$8.00**

A GENERAL HISTORY OF MUSIC, Charles Burney. The complete history of music from the Greeks up to 1789 by the 18th century musical historian who personally knew the great Baroque composers. Covers sacred and secular, vocal and instrumental, operatic and symphonic music; treats theory, notation, forms, instruments; discusses composers, performers, important works. Invaluable as a source of information on the period for students, historians, musicians. "Surprisingly few of Burney's statements have been invalidated by modern research . . . still of great value," NEW YORK TIMES. Edited and corrected by Frank Mercer. 35 figures. 1915pp. 5½ x 8½. 2 volumes.   T36 The set, Clothbound **$12.50**

JOHANN SEBASTIAN BACH, Phillip Spitta. Recognized as one of the greatest accomplishments of musical scholarship and far and away the definitive coverage of Bach's works. Hundreds of individual pieces are analyzed. Major works, such as the B Minor Mass and the St. Matthew Passion are examined in minute detail. Spitta also deals with the works of Buxtehude, Pachelbel, and others of the period. Can be read with profit even by those without a knowledge of the technicalities of musical composition. "Unchallenged as the last word on one of the supreme geniuses of music," John Barkham, SATURDAY REVIEW SYNDICATE. Total of 1819pp. 5⅜ x 8. 2 volumes.   T252 The set, Clothbound **$10.00**

HISTORY

THE IDEA OF PROGRESS, J. B. Bury. Prof. Bury traces the evolution of a central concept of Western civilization in Greek, Roman, Medieval, and Renaissance thought to its flowering in the 17th and 18th centuries. Introduction by Charles Beard. xl + 357pp. 5⅜ x 8.
T39 Clothbound **$3.95**
T40 Paperbound **$1.95**

THE ANCIENT GREEK HISTORIANS, J. B. Bury. Greek historians such as Herodotus, Thucydides, Xenophon; Roman historians such as Tacitus, Caesar, Livy; scores of others fully analyzed in terms of sources, concepts, influences, etc., by a great scholar and historian. 291pp. 5⅜ x 8.   T397 Paperbound **$1.50**

HISTORY OF THE LATER ROMAN EMPIRE, J. B. Bury. The standard work on the Byzantine Empire from 395 A.D. to the death of Justinian in 565 A.D., by the leading Byzantine scholar of our time. Covers political, social, cultural, theological, military history. Quotes contemporary documents extensively. "Most unlikely that it will ever be superseded," Glanville Downey, Dumbarton Oaks Research Library. Genealogical tables. 5 maps. Bibliography. 2 vols. Total of 965pp. 5⅜ x 8.   T398, T399 Paperbound, the set **$4.00**

GARDNER'S PHOTOGRAPHIC SKETCH BOOK OF THE CIVIL WAR, Alexander Gardner. One of the rarest and most valuable Civil War photographic collections exactly reproduced for the first time since 1866. Scenes of Manassas, Bull Run, Harper's Ferry, Appomattox, Mechanicsville, Fredericksburg, Gettysburg, etc.; battle ruins, prisons, arsenals, a slave pen, fortifications; Lincoln on the field, officers, men, corpses. By one of the most famous pioneers in documentary photography. Original copies of the "Sketch Book" sold for $425 in 1952. Introduction by E. Bleiler. 100 full-page 7 x 10 photographs (original size). 244pp. 10¾ x 8½
T476 Clothbound **$6.00**

THE WORLD'S GREAT SPEECHES, L. Copeland and L. Lamm, eds. 255 speeches from Pericles to Churchill, Dylan Thomas. Invaluable as a guide to speakers; fascinating as history past and present; a source of much difficult-to-find material. Includes an extensive section of informal and humorous speeches. 3 indices: Topic, Author, Nation. xx + 745pp. 5⅜ x 8.
T468 Paperbound **$2.49**

FOUNDERS OF THE MIDDLE AGES, E. K. Rand. The best non-technical discussion of the transformation of Latin paganism into medieval civilization. Tertullian, Gregory, Jerome, Boethius, Augustine, the Neoplatonists, other crucial figures, philosophies examined. Excellent for the intelligent non-specialist. "Extraordinarily accurate," Richard McKeon, THE NATION. ix + 365pp. 5⅜ x 8.   T369 Paperbound **$1.85**

THE POLITICAL THOUGHT OF PLATO AND ARISTOTLE, Ernest Barker. The standard, comprehensive exposition of Greek political thought. Covers every aspect of the "Republic" and the "Politics" as well as minor writings, other philosophers, theorists of the period, and the later history of Greek political thought. Unabridged edition. 584pp. 5⅜ x 8.
T521 Paperbound **$1.85**

PHILOSOPHY

THE GIFT OF LANGUAGE, M. Schlauch. (Formerly, "The Gift of Tongues.") A sound, middle-level treatment of linguistic families, word histories, grammatical processes, semantics, language taboos, word-coining of Joyce, Cummings, Stein, etc. 232 bibliographical notes. 350pp. 5⅜ x 8.
T243 Paperbound **$1.85**

THE PHILOSOPHY OF HEGEL, W. T. Stace. The first work in English to give a complete and connected view of Hegel's entire system. Especially valuable to those who do not have time to study the highly complicated original texts, yet want an accurate presentation by a most reputable scholar of one of the most influential 19th century thinkers. Includes a 14 x 20 fold-out chart of Hegelian system. 536pp. 5⅜ x 8.
T254 Paperbound **$2.00**

ARISTOTLE, A. E. Taylor. A lucid, non-technical account of Aristotle written by a foremost Platonist. Covers life and works; thought on matter, form, causes, logic, God, physics, metaphysics, etc. Bibliography. New index compiled for this edition. 128pp. 5⅜ x 8.
T280 Paperbound **$1.00**

GUIDE TO PHILOSOPHY, C. E. M. Joad. This basic work describes the major philosophic problems and evaluates the answers propounded by great philosophers from the Greeks to Whitehead, Russell. "The finest introduction," BOSTON TRANSCRIPT. Bibliography, 592pp. 5⅜ x 8.
T297 Paperbound **$2.00**

LANGUAGE AND MYTH, E. Cassirer. Cassirer's brilliant demonstration that beneath both language and myth lies an unconscious "grammar" of experience whose categories and canons are not those of logical thought. Introduction and translation by Susanne Langer. Index. x + 103pp. 5⅜ x 8.
T51 Paperbound **$1.25**

SUBSTANCE AND FUNCTION, EINSTEIN'S THEORY OF RELATIVITY, E. Cassirer. This double volume contains the German philosopher's profound philosophical formulation of the differences between traditional logic and the new logic of science. Number, space, energy, relativity, many other topics are treated in detail. Authorized translation by W. C. and M. C. Swabey. xii + 465pp. 5⅜ x 8.
T50 Paperbound **$2.00**

THE PHILOSOPHICAL WORKS OF DESCARTES. The definitive English edition, in two volumes, of all major philosophical works and letters of René Descartes, father of modern philosophy of knowledge and science. Translated by E. S. Haldane and G. Ross. Introductory notes. Total of 842pp. 5⅜ x 8.
T71 Vol. 1, Paperbound **$2.00**
T72 Vol. 2, Paperbound **$2.00**

ESSAYS IN EXPERIMENTAL LOGIC, J. Dewey. Based upon Dewey's theory that knowledge implies a judgment which in turn implies an inquiry, these papers consider such topics as the thought of Bertrand Russell, pragmatism, the logic of values, antecedents of thought, data and meanings. 452pp. 5⅜ x 8.
T73 Paperbound **$1.95**

THE PHILOSOPHY OF HISTORY, G. W. F. Hegel. This classic of Western thought is Hegel's detailed formulation of the thesis that history is not chance but a rational process, the realization of the Spirit of Freedom. Translated and introduced by J. Sibree. Introduction by C. Hegel. Special introduction for this edition by Prof. Carl Friedrich, Harvard University. xxxix + 447pp. 5⅜ x 8.
T112 Paperbound **$1.85**

THE WILL TO BELIEVE and HUMAN IMMORTALITY, W. James. Two of James's most profound investigations of human belief in God and immortality, bound as one volume. Both are powerful expressions of James's views on chance vs. determinism, pluralism vs. monism, will and intellect, arguments for survival after death, etc. Two prefaces. 429pp. 5⅜ x 8.
T294 Clothbound **$3.75**
T291 Paperbound **$1.65**

INTRODUCTION TO SYMBOLIC LOGIC, S. Langer. A lucid, general introduction to modern logic, covering forms, classes, the use of symbols, the calculus of propositions, the Boole-Schroeder and the Russell-Whitehead systems, etc. "One of the clearest and simplest introductions," MATHEMATICS GAZETTE. Second, enlarged, revised edition. 368pp. 5⅜ x 8.
S164 Paperbound **$1.75**

MIND AND THE WORLD-ORDER, C. I. Lewis. Building upon the work of Peirce, James, and Dewey, Professor Lewis outlines a theory of knowledge in terms of "conceptual pragmatism," and demonstrates why the traditional understanding of the a priori must be abandoned. Appendices. xiv + 446pp. 5⅜ x 8.
T359 Paperbound **$1.95**

THE GUIDE FOR THE PERPLEXED, M. Maimonides One of the great philosophical works of all time, Maimonides' formulation of the meeting-ground between Old Testament and Aristotelian thought is essential to anyone interested in Jewish, Christian, and Moslem thought in the Middle Ages. 2nd revised edition of the Friedlander translation. Extensive introduction. lix + 414pp. 5⅜ x 8.
T351 Paperbound **$1.85**

THE PHILOSOPHICAL WRITINGS OF PEIRCE, J. Buchler, ed. (Formerly, "The Philosophy of Peirce.") This carefully integrated selection of Peirce's papers is considered the best coverage of the complete thought of one of the greatest philosophers of modern times. Covers Peirce's work on the theory of signs, pragmatism, epistemology, symbolic logic, the scientific method, chance, etc. xvi + 386pp. 5 3/8 x 8.   T216 Clothbound **$5.00**
                                                                T217 Paperbound **$1.95**

HISTORY OF ANCIENT PHILOSOPHY, W. Windelband. Considered the clearest survey of Greek and Roman philosophy. Examines Thales, Anaximander, Anaximenes, Heraclitus, the Eleatics, Empedocles, the Pythagoreans, the Sophists, Socrates, Democritus, Stoics, Epicureans, Sceptics, Neo-platonists, etc. 50 pages on Plato; 70 on Aristotle. 2nd German edition tr. by H. E. Cushman. xv + 393pp. 5⅜ x 8.   T357 Paperbound **$1.75**

INTRODUCTION TO SYMBOLIC LOGIC AND ITS APPLICATIONS, R. Carnap. A comprehensive, rigorous introduction to modern logic by perhaps its greatest living master. Includes demonstrations of applications in mathematics, physics, biology. "Of the rank of a masterpiece," Z. für Mathematik und ihre Grenzgebiete. Over 300 exercises. xvi + 241pp. 5⅜ x 8.   Clothbound **$4.00**
                                                                S453 Paperbound **$1.85**

SCEPTICISM AND ANIMAL FAITH, G. Santayana. Santayana's unusually lucid exposition of the difference between the independent existence of objects and the essence our mind attributes to them, and of the necessity of scepticism as a form of belief and animal faith as a necessary condition of knowledge. Discusses belief, memory, intuition, symbols, etc. xii + 314pp. 5⅜ x 8.   T235 Clothbound **$3.50**
                                                                T236 Paperbound **$1.50**

THE ANALYSIS OF MATTER, B. Russell. With his usual brilliance, Russell analyzes physics, causality, scientific inference, Weyl's theory, tensors, invariants, periodicity, etc. in order to discover the basic concepts of scientific thought about matter. "Most thorough treatment of the subject," THE NATION. Introduction. 8 figures. viii + 408pp. 5⅜ x 8.
                                                                T231 Paperbound **$1.95**

THE SENSE OF BEAUTY, G. Santayana. This important philosophical study of why, when, and how beauty appears, and what conditions must be fulfilled, is in itself a revelation of the beauty of language. "It is doubtful if a better treatment of the subject has since appeared," PEABODY JOURNAL. ix + 275pp. 5⅜ x 8.   T238 Paperbound **$1.00**

THE CHIEF WORKS OF SPINOZA. In two volumes. Vol. I: The Theologico-Political Treatise and the Political Treatise. Vol. II: On the Improvement of Understanding, The Ethics, and Selected Letters. The permanent and enduring ideas in these works on God, the universe, religion, society, etc., have had tremendous impact on later philosophical works. Introduction. Total of 862pp. 5⅜ x 8.   T249 Vol. I, Paperbound **$1.50**
                                                                T250 Vol. II, Paperbound **$1.50**

TRAGIC SENSE OF LIFE, M. de Unamuno. The acknowledged masterpiece of one of Spain's most influential thinkers. Between the despair at the inevitable death of man and all his works, and the desire for immortality, Unamuno finds a "saving incertitude." Called "a masterpiece," by the ENCYCLOPAEDIA BRITANNICA. xxx + 332pp. 5⅜ x 8.
                                                                T257 Paperbound **$1.95**

EXPERIENCE AND NATURE, John Dewey. The enlarged, revised edition of the Paul Carus lectures (1925). One of Dewey's clearest presentations of the philosophy of empirical naturalism which reestablishes the continuity between "inner" experience and "outer" nature. These lectures are among the most significant ever delivered by an American philosopher. 457pp. 5⅜ x 8.   T471 Paperbound **$1.85**

PHILOSOPHY AND CIVILIZATION IN THE MIDDLE AGES, M. de Wulf. A semi-popular survey of medieval intellectual life, religion, philosophy, science, the arts, etc. that covers feudalism vs. Catholicism, rise of the universities, mendicant orders, and similar topics. Bibliography. viii + 320pp. 5⅜ x 8.   T284 Paperbound **$1.75**

AN INTRODUCTION TO SCHOLASTIC PHILOSOPHY, M. de Wulf. (Formerly, "Scholasticism Old and New.") Prof. de Wulf covers the central scholastic tradition from St. Anselm, Albertus Magnus, Thomas Aquinas, up to Suarez in the 17th century; and then treats the modern revival of. scholasticism, the Louvain position, relations with Kantianism and positivism, etc. xvi + 271pp. 5⅜ x 8.   T296 Clothbound **$3.50**
                                                                T283 Paperbound **$1.75**

A HISTORY OF MODERN PHILOSOPHY, H. Höffding. An exceptionally clear and detailed coverage of Western philosophy from the Renaissance to the end of the 19th century. Both major and minor figures are examined in terms of theory of knowledge, logic, cosmology, psychology. Covers Pomponazzi, Bodin, Boehme, Telesius, Bruno, Copernicus, Descartes, Spinoza, Hobbes, Locke, Hume, Kant, Fichte, Schopenhauer, Mill, Spencer, Langer, scores of others. A standard reference work. 2 volumes. Total of 1159pp. 5⅜ x 8.   T117 Vol. 1, Paperbound **$2.00**
                                                                T118 Vol. 2, Paperbound **$2.00**

LANGUAGE, TRUTH AND LOGIC, A. J. Ayer. The first full-length development of Logical Posivitism in English. Building on the work of Schlick, Russell, Carnap, and the Vienna school, Ayer presents the tenets of one of the most important systems of modern philosophical thought. 160pp. 5⅜ x 8.   T10 Paperbound **$1.25**

ORIENTALIA AND RELIGION

THE MYSTERIES OF MITHRA, F. Cumont. The great Belgian scholar's definitive study of the Persian mystery religion that almost vanquished Christianity in the ideological struggle for the Roman Empire. A masterpiece of scholarly detection that reconstructs secret doctrines, organization, rites. Mithraic art is discussed and analyzed. 70 illus. 239pp. 5⅜ x 8.
T323 Paperbound **$1.85**

CHRISTIAN AND ORIENTAL PHILOSOPHY OF ART. A. K. Coomaraswamy. The late art historian and orientalist discusses artistic symbolism, the role of traditional culture in enriching art, medieval art, folklore, philosophy of art, other similar topics. Bibliography. 148pp. 5⅜ x 8.
T378 Paperbound **$1.25**

TRANSFORMATION OF NATURE IN ART, A. K. Coomaraswamy. A basic work on Asiatic religious art. Includes discussions of religious art in Asia and Medieval Europe (exemplified by Meister Eckhart), the origin and use of images in Indian art, Indian Medieval aesthetic manuals, and other fascinating, little known topics. Glossaries of Sanskrit and Chinese terms. Bibliography. 41pp. of notes. 245pp. 5⅜ x 8.
T368 Paperbound **$1.75**

ORIENTAL RELIGIONS IN ROMAN PAGANISM, F. Cumont. This well-known study treats the ecstatic cults of Syria and Phrygia (Cybele, Attis, Adonis, their orgies and mutilatory rites); the mysteries of Egypt (Serapis, Isis, Osiris); Persian dualism; Mithraic cults; Hermes Trismegistus, Ishtar, Astarte, etc. and their influence on the religious thought of the Roman Empire. Introduction. 55pp. of notes; extensive bibliography. xxiv + 298pp. 5⅜ x 8.
T321 Paperbound **$1.75**

ANTHROPOLOGY, SOCIOLOGY, AND PSYCHOLOGY

PRIMITIVE MAN AS PHILOSOPHER, P. Radin. A standard anthropological work based on Radin's investigations of the Winnebago, Maori, Batak, Zuni, other primitive tribes. Describes primitive thought on the purpose of life, marital relations, death, personality, gods, etc. Extensive selections of original primitive documents. Bibliography. xviii + 420pp. 5⅜ x 8.
T392 Paperbound **$2.00**

PRIMITIVE RELIGION, P. Radin. Radin's thoroughgoing treatment of supernatural beliefs, shamanism, initiations, religious expression, etc. in primitive societies. Arunta, Ashanti, Aztec, Bushman, Crow, Fijian, many other tribes examined. "Excellent," NATURE. New preface by the author. Bibliographic notes. x + 322pp. 5⅜ x 8.
T393 Paperbound **$1.85**

SEX IN PSYCHO-ANALYSIS, S. Ferenczi. (Formerly, "Contributions to Psycho-analysis.") 14 selected papers on impotence, transference, analysis and children, dreams, obscene words, homosexuality, paranoia, etc. by an associate of Freud. Also included: THE DEVELOPMENT OF PSYCHO-ANALYSIS, by Ferenczi and Otto Rank. Two books bound as one. Total of 406pp. 5⅜ x 8.
T324 Paperbound **$1.85**

THE PRINCIPLES OF PSYCHOLOGY, William James. The complete text of the famous "long course," one of the great books of Western thought. An almost incredible amount of information about psychological processes, the stream of consciousness, habit, time perception, memory, emotions, reason, consciousness of self, abnormal phenomena, and similar topics. Based on James's own discoveries integrated with the work of Descartes, Locke, Hume, Royce, Wundt, Berkeley, Lotse, Herbart, scores of others. "A classic of interpretation," PSYCHIATRIC QUARTERLY. 94 illus. 1408pp. 2 volumes. 5⅜ x 8.
T381 Vol. 1, Paperbound **$2.50**
T382 Vol. 2, Paperbound **$2.50**

THE POLISH PEASANT IN EUROPE AND AMERICA, W. I. Thomas, F. Znaniecki. Monumental sociological study of peasant primary groups (family and community) and the disruptions produced by a new industrial system and emigration to America, by two of the foremost sociologists of recent times. One of the most important works in sociological thought. Includes hundreds of pages of primary documentation; point by point analysis of causes of social decay, breakdown of morality, crime, drunkenness, prostitution, etc. 2nd revised edition. 2 volumes. Total of 2250pp. 6 x 9.
T478 2 volume set, Clothbound **$12.50**

FOLKWAYS, W. G. Sumner. The great Yale sociologist's detailed exposition of thousands of social, sexual, and religious customs in hundreds of cultures from ancient Greece to Modern Western societies. Preface by A. G. Keller. Introduction by William Lyon Phelps. 705pp. 5⅜ x 8.
S508 Paperbound **$2.49**

BEYOND PSYCHOLOGY, Otto Rank. The author, an early associate of Freud, uses psychoanalytic techniques of myth-analysis to explore ultimates of human existence. Treats love, immortality, the soul, sexual identity, kingship, sources of state power, many other topics which illuminate the irrational basis of human existence. 291pp. 5⅜ x 8.
T485 Paperbound **$1.75**

ILLUSIONS AND DELUSIONS OF THE SUPERNATURAL AND THE OCCULT, D. H. Rawcliffe. A rational, scientific examination of crystal gazing, automatic writing, table turning, stigmata, the Indian rope trick, dowsing, telepathy, clairvoyance, ghosts, ESP, PK, thousands of other supposedly occult phenomena. Originally titled "The Psychology of the Occult." 14 illustrations. 551pp. 5⅜ x 8.
T503 Paperbound **$2.00**

DOVER BOOKS

YOGA: A SCIENTIFIC EVALUATION, Kovoor T. Behanan. A scientific study of the physiological and psychological effects of Yoga discipline, written under the auspices of the Yale University Institute of Human Relations. Foreword by W. A. Miles, Yale Univ. 17 photographs. 290pp. 5⅜ x 8. T505 Paperbound **$1.65**

HOAXES, C. D. MacDougall. Delightful, entertaining, yet scholarly exposition of how hoaxes start, why they succeed, documented with stories of hundreds of the most famous hoaxes. "A stupendous collection . . . and shrewd analysis, "NEW YORKER. New, revised edition. 54 photographs. 320pp. 5⅜ x 8. T465 Paperbound **$1.75**

CREATIVE POWER: THE EDUCATION OF YOUTH IN THE CREATIVE ARTS, Hughes Mearns. Named by the National Education Association as one of the 20 foremost books on education in recent times. Tells how to help children express themselves in drama, poetry, music, art, develop latent creative power. Should be read by every parent, teacher. New, enlarged, revised edition. Introduction. 272pp. 5⅜ x 8. T490 Paperbound **$1.50**

LANGUAGES

NEW RUSSIAN-ENGLISH, ENGLISH-RUSSIAN DICTIONARY, M. A. O'Brien. Over 70,000 entries in new orthography! Idiomatic usages, colloquialisms. One of the few dictionaries that indicate accent changes in conjugation and declension. "One of the best," Prof. E. J. Simmons, Cornell. First names, geographical terms, bibliography, many other features. 738pp. 4½ x 6¼. T208 Paperbound **$2.00**

MONEY CONVERTER AND TIPPING GUIDE FOR EUROPEAN TRAVEL, C. Vomacka. Invaluable, handy source of currency regulations, conversion tables, tipping rules, postal rates, much other travel information for every European country plus Israel, Egypt and Turkey. 128pp. 3½ x 5¼. T260 Paperbound **60¢**

MONEY CONVERTER AND TIPPING GUIDE FOR TRAVEL IN THE AMERICAS (including the United States and Canada), **C. Vomacka.** The information you need for informed and confident travel in the Americas: money conversion tables, tipping guide, postal, telephone rates, etc. 128pp. 3½ x 5¼. T261 Paperbound **65¢**

DUTCH-ENGLISH, ENGLISH-DUTCH DICTIONARY, F. G. Renier. The most convenient, practical Dutch-English dictionary on the market. New orthography. More than 60,000 entries: idioms, compounds, technical terms, etc. Gender of nouns indicated. xviii + 571pp. 5½ x 6¼. T224 Clothbound **$2.50**

LEARN DUTCH!, F. G. Renier. The most satisfactory and easily-used grammar of modern Dutch. Used and recommended by the Fulbright Committee in the Netherlands. Over 1200 simple exercises lead to mastery of spoken and written Dutch. Dutch-English, English-Dutch vocabularies. 181pp. 4¼ x 7¼. T441 Clothbound **$1.75**

PHRASE AND SENTENCE DICTIONARY OF SPOKEN RUSSIAN, English-Russian, Russian-English. Based on phrases and complete sentences, rather than isolated words; recognized as one of the best methods of learning the idiomatic speech of a country. Over 11,500 entries, indexed by single words, with more than 32,000 English and Russian sentences and phrases, in immediately usable form. Probably the largest list ever published. Shows accent changes in conjugation and declension; irregular forms listed in both alphabetical place and under main form of word. 15,000 word introduction covering Russian sounds, writing, grammar, syntax. 15-page appendix of geographical names, money, important signs, given names, foods, special Soviet terms, etc. Travellers, businessmen, students, government employees have found this their best source for Russian expressions. Originally published as U.S. Government Technical Manual TM 30-944. iv + 573pp. 5⅝ x 8⅜. T496 Paperbound **$2.75**

PHRASE AND SENTENCE DICTIONARY OF SPOKEN SPANISH, Spanish-English, English-Spanish. Compiled from spoken Spanish, emphasizing idiom and colloquial usage in both Castilian and Latin-American. More than 16,000 entries containing over 25,000 idioms—the largest list of idiomatic constructions ever published. Complete sentences given, indexed under single words —language in immediately usable form, for travellers, businessmen, students, etc. 25-page introduction provides rapid survey of sounds, grammar, syntax, with full consideration of irregular verbs. Especially apt in modern treatment of phrases and structure. 17-page glossary gives translations of geographical names, money values, numbers, national holidays, important street signs, useful expressions of high frequency, plus unique 7-page glossary of Spanish and Spanish-American foods and dishes. Originally published as U.S. Government Technical Manual TM 30-900. iv + 513pp. 5⅝ x 8⅜. T495 Paperbound **$1.75**

CATALOG OF

SAY IT language phrase books

"SAY IT" in the foreign language of your choice! We have sold over ½ million copies of these popular, useful language books. They will not make you an expert linguist overnight, but they do cover most practical matters of everyday life abroad.

Over 1000 useful phrases, expressions, with additional variants, substitutions.

Modern! Useful! Hundreds of phrases not available in other texts: "Nylon," "air-conditioned," etc.

The ONLY inexpensive phrase book **completely indexed**. Everything is available at a flip of your finger, ready for use.

Prepared by native linguists, travel experts.

Based on years of travel experience abroad.

This handy phrase book may be used by itself, or it may supplement any other text or course; it provides a living element. Used by many colleges and institutions: Hunter College; Barnard College; Army Ordnance School, Aberdeen; and many others.

Available, 1 book per language:

Danish (T818) 75¢
Dutch T(817) 75¢
English (for German-speaking people) (T801) 60¢
English (for Italian-speaking people) (T816) 60¢
English (for Spanish-speaking people) (T802) 60¢
Esperanto (T820) 75¢
French (T803) 60¢
German (T804) 60¢
Modern Greek (T813) 75¢
Hebrew (T805) 60¢

Italian (T806) 60¢
Japanese (T807) 60¢
Norwegian (T814) 75¢
Russian (T810) 75¢
Spanish (T811) 60¢
Turkish (T821) 75¢
Yiddish (T815) 75¢
Swedish (T812) 75¢
Polish (T808) 75¢
Portuguese (T809) 75¢

LISTEN & LEARN language record sets

LISTEN & LEARN is the only language record course designed especially to meet your travel needs, or help you learn essential foreign language quickly by yourself, or in conjunction with any school course, by means of the automatic association method. Each set contains three 33⅓ rpm long- playing records — 1½ hours of recorded speech by eminent native speakers who are professors at Columbia, N.Y.U., Queens College and other leading universities. The sets are priced far below other sets of similar quality, yet they contain many special features not found in other record sets:

* Over 800 selected phrases and sentences, a basic vocabulary of over 3200 words.
* Both English and foreign language recorded; with a pause for your repetition.
* Designed for persons with limited time; no time wasted on material you cannot use immediately.
* Living, modern expressions that answer modern needs: drugstore items, "air-conditioned," etc.
* 128-196 page manuals contain everything on the records, plus simple pronunciation guides.
* Manual is fully indexed; find the phrase you want instantly.
* High fidelity recording—equal to any records costing up to $6 each.

The phrases on these records cover 41 different categories useful to the traveller or student interested in learning the living, spoken language: greetings, introductions, making yourself understood, passing customs, planes, trains, boats, buses, taxis, nightclubs, restaurants, menu items, sports, concerts, cameras, automobile travel, repairs, drugstores, doctors, dentists, medicines, barber shops, beauty parlors, laundries, many, many more.

"Excellent . . . among the very best on the market," Prof. Mario Pei, Dept. of Romance Languages, Columbia University. "Inexpensive and well-done . . . an ideal present," CHICAGO SUNDAY TRIBUNE. "More genuinely helpful than anything of its kind which I have previously encountered," Sidney Clark, well-known author of "ALL THE BEST" travel books. Each set contains 3 33⅓ rpm pure vinyl records, 128- 196 page with full record text, and album. One language per set. LISTEN & LEARN record sets are now available in—

FRENCH	the set $4.95		GERMAN	the set $4.95
ITALIAN	the set $4.95		SPANISH	the set $4.95
RUSSIAN	the set $5.95		JAPANESE *	the set $5.95

* Available Sept. 1, 1959

UNCONDITIONAL GUARANTEE: Dover Publications stands behind every Listen and Learn record set. If you are dissatisfied with these sets for any reason whatever, return them within 10 days and your money will be refunded in full.

ART HISTORY

STICKS AND STONES, Lewis Mumford. An examination of forces influencing American architecture: the medieval tradition in early New England, the classical influence in Jefferson's time, the Brown Decades, the imperial facade, the machine age, etc. "A truly remarkable book," SAT. REV. OF LITERATURE. 2nd revised edition. 21 illus. xvii + 228pp. 5⅜ x 8.
T202 Paperbound $1.60

THE AUTOBIOGRAPHY OF AN IDEA, Louis Sullivan. The architect whom Frank Lloyd Wright called "the master," records the development of the theories that revolutionized America's skyline. 34 full-page plates of Sullivan's finest work. New introduction by R. M. Line. xiv + 335pp. 5⅜ x 8.
T281 Paperbound $1.85

THE MATERIALS AND TECHNIQUES OF MEDIEVAL PAINTING, D. V. Thompson. An invaluable study of carriers and grounds, binding media, pigments, metals used in painting, al fresco and al secco techniques, burnishing, etc. used by the medieval masters. Preface by Bernard Berenson. 239pp. 5⅜ x 8.
T327 Paperbound $1.85

PRINCIPLES OF ART HISTORY, H. Wölfflin. This remarkably instructive work demonstrates the tremendous change in artistic conception from the 14th to the 18th centuries, by analyzing 164 works by Botticelli, Dürer, Hobbema, Holbein, Hals, Titian, Rembrandt, Vermeer, etc., and pointing out exactly what is meant by "baroque," "classic," "primitive," "picturesque," and other basic terms of art history and criticism. "A remarkable lesson in the art of seeing," SAT. REV. OF LITERATURE. Translated from the 7th German edition. 150 illus. 254pp. 6⅛ x 9¼.
T276 Paperbound $2.00

FOUNDATIONS OF MODERN ART, A. Ozenfant. Stimulating discussion of human creativity from paleolithic cave painting to modern painting, architecture, decorative arts. Fully illustrated with works of Gris, Lipchitz, Léger, Picasso, primitive, modern artifacts, architecture, industrial art, much more. 226 illustrations. 368pp. 6⅛ x 9¼.
T215 Paperbound $1.95

HANDICRAFTS, APPLIED ART, ART SOURCES, ETC.

WILD FOWL DECOYS, J. Barber. The standard work on this fascinating branch of folk art, ranging from Indian mud and grass devices to realistic wooden decoys. Discusses styles, types, periods; gives full information on how to make decoys. 140 illustrations (including 14 new plates) show decoys and provide full sets of plans for handicrafters, artists, hunters, and students of folk art. 281pp. 7⅞ x 10¾. Deluxe edition.
T11 Clothbound $8.50

METALWORK AND ENAMELLING, H. Maryon. Probably the best book ever written on the subject. Tells everything necessary for the home manufacture of jewelry, rings, ear pendants, bowls, etc. Covers materials, tools, soldering, filigree, setting stones, raising patterns, repoussé work, damascening, niello, cloisonné, polishing, assaying, casting, and dozens of other techniques. The best substitute for apprenticeship to a master metalworker. 363 photos and figures. 374pp. 5½ x 8½.
T183 Clothbound $7.50

SHAKER FURNITURE, E. D. and F. Andrews. The most illuminating study of Shaker furniture ever written. Covers chronology, craftsmanship, houses, shops, etc. Includes over 200 photographs of chairs, tables, clocks, beds, benches, etc. "Mr. & Mrs. Andrews know all there is to know about Shaker furniture," Mark Van Doren, NATION. 48 full-page plates. 192pp. Deluxe cloth binding. 7⅞ x 10¾.
T7 Clothbound $6.00

PRIMITIVE ART, Franz Boas. A great American anthropologist covers theory, technical virtuosity, styles, symbolism, patterns, etc. of primitive art. The more than 900 illustrations will interest artists, designers, craftworkers. Over 900 illustrations. 376pp. 5⅜ x 8.
T25 Paperbound $1.95

ON THE LAWS OF JAPANESE PAINTING, H. Bowie. The best possible substitute for lessons from an oriental master. Treats both spirit and technique; exercises for control of the brush; inks, brushes, colors; use of dots, lines to express whole moods, etc. 220 illus. 132pp. 6⅛ x 9¼.
T30 Paperbound $1.95

HANDBOOK OF ORNAMENT, F. S. Meyer. One of the largest collections of copyright-free traditional art: over 3300 line cuts of Greek, Roman, Medieval, Renaissance, Baroque, 18th and 19th century art motifs (tracery, geometric elements, flower and animal motifs, etc.) and decorated objects (chairs, thrones, weapons, vases, jewelry, armor, etc.). Full text. 3300 illustrations. 562pp. 5⅜ x 8.
T302 Paperbound $2.00

THREE CLASSICS OF ITALIAN CALLIGRAPHY. Oscar Ogg, ed. Exact reproductions of three famous Renaissance calligraphic works: Arrighi's OPERINA and IL MODO, Tagliente's LO PRESENTE LIBRO, and Palatino's LIBRO NUOVO. More than 200 complete alphabets, thousands of lettered specimens, in Papal Chancery and other beautiful, ornate handwriting. Introduction. 245 plates. 282pp. 6⅛ x 9¼.
T212 Paperbound $1.95

THE HISTORY AND TECHNIQUES OF LETTERING, A. Nesbitt. A thorough history of lettering from the ancient Egyptians to the present, and a 65-page course in lettering for artists. Every major development in lettering history is illustrated by a complete alphabet. Fully analyzes such masters as Caslon, Koch, Garamont, Jenson, and many more. 89 alphabets, 165 other specimens. 317pp. 5⅜ x 8.
T427 Paperbound $2.00

LETTERING AND ALPHABETS, J. A. Cavanagh. An unabridged reissue of "Lettering," containing the full discussion, analysis, illustration of 89 basic hand lettering tyles based on Caslon, Bodoni, Gothic, many other types. Hundreds of technical hints on construction, strokes, pens, brushes, etc. 89 alphabets, 72 lettered specimens, which may be reproduced permission-free. 121pp. 9¾ x 8.   T53 Paperbound **$1.25**

THE HUMAN FIGURE IN MOTION, Eadweard Muybridge. The largest collection in print of Muybridge's famous high-speed action photos. 4789 photographs in more than 500 action-strip-sequences (at shutter speeds up to 1/6000th of a second) illustrate men, women, children—mostly undraped—performing such actions as walking, running, getting up, lying down, carrying objects, throwing, etc. "An unparalleled dictionary of action for all artists," AMERICAN ARTIST. 390 full-page plates, with 4789 photographs. Heavy glossy stock, reinforced binding with headbands. 7⅞ x 10¾.   T204 Clothbound **$10.00**

ANIMALS IN MOTION, Eadweard Muybridge. The largest collection of animal action photos in print. 34 different animals (horses, mules, oxen, goats, camels, pigs, cats, lions, gnus, deer, monkeys, eagles—and 22 others) in 132 characteristic actions. All 3919 photographs are taken in series at speeds up to 1/1600th of a second, offering artists, biologists, cartoonists a remarkable opportunity to see exactly how an ostrich's head bobs when running, how a lion puts his foot down, how an elephant's knee bends, how a bird flaps his wings, thousands of other hard-to-catch details. "A really marvelous series of plates," NATURE. 380 full-pages of plates. Heavy glossy stock, reinforced binding with headbands. 7⅞ x 10¾.
T203 Clothbound **$10.00**

THE BOOK OF SIGNS, R. Koch. 493 symbols—crosses, monograms, astrological, biological symbols, runes, etc.—from ancient manuscripts, cathedrals, coins, catacombs, pottery. May be reproduced permission-free. 493 illustrations by Fritz Kredel. 104pp. 6⅛ x 9¼.
T162 Paperbound **$1.00**

A HANDBOOK OF EARLY ADVERTISING ART, C. P. Hornung. The largest collection of copyright-free early advertising art ever compiled. Vol. I: 2,000 illustrations of animals, old automobiles, buildings, allegorical figures, fire engines, Indians, ships, trains, more than 33 other categories! Vol II: Over 4,000 typographical specimens; 600 Roman, Gothic, Barnum, Old English faces; 630 ornamental type faces; hundreds of scrolls, initials, flourishes, etc. "A remarkable collection," PRINTERS' INK.

Vol. I: Pictorial Volume. Over 2000 illustrations. 256pp. 9 x 12.   T122 Clothbound **$10.00**
Vol. II: Typographical Volume. Over 4000 speciments. 319pp. 9 x 12.   T123 Clothbound **$10.00**
Two volume set, Clothbound, only **$18.50**

DESIGN FOR ARTISTS AND CRAFTSMEN, L. Wolchonok. The most thorough course on the creation of art motifs and designs. Shows you step-by-step, with hundreds of examples and 113 detailed exercises, how to create original designs from geometric patterns, plants, birds, animals, humans, and man-made objects. "A great contribution to the field of design and crafts," N. Y. SOCIETY OF CRAFTSMEN. More than 1300 entirely new illustrations. xv + 207pp. 7⅞ x 10¾.   T274 Clothbound **$4.95**

HANDBOOK OF DESIGNS AND DEVICES, C. P. Hornung. A remarkable working collection of 1836 basic designs and variations, all copyright-free. Variations of circle, line, cross, diamond, swastika, star, scroll, shield, many more. Notes on symbolism. "A necessity to every designer who would be original without having to labor heavily," ARTIST and ADVERTISER. 204 plates. 240pp. 5⅜ x 8.
T125 Paperbound **$1.90**

THE UNIVERSAL PENMAN, George Bickham. Exact reproduction of beautiful 18th century book of handwriting. 22 complete alphabets in finest English roundhand, other scripts, over 2000 elaborate flourishes, 122 calligraphic illustrations, etc. Material is copyright-free. "An essential part of any art library, and a book of permanent value," AMERICAN ARTIST. 212 plates. 224pp. 9 x 13¾.   T20 Clothbound **$10.00**

AN ATLAS OF ANATOMY FOR ARTISTS, F. Schider. This standard work contains 189 full-page plates, more than 647 illustrations of all aspects of the human skeleton, musculature, cutaway portions of the body, each part of the anatomy, hand forms, eyelids, breasts, location of muscles under the flesh, etc. 59 plates illustrate how Michelangelo, da Vinci, Goya, 15 others, drew human anatomy. New 3rd edition enlarged by 52 new illustrations by Cloquet, Barcsay. "The standard reference tool," AMERICAN LIBRARY ASSOCIATION. "Excellent," AMERICAN ARTIST. 189 plates, 647 illustrations. xxvi + 192pp. 7⅞ x 10⅝.   T241 Clothbound **$6.00**

AN ATLAS OF ANIMAL ANATOMY FOR ARTISTS, W. Ellenberger, H. Baum, H. Dittrich. The largest, richest animal anatomy for artists in English. Form, musculature, tendons, bone structure, expression, detailed cross sections of head, other features, of the horse, lion, dog, cat, deer, seal, kangaroo, cow, bull, goat, monkey, hare, many other animals. "Highly recommended," DESIGN. Second, revised, enlarged edition with new plates from Cuvier, Stubbs, etc. 288 illustrations. 153pp. 11⅜ x 9.   T82 Clothbound **$6.00**

ANIMAL DRAWING: ANATOMY AND ACTION FOR ARTISTS, C. R. Knight. 158 studies, with full accompanying text, of such animals as the gorilla, bear, bison, dromedary, camel, vulture, pelican, iguana, shark, etc., by one of the greatest modern masters of animal drawing. Innumerable tips on how to get life expression into your work. "An excellent reference work,' SAN FRANCISCO CHRONICLE. 158 illustrations. 156pp. 10½ x 8½.
T426 Paperbound **$2.00**

THE CRAFTSMAN'S HANDBOOK, Cennino Cennini. The finest English translation of IL LIBRO DELL' ARTE, the 15th century introduction to art technique that is both a mirror of Quatrocento life and a source of many useful but nearly forgotten facets of the painter's art. 4 illustrations. xxvii + 142pp. D. V. Thompson, translator. 6⅛ x 9¼.   T54 Paperbound **$1.50**

THE BROWN DECADES, Lewis Mumford. A picture of the "buried renaissance" of the post-Civil War period, and the founding of modern architecture (Sullivan, Richardson, Root, Roebling), landscape development (Marsh, Olmstead, Eliot), and the graphic arts (Homer, Eakins, Ryder). 2nd revised, enlarged edition. Bibliography. 12 illustrations. xiv + 266 pp. 5⅜ x 8.   T200 Paperbound **$1.65**

STIEGEL GLASS, F. W. Hunter. The story of the most highly esteemed early American glassware, fully illustrated. How a German adventurer, "Baron" Stiegel, founded a glass empire; detailed accounts of individual glasswork. "This pioneer work is reprinted in an edition even more beautiful than the original," ANTIQUES DEALER. New introduction by Helen McKearin. 171 illustrations, 12 in full color. xxii + 338pp. 7⅞ x 10¾.   T128 Clothbound **$10.00**

THE HUMAN FIGURE, J. H. Vanderpoel. Not just a picture book, but a complete course by a famous figure artist. Extensive text, illustrated by 430 pencil and charcoal drawings of both male and female anatomy. 2nd enlarged edition. Foreword. 430 illus. 143pp. 6⅛ x 9¼.   T432 Paperbound **$1.45**

PINE FURNITURE OF EARLY NEW ENGLAND, R. H. Kettell. Over 400 illustrations, over 50 working drawings of early New England chairs, benches, beds cupboards, mirrors, shelves, tables, other furniture esteemed for simple beauty and character. "Rich store of illustrations . . . emphasizes the individuality and varied design," ANTIQUES. 413 illustrations, 55 working drawings. 475pp. 8 x 10¾.   T145 Clothbound **$10.00**

BASIC BOOKBINDING, A. W. Lewis. Enables both beginners and experts to rebind old books or bind paperbacks in hard covers. Treats materials, tools; gives step-by-step instruction in how to collate a book, sew it, back it, make boards, etc. 261 illus. Appendices. 155pp. 5⅜ x 8.   T169 Paperbound **$1.35**

DESIGN MOTIFS OF ANCIENT MEXICO, J. Enciso. Nearly 90% of these 766 superb designs from Aztec, Olmec, Totonac, Maya, and Toltec origins are unobtainable elsewhere! Contains plumed serpents, wind gods, animals, demons, dancers, monsters, etc. Excellent applied design source. Originally $17.50. 766 illustrations, thousands of motifs. 192pp. 6⅛ x 9¼.   T84 Paperbound **$1.85**

AFRICAN SCULPTURE, Ladislas Segy. 163 full-page plates illustrating masks, fertility figures, ceremonial objects, etc., of 50 West and Central African tribes—95% never before illustrated. 34-page introduction to African sculpture. "Mr. Segy is one of its top authorities," NEW YORKER. 164 full-page photographic plates. Introduction. Bibliography. 244pp. 6⅛ x 9¼.   T396 Paperbound **$2.00**

THE PROCESSES OF GRAPHIC REPRODUCTION IN PRINTING, H. Curwen. A thorough and practical survey of wood, linoleum, and rubber engraving; copper engraving; drypoint, mezzotint, etching, aquatint, steel engraving, die sinking, stencilling, lithography (extensively); photographic reproduction utilizing line, continuous tone, photoengravure, collotype; every other process in general use. Note on color reproduction. Section on bookbinding. Over 200 illustrations, 25 in color. 143pp. 5½ x 8½.   T512 Clothbound **$4.00**

CALLIGRAPHY, J. G. Schwandner. First reprinting in 200 years of this legendary book of beautiful handwriting. Over 300 ornamental initials, 12 complete calligraphic alphabets, over 150 ornate frames and panels, 75 calligraphic pictures of cherubs, stags, lions, etc., thousands of flourishes, scrolls, etc., by the greatest 18th century masters. All material can be copied or adapted without permission. Historical introduction. 158 full-page plates. 368pp. 9 x 13.   T475 Clothbound **$10.00**

* * *

A DIDEROT PICTORIAL ENCYCLOPEDIA OF TRADES AND INDUSTRY, Manufacturing and the Technical Arts in Plates Selected from "L'Encyclopédie ou Dictionnaire Raisonné des Sciences, des Arts, et des Métiers," of Denis Diderot, edited with text by C. Gillispie. Over 2000 illustrations on 485 full-page plates. Magnificent 18th century engravings of men, women, and children working at such trades as milling flour, cheesemaking, charcoal burning, mining, silverplating, shoeing horses, making fine glass, printing, hundreds more, showing details of machinery, different steps in sequence, etc. A remarkable art work, but also the largest collection of working figures in print, copyright-free, for art directors, designers, etc. Two vols. 920pp. 9 x 12. Heavy library cloth.   T421 Two volume set **$18.50**

* * *

SILK SCREEN TECHNIQUES, J. Biegeleisen, M. Cohn. A practical step-by-step home course in one of the most versatile, least expensive graphic arts processes. How to build an inexpensive silk screen, prepare stencils, print, achieve special textures, use color, etc. Every step explained, diagrammed. 149 illustrations, 8 in color. 201pp. 6⅛ x 9¼.   T433 Paperbound **$1.45**

PUZZLES, GAMES, AND ENTERTAINMENTS

MATHEMATICS, MAGIC AND MYSTERY, Martin Gardner. Astonishing feats of mind reading, mystifying "magic" tricks, are often based on mathematical principles anyone can learn. This book shows you how to perform scores of tricks with cards, dice, coins, knots, numbers, etc., by using simple principles from set theory, theory of numbers, topology, other areas of mathematics, fascinating in themselves. No special knowledge required. 135 illus. 186pp. 5⅜ x 8.
T335 Paperbound **$1.00**

MATHEMATICAL PUZZLES FOR BEGINNERS AND ENTHUSIASTS, G. Mott-Smoth. Test your problem-solving techniques and powers of inference on 188 challenging, amusing puzzles based on algebra, dissection of plane figures, permutations, probabilities, etc. Appendix of primes, square roots, etc. 135 illus. 2nd revised edition. 248pp. 5⅜ x 8.
T198 Paperbound **$1.00**

LEARN CHESS FROM THE MASTERS, F. Reinfeld. Play 10 games against Marshall, Bronstein, Najdorf, other masters, and grade yourself on each move. Detailed annotations reveal principles of play, strategy, etc. as you proceed. An excellent way to get a real insight into the game. Formerly titled, "Chess by Yourself." 91 diagrams. vii + 144pp. 5⅜ x 8.
T362 Paperbound **$1.00**

REINFELD ON THE END GAME IN CHESS, F. Reinfeld. 62 end games of Alekhine, Tarrasch, Morphy, other masters, are carefully analyzed with emphasis on transition from middle game to end play. Tempo moves, queen endings, weak squares, other basic principles clearly illustrated. Excellent for understanding why some moves are weak or incorrect, how to avoid errors. Formerly titled, "Practical End-game Play." 62 diagrams. vi + 177pp. 5⅜ x 8.
T417 Paperbound **$1.25**

101 PUZZLES IN THOUGHT AND LOGIC, C. R. Wylie, Jr. Brand new puzzles you need no special knowledge to solve! Each one is a gem of ingenuity that will really challenge your problem-solving technique. Introduction with simplified explanation of scientic puzzle solving. 128pp. 5⅜ x 8.
T167 Paperbound **$1.00**

THE COMPLETE NONSENSE OF EDWARD LEAR. The only complete edition of this master of gentle madness at a popular price. The Dong with the Luminous Nose, The Jumblies, The Owl and the Pussycat, hundreds of other bits of wonderful nonsense. 214 limericks, 3 sets of Nonsense Botany, 5 Nonsense Alphabets, 546 fantastic drawings, much more. 320pp. 5⅜ x 8.
T167 Paperbound **$1.00**

28 SCIENCE FICTION STORIES OF H. G. WELLS. Two complete novels, "Men Like Gods" and "Star Begotten," plus 26 short stories by the master science-fiction writer of all time. Stories of space, time, future adventure that are among the all-time classics of science fiction. 928pp. 5⅜ x 8.
T265 Clothbound **$3.95**

SEVEN SCIENCE FICTION NOVELS, H. G. Wells. Unabridged texts of "The Time Machine," "The Island of Dr. Moreau," "First Men in the Moon," "The Invisible Man," "The War of the Worlds," "The Food of the Gods," "In the Days of the Comet." "One will have to go far to match this for entertainment, excitement, and sheer pleasure," N. Y. TIMES. 1015pp. 5⅜ x 8.
T264 Clothbound **$3.95**

MATHEMAGIC, MAGIC PUZZLES, AND GAMES WITH NUMBERS, R. V. Heath. More than 60 new puzzles and stunts based on number properties: multiplying large numbers mentally, finding the date of any day in the year, etc. Edited by J. S. Meyer. 76 illus. 129pp. 5⅜ x 8.
T110 Paperbound **$1.00**

FIVE ADVENTURE NOVELS OF H. RIDER HAGGARD. The master story-teller's five best tales of mystery and adventure set against authentic African backgrounds: "She," "King Solomon's Mines," "Allan Quatermain," "Allan's Wife," "Maiwa's Revenge." 821pp. 5⅜ x 8.
T108 Clothbound **$3.95**

WIN AT CHECKERS, M. Hopper. (Formerly "Checkers.") The former World's Unrestricted Checker Champion gives you valuable lessons in openings, traps, end games, ways to draw when you are behind, etc. More than 100 questions and answers anticipate your problems. Appendix. 75 problems diagrammed, solved. 79 figures. xi + 107pp. 5⅜ x 8.
T363 Paperbound **$1.00**

CRYPTOGRAPHY, L. D. Smith. Excellent introductory work on ciphers and their solution, history of secret writing, techniques, etc. Appendices on Japanese methods, the Baconian cipher, frequency tables. Bibliography. Over 150 problems, solutions. 160pp. 5⅜ x 8.
T247 Paperbound **$1.00**

CRYPTANALYSIS, H. F. Gaines. (Formerly, "Elementary Cryptanalysis.") The best book available on cryptograms and how to solve them. Contains all major techniques: substitution, transposition, mixed alphabets, multafid, Kasiski and Vignere methods, etc. Word frequency appendix. 167 problems, solutions, 134 figures. 236pp. 5⅜ x 8.
T97 Paperbound **$1.95**

FLATLAND, E. A. Abbot. The science-fiction classic of life in a 2-dimensional world that is considered a first-rate introduction to relativity and hyperspace, as well as a scathing satire on society, politics and religion. 7th edition. 16 illus. 128pp. 5⅜ x 8.
T1 Paperbound **$1.00**

DOVER BOOKS

HOW TO FORCE CHECKMATE, F. Reinfeld. (Formerly "Challenge to Chessplayers.") No board needed to sharpen your checkmate skill on 300 checkmate situations. Learn to plan up to 3 moves ahead and play a superior end game. 300 situations diagrammed; notes and full solutions. 111pp. 5⅜ x 8.   T439 Paperbound **$1.25**

MORPHY'S GAMES OF CHESS, P. W. Sergeant, ed. Play forcefully by following the techniques used by one of the greatest chess champions. 300 of Morphy's games carefully annotated to reveal principles. Bibliography. New introduction by F. Reinfeld. 235 diagrams. x + 352pp. 5⅜ x 8.   T386 Paperbound **$1.75**

MATHEMATICAL RECREATIONS, M. Kraitchik. Hundreds of unusual mathematical puzzlers and odd bypaths of math, elementary and advanced. Greek, Medieval, Arabic, Hindu problems; figurate numbers, Fermat numbers, primes; magic, Euler, Latin squares; fairy chess, latruncles, reversi, jinx, ruma, tetrachrome other positional and permutational games. Rigorous solutions. Revised second edition. 181 illus. 330pp. 5⅜ x 8.   T163 Paperbound **$1.75**

MATHEMATICAL EXCURSIONS, H. A. Merrill. Revealing stimulating insights into elementary math, not usually taught in school. 90 problems demonstrate Russian peasant multiplication, memory systems for pi, magic squares, dyadic systems, division by inspection, many more. Solutions to difficult problems. 50 illus. 5⅜ x 8.   T350 Paperbound **$1.00**

MAGIC TRICKS & CARD TRICKS, W. Jonson. Best introduction to tricks with coins, bills, eggs, ribbons, slates, cards, easily performed without elaborate equipment. Professional routines, tips on presentation, misdirection, etc. Two books bound as one: 52 tricks with cards, 37 tricks with common objects. 106 figures. 224pp. 5⅜ x 8.   T909 Paperbound **$1.00**

MATHEMATICAL PUZZLES OF SAM LOYD, selected and edited by M. Gardner. 177 most ingenious mathematical puzzles of America's greatest puzzle originator, based on arithmetic, algebra, game theory, dissection, route tracing, operations research, probability, etc. 120 drawings, diagrams. Solutions. 187pp. 5⅜ x 8.   T498 Paperbound **$1.00**

THE ART OF CHESS, J. Mason. The most famous general study of chess ever written. More than 90 openings, middle game, end game, how to attack, sacrifice, defend, exchange, form general strategy. Supplement on "How Do You Play Chess?" by F. Reinfeld. 448 diagrams. 356pp. 5⅜ x 8.   T463 Paperbound **$1.85**

HYPERMODERN CHESS as Developed in the Games of its Greatest Exponent, ARON NIMZOVICH, F. Reinfeld, ed. Learn how the game's greatest innovator defeated Alekhine, Lasker, and many others; and use these methods in your own game. 180 diagrams. 228pp. 5⅜ x 8.
                                                                 T448 Paperbound **$1.35**

A TREASURY OF CHESS LORE, F. Reinfeld, ed. Hundreds of fascinating stories by and about the masters, accounts of tournaments and famous games, aphorisms, word portraits, little known incidents, photographs, etc., that will delight the chess enthusiast captivate the beginner. 49 photographs (14 full-page plates), 12 diagrams. 315pp. 5⅜ x 8.
                                                                 T458 Paperbound **$1.75**

A NONSENSE ANTHOLOGY, collected by Carolyn Wells. 245 of the best nonsense verses ever written: nonsense puns, absurd arguments, mock epics, nonsense ballads, "sick" verses, dog-Latin verses, French nonsense verses, limericks. Lear, Carroll, Belloc, Burgess, nearly 100 other writers. Introduction by Carolyn Wells. 3 indices: Title, Author, First Lines. xxxiii + 279pp. 5⅜ x 8.   T499 Paperbound **$1.25**

SYMBOLIC LOGIC and THE GAME OF LOGIC, Lewis Carroll. Two delightful puzzle books by the author of "Alice," bound as one. Both works concern the symbolic representation of traditional logic and together contain more than 500 ingenious, amusing and instructive syllogistic puzzlers. Total of 326pp. 5⅜ x 8.   T492 Paperbound **$1.50**

PILLOW PROBLEMS and A TANGLED TALE, Lewis Carroll. Two of Carroll's rare puzzle works bound as one. "Pillow Problems" contain 72 original math puzzles. The puzzles in "A Tangled Tale" are given in delightful story form. Total of 291pp. 5⅜ x 8.   T493 Paperbound **$1.50**

PECK'S BAD BOY AND HIS PA, G. W. Peck. Both volumes of one of the most widely read of all American humor books. A classic of American folk humor, also invaluable as a portrait of an age. 100 original illustrations. Introduction by E. Bleiler. 347pp. 5⅜ x 8.
                                                                 T497 Paperbound **$1.35**

Dover publishes books on art, music, philosophy, literature, languages, history, social sciences, psychology, handcrafts, orientalia, puzzles and entertainments, chess, pets and gardens, books explaining science, intermediate and higher mathematics mathematical physics, engineering, biological sciences, earth sciences, classics of science, etc. Write to:

Dept. catrr.
Dover Publications, Inc.
180 Varick Street, N. Y. 14, N. Y.